D1738729

The Dog
on the Bed

Also by Richard Teleky

FICTION

Winter in Hollywood
Pack Up the Moon
The Paris Years of Rosie Kamin
Goodnight, Sweetheart and Other Stories

NON-FICTION

Hungarian Rhapsodies: Essays in Ethnicity, Identity
and Culture

POETRY

The Hermit in Arcadia
The Hermit's Kiss

ANTHOLOGIES

The Exile Book of Canadian Dog Stories
The Oxford Book of French-Canadian Short Stories

RICHARD TELEKY

The Dog
on the Bed

A Canine Alphabet

Fitzhenry & Whiteside

Published in Canada by Fitzhenry & Whiteside, 195 Allstate Parkway, Markham, Ontario L3R 4T8

Published in the United States by Fitzhenry & Whiteside, 311 Washington Street, Brighton, Massachusetts 02135

www.fitzhenry.ca   godwit@fitzhenry.ca

10 9 8 7 6 5 4 3 2 1

Library and Archives Canada Cataloguing in Publication
Teleky, Richard
    Dog on the bed : a canine alphabet / Richard Teleky.
Includes bibliographical references and index.
ISBN 978-1-55455-219-1
    1. Dogs--Miscellanea. 2. Dogs--Humor. I. Title.
SF426.T44 2011   636.7   C2011-906613-0

Publisher Cataloging-in-Publication Data (U.S)
Teleky, Richard
    The dog on the bed : a canine alphabet / Richard Teleky.
[372] p. : photos. ; cm.
Includes bibliographical references and index.
Summary: An abecedarian that contains essays on the human-dog relationship, dog facts, dog lore, dogs in human culture and philosophy on dogs.
ISBN: 978-1-55455-219-1
1. Dogs. I. Title.
636.7 dc23 SF422.33.T454 2011

Fitzhenry & Whiteside acknowledges with thanks the Canada Council for the Arts, and the Ontario Arts Council for their support of our publishing program. We acknowledge the financial support of the Government of Canada through the Canada Book Fund (CBF) for our publishing activities.

 Canada Council   Conseil des Arts
for the Arts   du Canada

 ONTARIO ARTS COUNCIL
CONSEIL DES ARTS DE L'ONTARIO

Cover and interior design by Daniel Choi
Cover Image: *Precious - A Pug* (w/c on paper), Garstin, Alethea (1894-1978) / Private Collection / © Manya Igel Fine Arts, London, UK / The Bridgeman Art Library
Image on page 361: *Zoli*, author's photograph
Printed in Canada by Friesens

MIX
Paper from
responsible sources
FSC® C016245

For Rennie,
who can't read, but understands,
and
in memory of Zoli,
and Buster, Morgan, Max, and Spotty

CONTENTS

CAST OF CHARACTERS

If translations of Russian novels can include them, as can playwrights of every nationality, then I want to make use of a sensible convention as well. The dogs who appear in this book are:

The principal dogs:

Buster (1): Boston terrier
Buster (2): Boston terrier
Max: Wirehaired fox terrier
Morgan: Cavalier King Charles
    spaniel
Rennie: Pug
Spotty: Smooth-haired fox
    terrier
Zoli: Pug

Cameo appearances by:

Bramble: Cavalier King
    Charles spaniel
Bruno: Miniature poodle
Chico: Chihuahua
Cricket: Toy poodle
Daisy: Toy poodle
Diga: Pug
Eden: Japanese chin
Ennis: Black Labrador
Hector: Golden retriever
Jenny: Schnauzer and wheaten
    terrier mix
Oscar: Newfoundland
Phoebe: Mixed breed
Pixie: Chihuahua
Pudgy: Toy poodle
Sandy: Boxer
Willow: Chinese crested

I was born in the Year of the Dog, according to the Chinese system of astrology, which may account for the sympathy I have for dogs. Of course, I like to think that it does. At any rate, this book is the result of that bond, and of years of association with various dogs, wide reading about them, and connections with "dog people" (breeders, veterinarians, etc.). "Dog people," Chinese astrologers tell us, are supposed to be loyal and trustworthy, and I hope that I've earned the right to consider myself one.

My title comes from a French proverb: "There are two kinds of masters – those who admit that the dog sleeps on the bed, and those who don't admit it." I first heard this saying from Magda Csécsy-Sömjén, a professor of linguistics at the University of Nice, who regularly travelled between Europe and North America with her dog, Dolly. Perhaps it resonated with me because I remembered my mother frequently telling me, as a child, "Get that dog off the bed!" I've planned this book since 1995, when I brought home the first dog of my own, a pug named Zoli. In subsequent years I've read countless dog books, catching up on classics like Virginia Woolf's *Flush* and Konrad Lorenz's *Man Meets Dog* while following new titles and trends. We can learn a great deal about dogs not only by observing them but by reading about them too, and our dogs can benefit from that reading. People who genuinely love a dog as a dog – not as an emotional prop, a lifestyle accessory, or a child substitute – spend a lot of time thinking about how dogs take in their world. This often leads us to books, a good progression. Yet there have been days when it seemed that new books about dogs were being published faster than I could read them – or write my own – and *The Dog on the Bed* makes no claim to be comprehensive. But it is bookish, because that's the kind of person I am. As Groucho Marx once put it, "Outside of a dog, a book is man's best friend. Inside of a dog, it's too dark to read."

The Dog on the Bed is an alphabet of essays – an abecedarian – one short essay, at least, for each letter. The special nature of the abecedarian is that it's a meditation, a kind of philosophical ramble. The author of an alphabet book is a mediator of sorts, representing the general reader or the enthusiast. The genre has been used by a variety of writers, including M.F.K. Fisher (on food), Eleanor Perenyi (on gardening), Roland Barthes (on romantic love), Ezra Pound (on reading), Carlos Fuentes (an eclectic memoir), and Ambrose Bierce, who perfected it for that classic, *The Devil's Dictionary*. The form is a loose one, but it should be both informative and entertaining. Readers are free to read from cover to cover with growing momentum or jump in at essays of special interest, making individual versions of the book. This abecedarian, however, is *not* a how-to manual (there are enough of these on the market already), but rather an exploration of aspects of the mysterious bond between dogs and humans, and some of the ways in which it has been represented in our culture. There is an overall argument here, which runs through each letter of the alphabet: we are human because of our dogs. At almost every turn, the truly ancient human/dog bond has defined us as a species and our culture as well, from our early co-evolution to the way we've relied on dogs and how they have returned the attention. This bond is rich and messy, complex and even troubling – a mirror to our deepest desires and fears. How could it be otherwise?

Naturally my own dog stories will inform this book as a kind of leitmotif and mini-memoir. From my first dog, a smooth-haired fox terrier, through all the other dogs and breeds I've loved – wirehaired terriers, Boston terriers, Cavalier King Charles spaniels, and, of course, pugs – I'll record some of the interactions I've had that illustrate various points under discussion. Inevitably, some essays will not include personal material, but "dog people" like the anecdotal, and so dog books (like the writings of most ethologists, or specialists in animal behaviour) are full of anecdotes. I make no claim to the expertise of a dog specialist (if there is such a creature), but rather will bring to my subject a fiction writer's temperament, a literary critic's interest in the arts, a dog lover's fascination with a popular subject, and my own concerns and values, likes and dislikes. So curl up with your dog at your side, or on your lap, and jump in. – Richard Teleky

ACKNOWLEDGEMENTS

I'm especially grateful to Dr. Richard Medhurst, of the Rosedale Animal Hospital in Toronto, for kindly answering my endless questions since he first became the veterinarian to my dogs back in 1995, for his invaluable wise counsel as well as for reading this work in manuscript and commenting on it. For decades now I've had the good fortune to enjoy wonderful long conversations with my friend Dr. Lee Rainey, a professor of Chinese philosophy and religion – and a cat lover – and these pages reflect many of our talks, as well as her particular expertise. During the last stages of revision, when my pug Rennie required emergency eye surgery, Dr. Lionel Goldstein and Dr. Richard Klys of Toronto's Forest Hill Animal Clinic proved, again, that talented veterinarians can also be exemplary teachers. Thanks to Boris Castel, editor of *Queen's Quarterly*, who first published a longer version of my research about the dog artist Diana Thorne, and my great appreciation to the exacting Jennifer Hann for her research assistance. Special thanks to Richard Dionne for his support and enthusiasm, to Sarah Reid for her copyediting and thoughtful comments, to Pooja Tripathi for her careful production work, to

Daniel Choi for his handsome design, to Uma Subramanian for her meticulous proofreading and index, and to everyone else at Fitzhenry & Whiteside who helped to make this book possible (including, I'm tempted to add, the office cats, because animals – even if they're not dogs – always make an office a more humane place). Numerous friends and colleagues have shown the best kind of interest in my writing when they sent me an unexpected newspaper clipping, recommended a book or movie, shared a particular bit of expertise or one of their own dog stories (some appearing in these pages), or read a portion of my manuscript. I'm grateful to all of them, including: David Ayoub; Linda Beebe, Esquire; Barry Callaghan; Carole Carpenter; Mary Clark; Anita Cohen; Christopher Doda; Larry Fineberg; Frieda Forman; Mavis Gallant; Gail Geltner; Jason Guriel; the late Rose and Jules Hall; Suzanne Hively; Evan Jones; Yevgeniya Kalimbet; Jane Kessler; Audrey King; Lori Koenig, D.V.M.; Carol Krall; Harriet R. Logan; Marian Misters; Ilona Molnar; Mary Murdoch; Bo Rog, D.V.M.; Pam Salamone; Ian Sandler, D.V.M.; Mardel and Marc Sanzotta; William Secord; Nora Shulman; J.D. Singh; Penni Stewart; Teresa Stratas; Rosemary Sullivan; Noreen Talbot; Mark Tapia; William Toye; Felix Tyndel, M.D.; Marc Tyndel, computer wiz; Penelope Tzougros; Priscila Uppal; and Scott Wilson. Librarians at the Cleveland Public Library (main branch) and the Lakewood Public Library offered invaluable assistance, and the vertical files of the library of the Art Gallery of Ontario, the Boston Public Library, and the Cleveland Museum of Art Library were essential. I also received thoughtful assistance from the Canadian War Museum and the Curator of Parliament. Any errors, of course, are my own. Finally, I owe my deepest gratitude to my parents, who so very long ago taught me how to care for a dog. – RT

The Dog
on the Bed

The Dog
on the Bed

A Canine Alphabet

ANTHROPOMORPHISM

When you wake in the morning and the dog is asleep on the bed, the dog is the world. It appears to contain all of life – it breathes, it dreams, it needs, it wants, and it will soon be ready for the day – so that you are for a moment apart from your own cares, in tune with its essence, its being, and in this way you are apart from your world, subsumed. I don't mean this state of suspension, brief as it is, to sound mystical or spiritual, words easily tossed about. But a dog allows you to be both suspended from the world while more fully a part of it. As the dog yawns and stretches, you accept this contradictory pull, this tension. If you have a dog, you know what I mean. As the dog snuggles close, or yawns again, you may reach out to stroke its neck or scratch its ear, and the day has begun. All of this is instinctive and wordless, but we soon fall back into language, we've given names to things – to people, pets, feelings, even to the times of day – and suddenly we call the dog *this* or *that*, we stretch and climb out of bed and prepare to make order, summoning words to help us along, and the dog is no longer the world. The shift that has taken place leaves us in charge. The names we have given things count, appear true, and the dog is now a dog to be fed and let out. In an essential way we know he or she is somehow like us, but we, in control, are superior. And this is where we get into trouble.

Among people who study dogs and write about them, anthropomorphism is generally considered the cardinal sin. The word is a composite of two Greek roots, *anthro* for humanity, and *morph* for form. It involves attributing human qualities and emotions to non-human beings, and is something we humans, a self-centered lot, tend to do almost naturally. I think it's actually a form of metaphorical thinking, of combining two disparate things, or facets of them, to make a third thing. In this sense, it's an attempt at understanding, and even a way of knowing. How can we talk about animal consciousness? Do dogs have emotions? How much like humans are they? How much not like?

To begin even a tentative answer we need to look at our Judeo-Christian heritage. One of its pervasive ideas is the great chain of being, a concept that has evolved from ancient Greece and Aristotle's studies and classification of the natural world to modern times through religion, literature, and the arts, and even political thought and science. Put simply, in the great chain of being, humankind – once known as "man" – ranks above inanimate nature, such as rocks, and plants and "lower" animals. Above us are the angels, archangels, and seraphim. Humans have the potential to develop either their lower or higher nature. In this schema, a dog has fewer potentialities than a human being – it cannot read a book or cook a meal – so it is seen as a lesser being. Almost inevitably, species status took on religious significance in the Judeo-Christian tradition and made dogs metaphysically lesser – mere animals. That dogs and humans are both mammals, with significant commonalities, is easy to overlook. That dogs may fulfill their potentialities more successfully than many humans do is seldom contemplated. After all, we humans are closer to the angels, or so we like to think.

An example might be useful here. One summer I decided to drive from Toronto to the Shaw Festival, near Niagara Falls, for a matinee, which meant I would be away from home for most of the day and early evening. Rennie, my pug, who was then not quite two years old, of course needed someone to look after him, so I arranged for a student to dog-sit. I left just before lunch and, because of traffic problems on the return trip, didn't arrive home until nearly nine in the evening. I was told immediately that Rennie had been fine, had enjoyed the day, had played and napped, as I expected, but that around eight o'clock he went into the hallway and sat staring at the door, waiting. What, here, does *waiting* mean? In human terms we know, but for a dog? *Waiting* suggests a kind of understanding, a sense of order, habit, and appropriateness, even cause and effect. Was Rennie making an association between the darkening night sky and bedtime? Had he suddenly decided to miss me and his routine? Why hadn't he gone to the door earlier? Was he bored? What does it mean for a dog to be *bored*? Or, did he for some reason distrust the student who'd fed and walked him, attending to his needs without asking? What was going through his mind or head?

There is much to be said about dog consciousness, and new books about the subject now pile up yearly. Whether the writer is a specialist in the study of animal behaviour or a dog trainer, one issue comes up again and again: dogs are not people. On the other hand, books by memoirists, novelists, and humourists prefer to blur distinctions and occasionally remove them altogether. There's something to be learned from all of these approaches. Efforts to explain animals in scientifically credible terms have dominated much of the recent discourse about dogs – which means that observations and experiments are emphasized over anecdotes. But it's easy to forget that science is a system, a language, and that it is seldom value-neutral. Still, most scientists acknowledge that dog owners are prone to see, even invent, commonalities; they emphasize, instead, the need to recognize the dog's essential otherness.

In its most decadent manifestation, anthropomorphism involves treating a dog as if it were human, the *as if* aspect taking various forms. Speaking to a dog with baby talk, celebrating its birthday (which the dog doesn't anticipate), and dressing it in special clothes, like a doll or a toy, tells more about the dog's owner than about the dog itself. Yet dogs do respond to their own articles of clothing – some resist the confinement of a winter coat, others tolerate or welcome it. I have a friend whose mixed-breed, Phoebe, always perked up when a scarf was tied about her neck, as if she knew she looked dashing. Emphasizing a dog's difference, dress-up never humanizes animals but merely renders them cute, at best. The human impulse can be playful, possessive, sentimental, but the human is always in control, asserting superiority until the dog manages to get out of its costume. A dog dressed in human clothing is as much an illustration of the problems of human identity as an example of animal psyche – think of William Wegman's photographs of his various Weimaraners, which I'll discuss later.

The extreme opposite of anthropomorphism is not uncommon in people who write about dogs. In one of the pioneering studies, *Man Meets Dog* (1956), Konrad Lorenz shows a preference for dogs that are the most wolf-like, as if a tamed or domesticated creature were too far removed from its wild ancestry to deserve attention. We know that humans and dogs evolved beside each other, but some of us still hear the call of the wild. There's a kind of reverse snobbism here, and it also crops up in a more recent bestseller, *The Hidden Life of Dogs*, by Elizabeth Marshall Thomas. Though Marshall Thomas writes with sympathy of her pugs, her deepest engagement is with the dog pack she assembled on her farm in Virginia, which included Siberian huskies and even a dingo. An anthropologist, like Lorenz, she is naturally drawn to wildness, to the primitive. (Contrast the mundane names she gave her pugs – Violet and Bingo – with the more exotic names of her huskies and dingo: Windigo, Koki, Misha, Viva, and Fatima, and Rider for the Australian shepherd.) It would be easy to dismiss this stance as a professional bias, though an element of bravado may accompany it. The social anthropologist Donna Haraway shows a similar preference in her influential book *The Companion Species Manifesto: Dogs, People, and Significant Otherness* when she describes Great Pyrenees and Australian shepherds. At one point she claims, with a postmodern romanticism, that when she pets her partner's Great Pyrenees, "I also touch relocated Canadian gray wolves, upscale Slovakian bears, and international restoration ecology," and later she notes that in the world of adoption, small dogs and little girls are "the gold standard." These writers seem to suggest that there's more to learn about dog otherness from the larger breeds; that the love sponges such as pugs or spaniels are apparently less dignified because of their size and domestication. To avoid any hint of anthropomorphism, some writers appear to want wolf companions at their side.

But these are serious writers. Maybe they assume that lap dogs have in essential ways lost dogness and been perverted by breeding to satisfy overcivilized human desires; such dogs may seem like overly refined canine degenerates. This view is a sophisticated kind of anthropomorphism, I think, if one can overlook the contradictory combination of sophistication and anthropomorphism. It's not surprising to find anthropologists interested in evolution, and dog evolution makes for a rich and complicated subject. In fact, the process isn't over yet. (Even in the past century, specialized breeds have continued to evolve – the contemporary pug, for instance, has slowly been modified in appearance from the breed that was a favourite of Queen Victoria.) The desire for "wildness" may be part of the reason some people are attracted to pitbulls and Rottweilers. Perhaps without knowing it they want the status of owning something wild, or at least aggressive.

One of the most curious dog-book titles is *The Philosopher's Dog: Friendship with Animals*, by Raimond Gaita, a moral philosopher at the University of London. Anyone who has loved a dog will know that the relationship is a form of friendship. So, can moral philosophy help clarify the problems we have with anthropomorphism? As is the case with many philosophers – especially those who argue in a roundabout way or eschew the conventions of logical argument – Gaita avoids making his subject clear for several chapters, relying first on stories. But eventually he gets around to his real subject: what, he asks, does consciousness mean in a dog? Well, as far as I'm concerned, if the dog sitting beside me is looking around – if the dog isn't, in fact, dead – it's conscious. Sometimes you just have to see what's in front of you to answer a basic question. Gaita also asks if the dog is thinking, and here the matter becomes more complicated. *Thinking* is a human term for a human activity. A dog is an animal, so dog "thinking" has to mean something different. And an even deeper confusion emerges.

While dogs are animals, so are humans, though we like to ignore or forget this. What range of thinking is possible for animals? Shaped by our Western cultural assumption that humans are superior to other animals, the way we think about ourselves remains determined by that old great chain of being. But, as animals, dogs are wired to do certain kinds of things, to act in certain ways. And they do these well. The limitation seems to be that they do mainly what they're wired for, and not much else. As animals – we remind ourselves – humans are more complex. In fact, we are often ineffective (we needed to hunt in groups, not alone; we needed companions to watch the fire while we slept). Humans can, of course, do many things that other animals can't. Our glories include the ability to make art, record history, and so forth. But these virtues exist alongside faults or inefficiencies that are staggering: the tendency to make war, to betray one another, to delude ourselves. Gaita seems to have absorbed this great chain of being wholeheartedly, even when he chastizes some dog writers for their anthropomorphism. He wouldn't dress his dog in cute costumes, and objects to others doing so, but he is the macho flip side of the coin, bragging about his ease with killing animals.

One of the most interesting chapters in *The Philosopher's Dog* discusses the way we mourn an animal because of its distinctive, unique life. While this is in many ways true, I think that Gaita affirms individuality but not worth. Yes, each dog has a unique life, but we mourn the animals we're familiar with, the pets we've come to know and love, and even sleep beside: they are ours. Rarely do people mourn the death of a stranger's pet down the block, just as few people mourn the unfamiliar dead in the daily obituary pages of their newspapers. If we did, we might have a wiring that made us less prone to war and other violent recreations. Gaita's argument allows humans to mourn their dogs and still feel superior to them. Another British moral philosopher, the late Rush Rhees, is more helpful in his book *Moral Questions*, which includes a powerful chapter, "The Death of a Dog." Rhees argues that humans naturally give primary status to other humans, but, "Where I baulk is at the suggestion that *because* men have souls, they are of especial importance to God, so that we may conclude that other creatures, and notably animals, were created for the use and benefit of man."

Anthropomorphism, then, may be part of our human wiring. We see ourselves in our dogs, and when they act in reassuringly predictable ways, we compliment them ("good boy," "good girl") for pleasing us with their pseudo-humanity. How else could we speak to them? We're shaped by our language, by its richness as well as its limitations, and at the heart of any individual language is the sense that it is unique and even complete. While language evolves just as humans and dogs have, it's easy to forget that imperfection and error are its shadows. Many dog writers warn against anthropomorphism when they're actually opposing the limitations of language. (The term *dog writers* itself is a problem, and I'm using it, of course, in the sense of *mystery writers*, and not of dogs who write.) Some anthropomorphism is inevitable, and it's probably a matter of good will. If we didn't see ourselves – and our humanity – in our dogs, would we keep them close to us, at our sides?

ANTI-VIVISECTIONISTS

In 1946, the National Society for Medical Research created a new award: the Research Dog Hero Award. To be eligible, a dog had to be a surviving subject of experimental study in cancer research or heart surgery. This dubious award embodies one of the stranger moments in the conflict between vivisectionists and anti-vivisectionists.

Vivisection, or the dissection of live animals, has a long history. From the earliest centuries of medicine and surgery, its advocates have claimed innumerable benefits for humans and animals alike – our knowledge of the circulatory and nervous systems for a start. Back in the Roman era, Greek physicians such as Galen even gave public demonstrations of animal dissection, using pigs and dogs, among others, as their subjects. Such spectacles weren't done in the name of science but rather as illustrations of a physician's skill at a time when physicians were in competition with natural philosophers (those precursors of modern scientists) schooled in rhetoric. It may not have taken long for physicians to figure out sensational feats such as cutting the nerve to a dog's vocal cord, which would stop it from barking. As the centuries passed, vivisection continued – it even flourished. One example: in 1664, in order to study respiration, the natural philosopher Robert Hooke dissected a live dog at Oxford University to learn how its pulmonary system worked, though he later told his colleague Robert Boyle that he wouldn't perform another such experiment because of the dog's suffering.

By the end of the nineteenth century, which saw the popularization of Charles Darwin's theory of evolution, individuals banded together to protest vivisection; the result was polarizing controversy. These were also the years after the Civil War, when the United States was shifting from its agrarian roots to an industrial base, and the keeping of pets had begun to acquire a new meaning. Following the founding of the American Society for the Prevention of Cruelty to Animals in 1866, the American Anti-Vivisection Society was formed in 1883, and the New England Anti-Vivisection Society in 1895. Those opposed to animal experimentation gained an ally in the powerful newspaper publisher William Randolph Hearst. As well, anti-vivisectionists happened on a strategy that drew public attention and support by focusing on dogs as the subject of experimental research.

Americans, however, weren't the first to create such organizations, or to advocate the humane treatment of animals. The original Society for the Prevention of Cruelty to Animals was founded in Liverpool in 1833. Seven decades later, in 1911, playwright George Bernard Shaw took up the torch in his preface to *The Doctor's Dilemma*, his dramatic critique of the medical profession. Never one to mince words, he had this to say about vivisection: "From Shakespeare and Dr. Johnson to Ruskin and Mark Twain, the natural abhorrence of sane mankind for the vivisector's cruelty, and the contempt of able thinkers for his imbecile casuistry, have been expressed by the most popular spokesmen of humanity.... Not one doctor in a thousand is a vivisector, or has any interest in vivisection, either pecuniary or intellectual, or would treat his dog cruelly or allow anyone else to do it." Shaw goes on to dismiss the standard arguments in favour of vivisection – the pursuit of knowledge and its benefits – by reminding readers that if a scientist asked to torture a dog, "even those who say 'You may torture *a* dog' never say 'You may torture *my* dog.'"

Once dogs took on a central role in the controversy – a role they still play today – key issues ranged from the use of dogs from animal shelters and pounds in medical laboratories to the kidnapping of family pets for use as research subjects. Hearst popularized such stories in his newspapers and supported the anti-vivisection position with strong editorials. While dognapping wasn't as common as some feared, it wasn't entirely an urban myth either. Universities with medical schools have long been among the most prominent markets for animal subjects. In a study of twentieth-century biomedical research, Susan E. Lederer noted that in 1921 the Humane Society acquired a St. Louis animal shelter and refused to turn over stray dogs to the local medical schools. The dean of the Washington University School of Medicine challenged the legality of the decision and fought in public hearings for "the uninterrupted supply of pound dogs." In time, a law was passed ordering the shelter to sell the dogs to the medical schools for seventy-five cents apiece. Almost a century ago, yes, but experimentation is still a thriving matter. Eventually the Animal Welfare Act (AWA) was passed in 1966, an important piece of legislation addressing, in part, the use of animals in research and industry. It did not, however, outlaw vivisection.

If you happen to have an old encyclopedia nearby, look up the entry on vivisection. In the years following the Second World War, young North American parents were often persuaded to purchase home reference libraries as an aid to the education of their baby-boomer children, a moment in time now eclipsed by the Internet. I read the "Vivisection" entry in the 1949 edition of *The Encyclopedia Americana* and was struck by how sympathetic it was to the vivisectionist position. In fact, the anti-vivisection movement received two dismissive sentences in the vivisection entry; there were no entries on either the anti-vivisection movement or the prominent societies founded in the previous century. ("It is alleged that animal experimenters practice much needless cruelty, but even apart from this, some have taken the extreme view that any experiments on living animals, with the object of advancing medical and surgical knowledge, are, on moral grounds, unjustifiable.") Hearst did receive an entry that summarized his newspaper and magazine empire, noted accusations of yellow journalism and remarked on his luxurious ranch in San Simeon, California, but the entry bypassed his anti-vivisection editorial policy. However, this old encyclopedia may help explain the assumptions behind the Research Dog Hero Award of 1946. By the middle of the last century, dogs were part of the North American family, and the medical research establishment knew this and understood its grave implications.

ASTROLOGY

Every twelve years, anyone born in the Year of the Dog will see their lunar year in the ascendant according to the Chinese system of astrology. (Dog birth years include 2006, 1994, 1982, 1970, 1958, 1946, 1934, 1922, 1910, etc.) The other eleven figures in the cyclical zodiac are the boar, rat, ox, tiger, rabbit, dragon, snake, horse, sheep, monkey, and rooster, in that order, which makes dogs the only fully domesticated creature on the list, since tigers can't fairly represent the cat family (dogs, despite their wolf ancestry, are a separate species).

Dog people are thought to be faithful, loyal, honest, and reliable, qualities we certainly expect of our dogs. On the flip side, they can also be stubborn, moody, eccentric, and fretful. Yet, during the last celebration of the dog's lunar year (2006), Chinese officials were expecting a baby boom because a child born in the Year of the Dog would be so admired that many couples planned to have a child during that time. Although the Chinese historical ambivalence about dogs still allows for dog farming, and pet ownership is a relatively recent phenomenon in both mainland China and Taiwan, globalization may be changing old customs. Many North American Chinatowns have learned to celebrate the New Year holiday while marketing it, too, with doggy mementos to preserve the occasion. As acquisitive as the next guy, after a dim-sum lunch I bought a small metal pendant stamped with a dog that appears to be scratching itself. Astrological forecasters warned me to avoid sharp objects, watch out for my gallbladder, and not to start a new business or gamble or speculate.

Not unlike the Western zodiac, which has Eastern roots, the Chinese zodiac is a blend of folklore and folk religion with tradition, superstition, and even philosophy. Based on the lunar cycle (unlike the Western solar system), Chinese astrology follows a larger, sixty-year cycle. This means that the appearance of an animal every twelfth year will have a special significance. The animals are more than sentimental images; they represent a commentary on the nature of the universe and the yin (feminine) and yang (masculine) forces of all life. The assumption is that astrology can show an individual how to balance the ebb and flow of his or her own yin and yang, because an individual life reflects the cycle of the natural world. Astrology, it's worth remembering, embodies an agrarian, pre-industrial view of the world. As well, the five elements of the Chinese system – wood, fire, earth, metal, and water – are also linked to different animals. Earth is associated with the dog, ox, dragon, and ram; the dog's other associations include the colour yellow, sweet-tasting food, and the emotion of desire. More interesting is the fact that the dog takes five different forms within the sixty-year cycle, which come around in the following order: dog on guard (1934, 1994); sleepy dog (1946, 2006); dog going onto the mountain (1958, 2018); temple dog (1910, 1970); and family dog (1922, 1982), with different meanings, or variations on the dog theme, for each of the dogs in ascent. Of course the system is more elaborate than my sketch of it, but as a sleepy dog, I'm supposed to like cashew nuts, and that, at least, is true.

BEDS

Where should the dog sleep? Pet shops display a variety of beds in various price ranges and materials, and catalogues such as L.L. Bean's offer attractive mail-order choices. Stuffed with polyfoam or "high-loft polyfil," and covered with washable cotton or fleece or polyester blends, these cushions are designed with an array of patterns, from stripes to faux leopard.

Canine luxury is a big business, although it's actually a niche business of human luxury, since most dogs prefer to jump up onto your bed, and, if unwelcome, are content to sleep just about anywhere warm.

Perhaps our dogs carry an ancient memory in their DNA, since it appears that in their evolution from wild wolves to domesticated ones and then into proto-dogs, they shared sleeping areas with early humans, warning them of predators and even curling up for warmth. Anthropologists have long noted this old sleeping practice, and it wasn't only the dogs who wanted to keep warm. Without central heating – in fact, without dwellings – humans faced the harsh climates of plains or forests or deserts, with bitter nights. Is a sleeping memory also coded in human DNA? Anyone with children knows that they have to be taught to keep the dog off the bed. But it is not only children who call the dog up to their side. Vilmos Csányi, chair of the department of ethology at the leading university in Budapest, noted that in an informal study, fifty percent of the people questioned admitted that their dog slept on the bed, although they often seemed embarrassed by it. People today, of course, don't need dogs at their side to keep them warm. But the close association continues, and has evolved into a change in the status of domestic dogs. In a 2006 Pew Research Center poll of dog and cat owners, 80 per cent of all men and 89 per cent of all women said that they regarded their dogs as family members.

In one of the classic dog stories, Eleanor Atkinson's *Greyfriars Bobby* (first published in 1912, and based on a Scottish legend), the Skye terrier, Bobby, whose love is "unpurchaseable," has bonded deeply with a elderly shepherd, Auld Jock, now living in Edinburgh, and ill with age and years of hardship. In an early scene, Auld Jock collapses in a rainy cul-de-sac, and Bobby draws close to him: "Therefore, when Auld Jock lay down again and sank, almost at once, into sodden sleep, Bobby snuggled into the hollow of his master's arm and nuzzled his nose in his master's neck." Several pages later Bobby accompanies Auld Jock to the nasty, dank room he calls home, where animals are forbidden. Out of fear for his pet, Jock scolds the dog for barking, then recites the Twenty-third Psalm and "stooped and lifted Bobby into the bed. Humble, and eager to be forgiven for an offence he could not understand, the loving little creature leaped into Auld Jock's arms and lavished frantic endearments upon him. Lying so together in the dark, man and dog fell into a sleep that was broken by Auld Jock's fitful coughing..." Jock dies, of course, in a heart-tugging scene that runs for several pages, offering his loyal dog one last bun "between strangled breaths: 'Puir – Bobby! Gang – awa' – hame – laddie!'" and after taking one last look at his master, Bobby "stretched himself upon the hearthstone below the bed." This scene, straight out of Victorian melodrama, may not appeal to readers with a taste for postmodern style, yet dogs, by their very nature, are timeless, and refuse to follow fashion or be modern, let alone postmodern. Bobby, naturally – even inevitably – sleeps beside Auld Jock.

My own nightly routine usually includes reading in bed for an hour or so before I turn out the lights. Some nights, if I chose to read in the living room instead, Zoli would go off to bed by himself. In fifteen minutes he'd return, stand in the doorway and stare patiently. If I kept reading, he would return to bed, only to come back in another five minutes. He may simply have been bothered by the variation in our regular pattern, but he couldn't rest comfortably until I joined him, and I saw a more persistent expression in his eyes. After his second or third visit I usually got the message – we had trained each other well. When Zoli died, I hated reading alone in bed, and stayed in my favourite chair. Rennie, my new dog, also sleeps on the bed, but if he decides it's time to go into the bedroom by himself, he curls up and stays put even if I'm not there. I tell this story (and also Atkinson's) because an interview in the *New York Times Magazine* made me think about beds and ownership. Cesar Millan, who advertises himself as a dog trainer to the stars, has his own television show and bestselling training guide. When asked if he thought it was appropriate for a dog to sleep on the bed with its owner, he replied: "Yes, because a dog pack sleeps together. But the thing is, you have to invite the dog into your bed." His reply misses an important point – if the dog sleeps on the bed, isn't it also his bed? Where else would he go for a nap when left alone in the house? What place of rest belongs to him? Like many trainers, Millan sees the dog as something in need of "control," a word he uses frequently. I'm not suggesting that a pet dog should be left completely to its own desires, but surely a dog's sleeping arrangements reflect something more than its pack-animal, genetic heritage.

Some reservations about letting the dog on the bed may come from a fear of dirt or germs, yet in the winter of 2003, when my mother spent several weeks in a hospital run by the esteemed Cleveland Clinic, Zoli was allowed to visit her with me and sleep beside her on the bed. That winter he had cancer, and had already survived several surgeries and chemotherapy treatments, but when I informed the nursing staff of his condition – to protect everyone – they spoke with their superiors who did not object to his visits. No,

I think the problem is not about dirt. Beds are associated not only with rest and sleep but with sex, and this connection makes some people uncomfortable. One summer, while staying in Ogunquit, Maine, with Zoli, I ordered breakfast from a waiter, a man in his sixties, who said that he'd seen my pug the day before. He went on to explain that he had an elderly dog with arthritis who was now unable to jump up to the bed, where she had always slept beside him. "She's the best sleeping companion I've ever had," he said, suddenly smiling self-consciously, as if he'd revealed too much. But I knew he hadn't, and told him about a catalogue offering steps that older pets can use to climb onto furniture.

Close to the experience of most people, I believe, is a scene from John Steinbeck's *Travels with Charley (in Search of America)*. At one point during his road trip in the 1960s, a tired Steinbeck imagines a conversation with his restless poodle, and, looking at the dog, who slowly wags his tail in reply, Steinbeck finally says, "Come in up on the bed, Charley. Let's be miserable together." Consolation is the key to understanding this scene, for man and dog alike. I suspect that the vast majority of people who allow a dog to sleep on the bed are, like our prehistoric forebears, simply enjoying a night of peaceful canine company after the work of the day.

BOOKS

North America is awash with best-of lists, from the American Film Institute's Hundred Best Movies to Reader's Choice pages in alternative newspapers across the continent. In this spirit, I'm going to offer my own list of the twenty-five essential dog books. While lists of this kind are inevitably subjective, and, of course, have omissions, that's part of their appeal – they can begin debate. And

I'm glad to add that two of the titles were published as I completed mine, which proves that there is no last word about dogs.

First, some background thoughts. Like many bookish dog owners, I'd read several breed books and also a number of training manuals before deciding on a pug. Watching a dog grow out of puppyhood made me curious about dog development in general, and so I read and read. This all took place during a time of change in my own life. After fifteen years as an editor, I left the publishing world to teach and to write my own books. This career change coincided with a sharp decline in my father's health. In order to help take care of him, I travelled frequently between Toronto and Cleveland, with Zoli always at my side. After my father's death, my mother gradually slipped from bereavement into old-age dementia, and I had to keep her safe and comfortable while looking for a good assisted-living home. Meanwhile, I was also travelling to promote my books, with a schedule that meant I always had a packed suitcase ready for departure. Throughout this time Zoli was more than a companion; he became my portable home. In order to understand him better – at least initially – I read the classic dog books as well as newly published titles. Through all my reading I felt there was more to be said. Writers who are dog owners, like writers who are gardeners or hobbyists of any sort, want to place their own experience in the context of everything that has been written about their passion. This means that a writer's book about dogs is likely to be more idiosyncratic than a professional's in the field. Non-specialist writers can afford to share their likes and dislikes, to go out on a limb, and they have sometimes even directed me to other books.

The books listed here have been chosen for a variety of reasons. They teach and they entertain, but they do much more than that – they tell stories worth hearing; they're books I've returned to, books I've given as gifts, books with passages that make me phone a friend who might enjoy hearing them. Some books on the list are acknowledged classics, while others are less well-known, but there is an absence of the glib, humorous books that publishers regularly pump out. (The exigencies of the publishing industry mean that the dog books most widely promoted tend to be the mostly easily promoted, even if they're mediocre.) If my list has a literary bias, so be it. Most bookstores gather dog titles together in one section, but when faced with shelves of titles, where to begin? If there's a specific need, that's a partial answer. Choosing a breed, for example, can be helped by any number of breed books as long as you remember that the book exists both to sell the breed and itself. I haven't included any of them here because they're easily available, and most people find what they need in them by scanning their pages in a library or bookstore aisle. The twenty-five books I've chosen are for reading, not quick consultation. On various occasions I've tried to prune the list back to ten titles, or twelve, or to a baker's dozen, but after reading hundreds and hundreds of books about dogs, I wouldn't want to be without any of these. In alphabetical order by author, they are:

Ackerley, J. R., *My Dog Tulip*
Atkinson, Eleanor, *Greyfriar's Bobby*
Bakis, Kirsten, *Lives of the Monster Dogs*
Bonaparte, Marie, *Topsy: The Story of a Golden-Haired Chow*
Burnford, Sheila, *The Incredible Journey*
Coppinger, Raymond, and Lorna Coppinger, *Dogs: A Startling New Understanding of Canine Origin, Behavior & Evolution*
Coren, Stanley, *How Dogs Think*
Csányi, Vilmos, *If Dogs Could Talk: Exploring the Canine Mind*
de la Roche, Mazo, *Portrait of a Dog*
Derr, Mark, *Dog's Best Friend: Annals of the Dog-Human Relationship*
Déry, Tibor, *Niki: The Story of a Dog*
Dutourd, Jean, *A Dog's Head*

Grenier, Roger, *The Difficulty of Being a Dog*
Hornung, Eva, *Dog Boy*
Horowitz, Alexandra, *Inside of a Dog: What Dogs See, Smell,
    and Know*
Knight, Eric, *Lassie Come-Home*
London, Jack, *The Call of the Wild*
Lorenz, Konrad, *Man Meets Dog*
Mann, Thomas, *Bashan and I*
Marshall Thomas, Elizabeth, *The Hidden Life of Dogs*
Masson, Jeffrey Moussaieff, *Dogs Never Lie About Love:
    Reflections on the Emotional World of Dogs*
O'Hagan, Andrew, *The Life and Opinions of Maf the Dog and
    of his friend Marilyn Monroe*
Terhune, Albert Payson, *Lad: A Dog*
Woolf, Virginia, *Flush*
von Arnim, Elizabeth, *All the Dogs of My Life*

I'll have much more to say about these titles, and numerous others, in the course of this book, but for now, anyone who sets out with this list in hand has great reading ahead.

BREEDS

Dog breeds, like so many things, are subject to fashion. Boston terriers were popular in the 1920s, wirehaired fox terriers in the 1930s, cocker spaniels in the 1950s, soft-coated wheaten terriers in the 1980s, Labrador retrievers in the 1990s. A movie or television show can create a demand overnight. *Lassie* once popularized collies and *Frasier* was a similar boon to breeders of Jack Russells, just as pugs became hot after one appeared as a talking creature from outer space in *Men in Black* (1997). I well remember that swing in fashion because Zoli came into my life in 1995, when pug sightings were rare.

Right now the fashion is for bigger breeds. The problem is that most people can't or won't manage them. Several years ago a friend and I visited an animal shelter in Charlotte County, Florida, where the young manager explained that they had a serious problem common to dog pounds across the country: the small dogs were the first to be adopted, and next the mid-sized. Meanwhile, people kept acquiring larger dogs and then dropping them off like discarded clothing because they were too much work or trouble. The situation takes an especially nasty turn when university students acquire a large dog during the school year but, once summer vacation arrives, dump the pet in a shelter if it's lucky, or too often abandon it along some highway. A dog of any breed is, first of all, an animal. It has needs that are immediate and essential. Breed books offer glossy pictures, and televised dog shows like the Westminster Dog Show, sponsored by the American Kennel Club, or the Eukanuba Dog Show, present coiffed creatures at their most becoming – but don't be taken in. Dogs are work if they're looked after with any care. As well, the nature of the dog – its genetic background, its special features – in the sense what it's been bred for, should be a matter of consideration to any prospective owner.

At the end of his excellent book about collies, *Eminent Dogs, Dangerous Men: Searching through Scotland for a Border Collie*, Donald McCaig, a sheep farmer in Virginia, included "A Note to the Reader" that I want to quote: "If this has persuaded you to buy a Border Collie for a pet, I have done you and your dog a disservice. If you don't have work for a Border Collie, or time to train it properly, your bright young Border Collie will invent his own work, and chances are you won't like it. There are dozens of dog breeds bred to be good pets. If a pet is what you seek, you should choose among them." This is more than sensible advice; it shows McCaig's love of dogs, and not just his own. Anyone who still dreams of a border collie in a city or suburban backyard need only turn to chapter five of Thomas Hardy's Victorian novel *Far from the Madding Crowd*, where an unsupervised collie runs wild and leads a flock of two hundred sheep, many of them pregnant, over a precipice to their death. Although the distracted shepherd has lost his livelihood, "The dog came up, licked his hand, and made signs implying that he expected some great reward for signal services rendered." I rest my case.

But we are bombarded with subtle and not-so-subtle messages about the desirability of large dogs all the time. The jacket cover of Cesar Millan's popular *Cesar's Way* is a good example. In the book, Millan explains that the dog who serves as the family dog in his life, the dog he frequently takes home from his Dog Psychology Center in Los Angeles, is a French bulldog named Scarlett – one of the smaller breeds. Scarlett, however, isn't included in the cover photograph. Instead, Millan smiles at the camera with four large-breed dogs: a Weimaraner, a German shepherd, a pitbull, and a yellow Lab. Big dogs are butch, they're macho, they prove something. I'm not suggesting that everyone should run off to buy a teacup poodle, but the choice of a breed isn't only a matter of common sense, it has a moral dimension to it. If you can't give the dog what it needs, leave it alone.

We tend to think of dog breeds as permanent and immutable, overlooking the role humans have played in shaping them. Many of the standards for the most popular breeds as we know them weren't set until the late nineteenth century, the time of Darwinism and the founding of the British Kennel Club in 1873. I want to mention two examples to illustrate the importance of single individuals to breed standards and preservation. Cavalier King Charles spaniels have been around since the Stuart courts in seventeenth-century England, when Charles II's name was associated with the floppy-eared, gentle-eyed spaniels. With their silky, chiffon-like coats, Cavaliers are particularly beautiful dogs, and in my experience people usually assume that any Cavalier is a female, especially when one tosses its head in a gesture worthy of Garbo. These short-nosed toy dogs lost their popular royal status to the pugs of the court of William IV, although the red-and-white Blenheims continued to hold the affection of the Dukes of Marlborough. In the years I spent with Morgan and Zoli, people who knew British history – and dogs – often remarked about my companions, and I would explain that I really wasn't a diehard monarchist; I just liked these two breeds.

By the start of the twentieth century, a flat-faced toy spaniel, known as the King Charles spaniel, dominated, while the short-nosed Cavalier had all but vanished. In 1926, a self-made American millionaire, Roswell Eldridge, of Long Island, New York, went to England in search of the older Cavaliers and advertised for a breeding pair of "Blenheim spaniels of the Old Type" at the Crufts Dog Show, even offering a prize for them. Eldridge never found his dream dogs, the elegant spaniels he admired from European paintings, but his advertisement caused a British dog breeder, Amice Pitt, to accept the challenge; she won Eldridge's prize a year later. Clubs were soon devoted to the "old type" of spaniel and by 1929 the breed standard was acknowledged by the Kennel Club. But it took several decades before additional breeders were producing dogs that met the standard, and it wasn't until 1952 that the first imported Cavaliers arrived in the United States. So the Cavaliers you spot walking on the street – and their owners and admirers – owe a debt to Eldridge and Pitt. Most Cavalier breed books tell some of this story, as if to assure prospective buyers that the breed has a patrician lineage.

Such breed dedication is not only a Western phenomenon. In Japan, one man – Morie Sawataishi – was almost single-handedly responsible for preserving the Akita from extinction. His story is a fascinating one, with a similarity to Eldridge's in that notions of social class may have had a role in each man's fascination with his favoured breed. The Akita is an ancient dog, indigenous to Japan and associated with the samurai-warrior tradition. The breed was well known because of the unusual behaviour of a loyal Akita named Hachi-ko, who belonged to a professor at Tokyo University. After its owner died in 1924, the dog returned daily for nine years to the train station and waited to greet his master as commuters got off the afternoon train. Eventually postcards of Hachi-ko were sold and a bronze statue of the dog was placed where Hachi-ko had stood in wait. A propaganda song was even written for children, teaching them, by implication, the importance of loyalty to the emperor. Nearer than many other breeds to their wolf ancestry, Akitas can be difficult to handle and are known for intense loyalty. Helen Keller owned and loved one, as did Nicole Simpson – in fact, it was her pet Akita's barking that eventually drew a neighbour to discover her murdered body, which led to the infamous trial of her ex-husband O. J. Simpson.

During the Second World War, the survival of the Akita breed was threatened when severe poverty made pet-keeping unacceptable in Japan. Akitas were not considered stylish: the most admired breeds in 1920s and 1930s Japan had been the German shepherd and the dachshund, which reflected the esteem then held by the upper classes and intelligentsia for all things German. Many Akitas were slaughtered for food or for their coats, which were used to line soldiers' jackets. At this unlikely moment, Morie Sawataishi – not a dog lover – took pity on the breed and stubbornly acquired one, his first dog. In time, as Martha Sherrill relates in *Dog Man*, he restored the Akita to a place of prominence in Japanese culture while also founding a line of superior dogs. Living in northern Japan, in a region known as snow country, Sawataishi was the kind of eccentric who rejected modernity for artisanal tradition, and his life as an engineer in an out-of-the-way corner of the world allowed him to pursue his fancy. Like Eldridge and Pitt before him, he gave his energies to a specific breed, and its persistence can be regarded as his legacy.

One might hope that all breeders care about the future homes of their dogs, and many do. When I arranged to buy Zoli from Noreen Talbot, a well-regarded breeder in Thunder Bay, Ontario, I'd researched pug breeders, and Noreen was known for healthy, good-tempered dogs. In one of the many long-distance phone chats we had, I mentioned that the dog would be regularly accompanying me to campus and on frequent road trips. "Do you have air conditioning?" she asked. I didn't, then, and she said she wouldn't sell a pug to someone whose car lacked it; it wouldn't suit a flat-faced (or brachycephalic) animal. Since I planned to get a new car that summer, I moved the date forward several months and we had an agreement. That's the kind of breeder to trust, someone who knows how and when to say no. And someone you can call over the years if problems crop up, or if you simply want to talk about your dog to a person who should be curious about his or her progress.

I was lucky to find another good breeder after Zoli died. In those unhappy months I was of two minds about getting another dog, but I knew that the time was right from a practical point of view – I had the long summer ahead to train a new puppy. Several friends and my vet urged me to consider another breed – they were concerned that another pug would suffer in comparison, a risk that dog books also raised. I considered a Boston terrier, but they're prone to mast-cell tumours (the kind of cancer Zoli had died of); then French bulldogs, Tibetan spaniels, even Cavalier King Charles spaniels, but their potential heart problems gave me pause. I'll say more about my search later, in "Second Dogs," but I soon admitted that any new dog had to be a pug. Today, even when I make the occasional slip and call Rennie by Zoli's name, I know the difference.

This reminds me of a story told by my friend Teresa Stratas when we were discussing names for our new dogs. Pip was my initial choice for Rennie, although training books suggest using a two-syllable name, with different vowels in each syllable, to catch the dog's attention easily. But Pip had a bright edge to it that I liked. Teresa said that Rudolf Bing, the former general manager of New York City's Metropolitan Opera, had always named his dogs Pip, and all of them were dachshunds – one after the other. One day Teresa asked if he didn't confuse the dogs with each other, but Bing insisted he could easily tell them apart, though Teresa thought they were all pretty similar. If you love a dog and have happy associations with its breed, the differences are as clear as day from night.

CHILDHOOD DOGS
AND CHILDREN'S DOG BOOKS

The year 1866 saw the founding of the American Society for the Prevention of Cruelty to Animals, and nine years later, in 1875, the American Society for the Prevention of Cruelty to Children was founded – dogs, in a very real sense, came first. Since then, children and dogs have been linked together as inevitably as Timmy and his collie Lassie, Eloise and her pug Weenie, and Dick and Jane and their terrier Spot. But before saying more about this historical association, I want to join the story myself. "A boy needs a dog" – that was what Uncle Jules and Aunt Rudie said when, sometime around my sixth birthday, they gave me a black-and-white, smooth-haired fox terrier. Of course I named him Spotty, with a child's literalness. Jules, an engineer, was in charge of building a new reservoir, and one of the men working for him bred fox terriers and had a recent litter. Spotty wasn't the first dog in my life, but he is the one I remember best, the dog who started me out on dog love.

My mother's family had always had Boston terriers, a classic

American dog of the 1920s and 1930s that has recently returned to the list of fashionable dogs of the day. Except for one Boston called Princey, the others were all named Buster. Buster (1), as I think of him, was my grandmother's dog, a runt she'd raised from puppyhood. My grandparents lived in the suite above us, in a duplex near Shaker Square and the old Hungarian neighbourhood. When I was brought home from the nearby hospital – my grandmother's first grandchild – a crisis ensued, though I had no knowledge of causing it. Nine-year-old Buster was jealous. He didn't bite, he sulked. As family legend goes, the dog found me tolerable when I was kept downstairs, but when Grandma took me up to her suite and I trespassed on Buster's territory, he'd had enough. One day he simply left home – walked out of the yard onto East Boulevard and vanished. My family searched the neighbourhood for weeks, hoping for a sight of him and wondering if an unknown motorist had spotted the missing dog and adopted him. My life, therefore, began with a blot on it: my existence caused such stress to a loving animal that it ran away from a good home. Ethologists might say that I'd violated his sense of rank order. I have several old black-and-white pictures of him, from around 1940, with my mother and her sister taking him for a walk in one of the city's parks. No one ever heard of Buster again. This story has always troubled me, so I'm paying a small debt to that poor dog by telling it here, the only thing I can do.

Sandy came next, a boxer puppy that my father brought home. Sandy didn't last long, but his exit wasn't painful. Our large backyard had half a dozen fruit trees, including several generous peach trees that dropped some of their fruit on the lawn. Sandy had a taste for peaches but was allergic to them; the vet's bills mounted. One day, after taking the ill dog to the doctor in a taxi, my mother told my father that he had to choose: either the dog went or she would. He soon found Sandy a home in the country with a family from his workplace. And then Spotty arrived, a dog who liked to sit under the dining-room table when we'd put up the tracks for the Lionel train set and watch its cars circling about him, who tolerated my sister dressing him up in her doll clothes, who crowed like a rooster when he'd been left alone for the day and someone finally came home – a keen watchdog and ideal family pet, with a way of making each of us feel like his favourite.

We're often told that children and dogs have a natural affinity. As long as a child is introduced to a dog in a safe setting, a bond of value to both might grow between them. I'm often surprised by the young parents who allow their small children to run up to an unfamiliar dog on the street, hands outstretched. I'm careful at that point to keep any dog I'm walking on a short leash, and I even bend down to caution the child that sticking one's hand in a dog's face isn't the best way to get acquainted. In fact, I'm addressing the parents.

The association of dogs and childhood is not only a North American phenomena, and I don't want to leave that impression. During the Russian Revolution, when the Tsar and his family were imprisoned in Siberia, the childrens' dogs accompanied them, even to the moment of execution on July 17, 1918, and to subsequent burial. As Frances Welch recounted in *A Romanov Fantasy*, the young Tsarevich Alexis's male dog Joy survived the shootings and was rescued from the murder site by Mikhail Letemen, a seventeen-year-old Bolshevik who took the pet home with him. Spotted there by a White army officer, he was retrieved by pro-Tsarist sympathizers, Letemen was executed, and Joy was "dispatched to England to pass his twilight years with a distinguished Russian family in Windsor." It's amazing to think that Western political leaders had not been able to rescue Russia's Imperial family but people somehow managed to save one of their dogs. In a lighter vein, when the Belgian writer Georges Remi created his popular comic-book hero Tintin (under his pseudonym Hergé – the French pronunciation of the initials R.G.)

he naturally gave the boy a canine companion – Snowy, a small, white mutt – who accompanied him on his global adventures. The twenty-three books in the series, many in translation, have delighted children and adults alike, and have even resulted in a cottage industry referred to as "Tintinologists." I've always liked the cartoon frames that include Snowy; without him, Tintin seems too hyper for me.

One of the lessons dogs can teach – the parallel child/dog need for connection and refuge – was powerfully caught in a photograph taken by Ettore Malanca of some Romanian lost boys, as they were called, the children who lived in Bucharest's streets after the fall of Nicolae Ceausescu's corrupt government. Many of them suffered from AIDS, and it was believed that 85 per cent of the street children were boys. They made space for themselves in sewers, train terminals, and rail yards, and managed to survive in a horrific state of brutality, nothing like J.M. Barrie's *Peter Pan* fantasy of boys adventuring alone, and the Darlings' doggy nanny Nana, a Newfoundland.

These photographs, published in 1998, include a poignant yet disturbing night image of several boys huddled together on baggage carts behind the North Station, a mangy white dog curled up with them, his paw resting on one child's running shoes. Dog and boys are lost in sleep space, and we can only wonder what they dream of as their bodies give each other warmth. The single full face in the photograph belongs to the dog (one boy does appear in shadowy profile) and the dog, who looks like it needs a bath and good brushing, adds a special note of rebuke to the image – you wouldn't, it seems to ask, allow even a dog to live like this?

All dog lovers remember their childhood dogs, and family stories like mine go with the territory. As adults, some people seek out the same breed, some are content to enjoy fond memories, and others write books about their dogs. We're all, in a sense, children

Homeless boys and their dog, from Ettore Malanca's photographic series *The Romanian Lost Boys*. This image originally appeared in the *New York Times Magazine* on May 10, 1998.

of the Romantic era – we feel nostalgia for an "innocent" past and cultivate our memories. No longer living a communal agrarian life, we're cut off from each other in cities or suburbs. This is the social phenomena caused by the Industrial Revolution, which replaced the natural cycle of seasonal time with the clock-time of the urban work world. Childhood as we think of it was a creation of the nineteenth century. A child was no longer another pair of hands to help out on the farm, but a special creature, young and innocent (until Freud). In time, laws were passed regulating child labour and education; books were created to capitalize on a new market; and children emerged as a force to be reckoned with – to be trained, subdued, socialized. Animals could help. In the long flow of human history, the special bond between children and dogs is relatively new.

The Industrial Revolution changed more than the daily realities of work. Culture changed with it. In Europe, folklorists like the Grimm brothers collected the old stories that we now call fairy tales, and their compilations became part of the new book publishing for children. Many of these tales involved animals, and not always domestic ones. Early collections of animal fables by Aesop or La Fontaine were considered good teaching tools, as were later story collections by Rudyard Kipling and Ernest Thompson Seton, because animals can stand in for humans in situations with moral implications. As a result of their dependent position, children, like dogs, naturally exaggerate an adult's power; by contrast, adults can underestimate the stresses of childhood, those years imperfectly remembered. While a dog might have gotten in Tom Sawyer's way, and the March sisters didn't need a dog to help them become women, adventure stories such as Jack London's *The Call of the Wild* and Eleanor Atkinson's *Greyfriars Bobby* showed the opposite. (Louisa May Alcott did include a dog character in *Under the Lilacs*, a white standard poodle named Sancho who accompanies the boy hero on his adventures after they escape their hard life in a travelling circus.) During Alice's initial adventures in Wonderland, Lewis Carroll's heroine eats a piece of cake that causes her body to shrink. Soon she meets an enormous puppy and, stick in hand, plays with him for a while. But she continues on in her wanderings alone, though with some regret – "I should have liked teaching it tricks very much, if – if I'd only been the right size to do it." Dog-less classics like Francis Hodgson Burnett's *The Secret Garden* are often about neglected, homeless children, and dogs – who need a home and care – would interfere with the story line. The exception is Sandy in Harold Gray's Depression-era comic strip *Little Orphan Annie*. An attentive dog, Sandy listens to Annie's plans and woes with intense concern and the occasional "Arf." The comic-strip form, looser than the conventions of a novel, gave Gray an enviable freedom.

By the early years of the twentieth century, publishers had successfully targeted the new market with titles of varying quality, producing only a few classics still read today. But I want to admit that as a child-reader I was never drawn to animal stories, which struck me as too obviously preachy, a Sunday-school lesson in another form. Dogs in books, unlike the dogs in my life, were always teaching a lesson. They were so noble, so didactic, so insufferably right. I had yet to understand the genuine lessons to be learned by living with a dog.

There are, however, a few exceptions, and I was glad to discover them as an adult. The best are by Albert Payson Terhune (1872– 1942), who was also a breeder of collies in Wayne, New Jersey (his kennels are now open to the public at the Terhune-Sunnybank Park). Many of Terhune's novels, which are often made up of linked stories, first saw serial publication in magazines such as the *Saturday Evening Post* and the *Ladies' Home Journal*, alongside stories by F. Scott Fitzgerald. Yet does anyone but an oddball read him today? I've mentioned Terhune to readers of all ages but only those well over fifty remembered tattered copies of his books from their childhood. (In her memoir, *1185 Park Avenue*, novelist Anne Roiphe recalls reading Terhune's novels in the 1940s and her disappointment when her parents finally bought her a dog – not one of Terhune's elegant collies but a small dachshund.) Educated at Columbia University, Terhune became a freelance writer and produced eighteen books (including one co-written with Sinclair Lewis) before he turned to dogs. His first collie title, *Lad: A Dog* (1919), is still his best remembered, and it surely influenced Eric Knight's *Lassie Come-Home* (1940). Like all of Terhune's collie books, *Lad* is fast-paced, heart-tugging and honest. Most remarkably, it tells the story of an actual dog from his point of view, often juxtaposing the reasons for human actions with the dog's interpretation of them. We see Lad's world through his eyes, and just as Terhune's human characters do, we come to understand something of canine logic. Terhune probably didn't want to keep repeating himself, although he wrote more than a dozen collie novels, varying the setting from the American east coast to Scotland (*A Highland Collie* is the best of these), perhaps

Jacket cover for the novel *His Dog* by Albert Payson Terhune (1922), artist unknown.

to keep his public – and himself – interested.

One of Terhune's few books that isn't a collie saga, *A Dog Named Chips* (1931), tells the story of a mixed-breed scrapper.

Devoted to his "own-your-own-soulism," Chips runs away from his humble river-shack origins in search of the good life and along the way lives with a variety of Dickensian eccentrics, from a social-climbing nouveau-riche family to a multi-millionaire and her household in a Philadelphia mansion. The book is a lively social satire with, for its day, some genuine surprises, including a cross-dressing maid who is actually a male jewel thief in disguise. Often spoiled but always tolerant of those who appreciate him, Chips has little in common with the noble dogs that would make a saint pause. If there's moralizing here, it's balanced by a disavowal of sentimental pieties (as the old butler Jerram says, "There's all sorts of lies – all manner of lies, miss – floating around this world. And the silliest of those lies is about dogs. But of all the crazy lies ever told about dogs, the craziest is the lie about their knowing good folks from bad folks, and that you can trust a man a dog takes to.").

There are only a few other books like Terhune's that an adult can read without cringing or to recapture that child-like pleasure of being taken care of by a book. Children sometimes adopt books written for adults, like Farley Mowat's *The Dog Who Wouldn't Be*. A memoir of growing up outside Saskatoon in the 1930s with Mutt, the family dog, as well as several pet owls, this dry-eyed evocation of childhood deserves to regain its original adult audience. Sheila Burnford's *The Incredible Journey* (1961) is another book that lacks the sentimental or didactic edge which spoils too many books for children. For a generation of readers following mine, the classics may be Fred Gipson's *Old Yeller* (1956), Wilson Rawls's *Where the Red Fern Grows* (1961), and William Howard Armstrong's *Sounder* (1969). These titles, however, are on the way to becoming historical curiosities. During a talk with Jane Kessler of Appletree Books in Cleveland Heights – one of those vanishing independent booksellers – she said that for the last twenty years or so there have been only a few orders for what are now called "middle-grade books" about dogs, though occasionally someone requests

The Incredible Journey. Horse classics like Anna Sewell's *Black Beauty* still sell, but dogs are out of fashion except in picture books for pre-readers, and even in this market they're less popular than dragons. Several children's librarians have confirmed Kessler's remarks. When borrowers look for *Sounder*, it's usually on a class list of required reading. A few "recent" classics may have emerged, with Gordon Korman's *No More Dead Dogs* (2000) the main contender. Korman's book features a sarcastic middle-school hero who hates dog books "because the dog always dies. Go to the library and pick out a book with an award sticker and a dog on the cover. Trust me, the dog is going down." This sitcom-like creation emphasizes a school play performed on rollerblades and movie stars like Julia Roberts rather than dogs. If it counts as a classic, we've come to the end of a tradition. On the other hand, Kessler was glad to say that dog books for adults "sell like mad." I suspect this has less to do with a devotion to dogs than to a desire to escape the demands of daily life, which reading about dogs can offer.

When I asked my recent university students if they'd read any of these books, I was met with blank stares; some feel nostalgia for Harry Potter. The reputed best-selling children's book of all time was published in 1942 by Little Golden Books: *The Poky Little Puppy* by Janette Sebring Lowrey, illustrated by Gustav Tenggren. I vaguely recall reading it as a child and the story's pretty lame, but perhaps the notion of one puppy missing from a litter of five, a puppy who has vanished through a hole under a fence, connects with early-childhood fears of loss and abandonment. While dogs are ideal subjects for illustration, they can become a problem in chapter books for older children, where they have to fit into the plot. There's no dog in the first thirteen volumes of the Nancy Drew series until 1937 and *The Whispering Statue*, when a small stray terrier causes a commotion that starts up the mystery. Although Nancy names him Togo, and eventually adopts him, he remains a feature of that title alone. The Hardy Boys series also lacks a dog, since one might get in the way of the brothers' adventures. In subsequent years, dog books proliferated; they now come out fast and furious, and a new category – the training guide for children, which examines the dog/child connection – exists alongside picture and chapter books. A title like Jan Craighead George's *How to Talk to Your Dog* is a recent example. The desire to teach and socialize while entertaining remains strong. In Colin Thompson's *Unknown*, for example, the setting is a dog pound where abandoned pets are named after the tags over their cages: Unknown is the protagonist, accompanied by Owner Died, Grown Too Large and Unwanted Christmas Gift. Didactic, yes, but unfortunately true.

COMMUNICATION

I live alone, almost. Friends visit, sometimes for the weekend; one comes annually for a fortnight. Yet solitude is not the case. For the past sixteen years a dog has lived with me – first Zoli, for nine years, and now Rennie. And a lot of communication goes on, some with language, much without.

In the summer of 2004, newspapers across North America were filled with stories of a recent German discovery, reported in the American journal *Science*, that dogs may have a vocabulary of up to two hundred words. The sole dog studied was a nine-year-old border collie named Rico, and the research took place under Dr. Julia Fischer at the Max Planck Institute for Evolutionary Anthropology in Leipzig. Rico was able to identify and fetch about two hundred items – mostly children's toys – which meant he had a vocabulary similar to that of a trained ape or parrot. Additional experiments with new toys showed that he had the vocabulary of a human three-year-old, though it was centred on nouns/objects.

Further experiments are underway with more complex language, including entire phrases and commands. As well, Dr. Fischer planned to study other border collies and breeds, since Rico's behaviour alone provided insufficient information about language acquisition by dogs and humans.

While issues of dog training may come to mind, as well as matters of canine intelligence, I'm interested in the act of communication. Language is the main tool people have for telling each other their thoughts, desires, fears, and affections, but why should it be the same for dogs? Yes, dogs can understand a range of words and commands, especially for things that interest them. Rennie knows *breakfast, lunch, dinner, supper, treat* and other variations on the theme of food. This doesn't surprise me – pugs, it seems, live to eat, and I sometimes jokingly call him a stomach on a leash. (Zoli had the same hearty appetite, which means, I suppose, that we've moved from a singular anecdote to a generalization about a breed.) The average dog is assumed to understand forty to eighty words and commands, with tone of voice an important factor in word recognition. Since dogs have ears and complex hearing systems, it makes sense that they use them. They have eyes that suit their needs as well, and use those to recognize hand signals and facial and body expressions, types of non-verbal communication. Their legendary noses also let them read their world. In fact, all of the senses that serve communication between people are shared by dogs. But there are differences. Though dogs have ears, I've never known one to show musical preferences – Bach or Puccini, Sinatra or Nina Simone, it never seems to matter. Their eyes, though, do allow them to recognize other dogs on television, even when they're not barking, and Zoli must have had special powers of abstraction because he watched the cartoon dogs in Disney's *Lady and the Tramp* as if he'd seen them earlier that day on the street. In other words, dogs use their senses to take in information, but not everything that interests people. Communication is partly about reception, and dogs are good receivers in selected categories.

Among the pseudo-scientific Nazi experiments that took place during the Second World War, one deserves mention here. Historian Jan Bondeson recounts it in his striking survey of peculiar dog lore, *Amazing Dogs: A Cabinet of Canine Curiosities*. Well known as a dog lover and prone to lunatic beliefs, Adolf Hitler sponsored a canine school where attempts were made to teach carefully selected dogs to talk with humans and also to read. Margarethe Schmitt, who ran the school near Hanover, even claimed that some of the dogs could speak a few words. When one was asked "Who is Adolf Hitler?" it allegedly replied, "*Mein Führer!*" While such experimentation may eerily seem to foreshadow studies later pursued by some contemporary psychologists, it evolved out of Nazi beliefs about a master race and their high opinion of canine intelligence, and was meant to serve sinister goals. Bondeson asks, "Were the Nazis trying to develop a breed of super-intelligent canine storm-troopers, capable of communicating with their human masters of the Herrenvolk?" We can easily guess the answer.

In his eclectic history of the typewriter, Darren Werschler-Henry, a professor of communications, relates the more innocent yet bizarre experiments of Elisabeth Mann Borgese, daughter of the Nobel Prize–winning German novelist Thomas Mann, and her English setter, Arlecchino. During the 1960s, for reasons that were never made clear, she taught the dog to type with his nose on a specially constructed electric typewriter. It took a year of encouragement and raw hamburger before he could type twenty words, however they included many typos. Of course Arlecchino couldn't record his own thoughts, whatever they were, and when encouraged to do so the dog hit the typewriter with his paw – a sensible reaction, all said. Undaunted, Borgese sent pages of her dog's typing to a poetry critic, who claimed that the dog showed "a definite affinity with the 'concretist' groups in Brazil, Scotland, and Germany."

While dogs don't intentionally write poetry, they also appear not to distinguish between languages they've heard frequently or been trained with. Occasionally, I spoke to Zoli in French and Hungarian, as well as in English (my own experiment), and he heard no difference between "good dog" and "*jó kutya*," its Hungarian equivalent. On a more serious level, in the spring of 2007, sixteen service dogs that had been trained in Israel for two months, along with their handlers – eight California policemen – returned to the United States to begin their bomb-sniffing tasks, searching for explosives and other signs of terrorism. The dogs had "studied" (a perfectly suitable word) under the auspices of Pups for Peace, a non-profit organization that has funded and trained anti-terrorism dogs since 2002. Josh Richman told their story in *The Forward*, and it's a fascinating one. While the dogs now live and work in an English-speaking environment, they respond to directions given in Hebrew that were taught to their American handlers as well. The training project received financial support of more than $400,000 from the California Governor's Office of Homeland Security, from federal grant money – a not insignificant fact. And it is likely to be followed by further links between Pups for Peace and U.S. law-enforcement agencies. What amazes me is that no bureaucrat objected to teaching American dogs Hebrew, or any language other than English.

Communication between people and dogs may appear simple on the surface, but when all the senses are taken together, it is actually an elegant, non-verbal exchange. Touch is an element that enhances it. Except for quick hugs, cheek kisses, hand shakes and the like, people rarely touch each other unless they've already established a connection, while in intimate relations touching is often a prelude to sex or an act of consolation. When you pet or stroke your dog in prolonged physical connection, the exchange defies words. It's now a commonplace that touching a beloved pet can lower one's blood pressure and heartbeat, and relieve stress, but how do we explain this? Comfort, familiarity, consolation again – no single word or notion is adequate to sum up this process. While it's important for safety's sake that dogs learn some key words and phrases (*no* and *drop it* come to mind), it's equally important that dog owners learn to interpret non-verbal signs and behaviour – a delicate balance. A dog teaches people how *not* to use words, and how to trust and rely on other ways of sharing ourselves. There's relief in the knowledge, which itself resists language, and pleasure in non-verbal communion that exists so deeply and intensely that it can for a time take us out of ourselves. Dogs may be healing to us in part because they're wordless – they make us look at, and feel, essentials. This sense of silent rest, I think, is one of the main reasons why dogs comfort us, and even lower our blood pressure. Too often we're overwhelmed by words and their demands coming at us from every direction, so the chance to communicate without them is a relief from the burden. Dogs often sense what we're about to say before we speak, also a relief. For people who live alone with a dog, the shared silence takes on deeper meaning. For those who are surrounded by family – and words – silent communication can sometimes seem like a privilege, even a reward.

CRUELTY

Borrowing from the well-known sonnet by Elizabeth Barrett Browning, "How do I harm thee, let me count the ways..." To begin with the more obvious kinds of cruelty humans have thought to inflict on dogs, we've created puppy mills, battered dogs, neglected dogs in our care in pet shops and animal shelters, dognapped other people's pets, abandoned dogs we couldn't learn to handle or lost interest in, organized dog fights and trained dogs for them, exploited dogs in "sports" such as racing, used dogs in pharmaceutical and cosmetic experiments, intentionally – and sometimes unintentionally – poisoned dogs with a variety of substances (in Toronto, Ontario, in 2004, fourteen dogs in Riverdale and Withrow parks ate hot dogs laced with a pesticide that was banned in the United States but still available in Canada). In Italy's Tuscany region, humans regularly poison dogs so they won't interfere with the annual truffle hunt – in 1999, for example, the Scottish novelist Muriel Spark, who then lived in Tuscany, found her dog Mungo one of the victims. To my litany I'll add just a few of the more outrageous examples of individual cruelty: in Shelburne, Ontario, in 1996, a woman in her sixties dragged her Irish setter behind her moving car to discipline it (the dog recovered and the woman claimed it loved her); in June 2001, during an episode of road rage, a man in San Jose, California, reached into another car, grabbed the driver's bichon frise, and threw it into the traffic, where it was struck and killed; in Lorain, Ohio, a terrier-mix puppy was set on fire and thrown from a moving car. This list quickly becomes an indictment of our much-valued humanity.

The subject of cruelty to animals is too vast to address here, but I want to draw attention to the way we think about – and write about – the subject. As a species, humans can be slow to acknowledge cruelty to animals, or to take the subject seriously. Just after American Thanksgiving in November 2000, the *New York Times Magazine* ran on its last page an article by Ernesto Quiñonez, entitled "Dog Days," under the series heading *Lives*. In his short essay Quiñonez told how, as a child in Spanish Harlem, he wanted to be a "revolutionary thief," so after a brief period of shoplifting he went down to the prosperous Upper East Side and kidnapped small dogs, waiting to see posters and flyers offering rewards for their recovery, which he gladly collected. "I have no regrets," the author told us, and though he became a published novelist, apparently he had never read Virginia Woolf's *Flush*, which tells of a London slum not far from the home of Victorian poet Elizabeth Barrett Browning that produced local thugs who also turned to dognapping – even, on occasion, sending along an animal's ear if the ransom wasn't offered speedily enough. Perhaps readers were supposed to feel sorry for Quiñonez for what must have been a difficult childhood. I didn't buy it then and I don't now. Quiñonez remained proud of his childhood behaviour and explained it away too glibly ("The country was in recession, New York City was losing jobs," etc.). By Quiñonez's logic, Muriel Spark's poisoned dog was the byproduct of local economic development, and the man who threw the bichon frise into oncoming traffic may have suffered an especially stressful work day.

While we can't fully explain human cruelty, at least we have sometimes legislated against it, and enforced the laws. Stories of cruelty by breeders, even those registered with the American Kennel Club, who should know better, regularly crop up on the evening TV news, only to fade by the next morning. Laws are talked about, briefly. In the spring of 2007, for example, a proposed law regulating puppy mills and puppy sales was making its way through the Ohio House and Senate. By 2007, I would have thought that anyone who had ever read a newspaper knew that such a law was necessary, that breeding kennels ought to be regularly inspected, that breeders need to be monitored, that the health and safety of dogs was a legitimate concern – no, an obligation. Pet stores as well ought to be required to certify that their pets are healthy and their breeders are responsible. In 2005, the chief investigator for the Ontario Society for the Prevention of Cruelty to Animals, an advocate of stronger anti-cruelty laws in Canada, gave a newspaper interview in which he referred to a puppy mill as "a concentration camp for dogs." While the term is an upsetting one, it should be.

The Ohio legislation was not controversial, unlike a proposed California law hotly debated during the same summer. This bill, proposed by Assemblyman Lloyd Levine, required that Californians spay or neuter their pets or face significant fines. Pet owners went berserk, but few of them wanted to discuss the larger issues. According to the *Los Angeles Times*, "454,000 unclaimed cats and dogs are put to death each year in California shelters at a cost of about $300 million." Beside the monetary cost, imagine euthanizing that number of pets! Amendments to the proposed law exempted working dogs, show dogs and breeders' dogs, yet objections mounted, including those of Bob Weatherwax, owner of the current Lassie (the ninth generation of the canine film family), at a hearing about the legislation, with Lassie beside him. At stake, along with the "rights" of individual pet owners, are the health and welfare of hundreds of thousands of dogs – millions, in fact – as the years pass. Precise figures for the number of dogs euthanized annually in North America are difficult to come by, but some estimates suggest the number is over two million. In 1997, the National Council on Pet Population Study and Policy suggested that 56 per cent of all dogs entering animal shelters were euthanized.

Cruelty can begin inadvertently, with good intentions. If common sense isn't enough of a guide, try to put yourself in a dog's place and see if that might clarify things. I have neighbours who work all day and leave their cocker spaniel locked in the basement, although they say that they have an old, upholstered easy chair down there for her to sleep on. Dogs need more than a cold basement, even if there's fresh water *and* an easy chair. If these people spent one day locked in their own basement, they might better understand why their solution to dog care borders on cruelty. Unattended dogs locked in a hot car, dogs left tied in a sunny backyard, unleashed dogs on busy city streets–these are all potentially dangerous situations, and raise issues of canine rights (discussed elsewhere) because carelessness can be a form of cruelty. When the Disney Studios released a remake of *101 Dalmatians* in 1997, the breed became, overnight, a popular gift for Christmas, and many breeders were only too glad to make a fast buck. By the following year, when the puppies had grown, animal shelters across North America reported an increase in abandoned dalmatians. Any parent should have anticipated the needs of a large and potentially difficult dog – buying one, making it a part of one's family, and then dropping it off at an animal shelter is a form of cruelty too, if less dramatic than raising dogs for illegal dogfighting.

A "sport" where millions of dollars are waged annually, dogfighting periodically hits the newspapers. But objections to the use of animals in "sport" are not unique to our time. The sixteenth-century French writer Michel de Montaigne, who is credited with inventing the modern essay form, expressed grave reservations in "On Cruelty." Citing the ancient Roman training of gladiators, he wrote that men first learned to kill animals before progressing to each other. And he went further, concluding that men given to animal bloodshed had "an inborn propensity to cruelty," almost anticipating the work of some contemporary psychologists (though they might dispute the propensity as "inborn"). "Watching animals playing together and cuddling each other is nobody's sport," he noted, but "everyone's sport is to watch them tearing each other apart and wrenching off their limbs." There are a lot of things we humans have refused to learn since Montaigne wrote those lines, first published in the 1580s, and the proper role of animals in our "sport" is one of them.

During the first week of June 2007, the most-viewed article on Newsweek.com was "Going for the Throat," about the growing "underground world" of dogfighting. Little more than a month later, a nineteen-page federal indictment was served against Atlanta Falcons quarterback Michael Vick. The charges of running a dog fighting operation in rural Virginia, through Bad Newz Kennel, were shocking and grisly. Among the details, Vick and several associates allegedly killed eight dogs "by various methods, including hanging, drowning, and slamming at least one dog's body to the ground" because they hadn't proved to be vicious enough in pre-fight testing sessions. Fortunately, more than fifty dogs were rescued from Vick's property.

But what concerns me is the way Vick's story was reported by the press, usually in the Sports sections of newspapers, as if the subject had little to do with cruelty to animals, or as if the dogs were a secondary matter. Although *The New York Times* had run a disturbing article about dogfighting titled "A Brutal Sport Is Having Its Day Again in Russia" on the front page of its February 9, 2007 edition, it printed Clifton Brown's story about the NFL star – "Vick Faces Federal Charges on Dogfighting" – on the first page of "SportsWednesday," in the separate Business section. As if the indictment wasn't about dog abuse, several days later William C. Rhoden of the *Times* followed with his thoughts in "An Elusive Quarterback Takes His Hardest Hit," concluding: "How do young newly created millionaires react when wealth allows them to indulge their dark side[?]." Rhoden reminded his readers of Vick's presumption of innocence, and called the indictment "the greatest loss of his career." Perhaps Rhoden felt sorry for Vick, but I wonder if he would have had the same sympathy for a young, newly rich lawyer or dentist or writer, who one evening hung his pet collie, indulging his "dark side." While *USA Today* ran a strong editorial ("Window on a cruel world: Law enforcement, weak penalties allow dogfighting to flourish"), it also published on the front page of the same edition Skip Wood's piece, "Quarterbacks face harsh reality: Pressure to win now – or else," as if football players are the only people on the planet to work under pressure. And on CNN, several news anchors, seemingly oblivious to the ethical issues involved, chortled among themselves about angry dog lovers who were "a powerful lobby" and sometimes considered their dogs to be part of their families. My point is that we don't truly regard cruelty to dogs as a crime, even though dogfighting is illegal in every state in the U.S. and a felony in all but two. In the immediate days after Vick's indictment, he wasn't suspended by the NFL; eventually he was, as allegations about gambling were also mentioned.

When Vick accepted a plea bargain a month later, in late August, it was often acknowledged by sportscasters that he had done something wrong "but...." The *but* suggested that Vick was going to pay with his future, perhaps jail time and financial loss; the injured dogs were seldom mentioned, and cruelty to animals was set aside. If Vick was admonished, it was for breaking the law, as if in this instance the law had no content. Perhaps only a few journalists bothered to read the prosecutor's indictment and the horrors it detailed. One friend who follows football even remarked that she was glad "the Feds" were responsible for the investigation – had it been solely a local matter, it might have been swept under the rug. In December 2007, Vick was sentenced to a jail term of twenty-three months, one month less than the maximum allowed. Since his release, Vick has worked with the Humane Society to raise consciousness about animal cruelty. Whether this association is a public-relations gimmick to revive his career, or a genuine new understanding of the value of canine life – or some of each – is not for me to say. In his book *The Bond: Our Kinship with Animals, Our Call to Defend Them*, Wayne Pacelle, the president and CEO of the Humane Society of the United States, discussed his work with Vick, who has visited high-school students and urged them to eschew the world of dogfighting. Pacelle wrote, "Whatever was in Michael's heart, whether or not he really was now a changed man, the things he had done had made him an agent of change in the world he had chosen."

Dogfighting is not a uniquely American pastime (it is legal in Japan), and the notion of what constitutes a sport needs to be rethought everywhere. In 2004, to considerable protest, the House of Commons of the British Parliament, in a 356-to-166 vote, outlawed the revered "sport" of hunting with hounds. Such a vote took courage because the tradition is an old one, as attested to by the hounds in medieval tapestries and on the pages of illuminated manuscripts. Supporters of the ban cited cruelty to dogs, opponents cited their own civil liberties. Debates about various amendments between the Commons and the House of Lords dragged on for several years, with no agreement likely. As the parliamentary session came to an end in November 2007, the banning bill received Royal Assent, becoming the 2004 Hunting Act. Hunts, as you might expect, have continued, with hunters claiming to follow the law and critics claiming they aren't. Closer to home, the matter of training greyhounds for dog racing periodically hits the press (dog racing is not illegal in the United States), occasionally with articles about greyhound adoption or the closing of dog tracks. Although Greyhound Pets of America, an industry-funded organization, attempts to find homes for aging or unwanted dogs, reports suggest that every year hundreds are killed. After all, how many people would be willing to adopt a large older dog, especially one with the medical problems dog racing can cause? This "sport" isn't found only in rural backwoods – there are popular tracks in Connecticut and New Hampshire, to name several states – and dog racing is nothing like the agility trials some dog owners enjoy with their dogs. For most people caught up in greyhound racing, the sport is about money. But while dog racing is also legal in Canada, dog-track betting is not.

Humans have often terrorized dogs, and continue to do so, even using dogs to terrorize each other for entertainment. On April 20, 2010, the Supreme Court of the United States, in an eight-to-one decision, overturned a federal law that criminalized the creation or sales of dogfight videos and other portrayals of animal cruelty. Despite legal complexities and the free-speech issues involved, you don't have to be a card-carrying member of People for the Ethical Treatment of Animals (PETA) to object.

DEATH

There is no way, finally, to protect your dog or yourself from death. In one of my favourite dog books, *The Difficulty of Being a Dog*, Roger Grenier, seventy-nine years old when his book was first published in France, had this to say: "Each day, by the brevity of its life, our pet tells us, I shall soon be dead. In the deepest sense, these familiar creatures are part of the hurt of living. Because dogs inflict the suffering of loss upon us, the French sometimes call them 'beasts of sorrow,' *bêtes de chagrin*." The original title of Grenier's short book was *Les larmes de Ulysses (The Tears of Ulysses)* and it captures the moment when Ulysses returned home to Ithaca and was recognized only by his dog Argus. We weep for our dogs, in part, because no one knows us as they do. In his discussion of the ancient Egyptian veneration of animals, the Greek writer Herodotus observed in his *Histories*, in the fifth century B.C.E., these mourning customs: "Egyptians are overcome by intense grief. All those who live in a household where a cat has died a natural death shave their eyebrows. For the death of a dog, however, they shave their entire head and body." While cats were embalmed and taken for burial to the city of Boubastis, dogs were buried in sacred tombs in their own cities. Allowing for confusion and even hyperbole on Herodotus's part, mourning a pet has never been easy.

What else can we feel but loss? I know several people who've said that after the death of a beloved dog, they would never get another pet because they couldn't face such a painful loss a second time. And I'm sympathetic to this distress. There is nothing quite as isolating as the death of your dog companion. After my pug Zoli died on the last day of March 2004, a veterinarian at Toronto's Emergency Hospital took me aside and said that she wanted to offer a word of advice. She suggested that I avoid talking about Zoli with anyone who wouldn't understand the nature of my loss, and even steer clear of people who didn't love animals. "They'll only make things worse," she cautioned.

I remember every detail of the last week of Zoli's life. The nature of his illness – the culmination of half a year of malignant mast-cell tumours – is something I'll write about elsewhere. But like cancer in humans, the disease in dogs can appear in remission and then, suddenly, life turns upside down. Near the end of that March I had my first night out since Zoli had been diagnosed with cancer the previous fall. A mediocre symphony concert only annoyed me and I hurried home to find Zoli at the door, tail wagging, and greeting me with his customary enthusiasm. But he couldn't calm down, he was restless and appeared to have some kind of stomach upset. Finding the right food for him had been a concern for several months, and I kept offering reassuring words and pats. We even took several short walks, but they made no difference. Just after midnight I decided to take him to the downtown branch of Toronto's Emergency Hospital, where Jon Forbes, the kind, soft-spoken vet on call, examined him, heard his medical history, and suggested that we could go home; if Zoli's symptoms didn't let up, we should return. Two hours later we were back at the hospital, and after an hour of tests Zoli was diagnosed with severe pancreatitis.

In the next days I learned about pancreatitis, which is essentially an inflamation of the pancreas. Pancreatitis in dogs, as in humans, is not necessarily fatal, though it can be. Rural dogs commonly acquire the disease after eating the carcass of a dead bird found in the woods. What's important to say here is that events run a course you can't predict or control. Zoli, I was told at first, had a good chance of recovery; but his elevated pancreatic levels were slow to respond to the appropriate treatment, which included various medications and several plasma transfusions. I felt numb. Had his increased liver enzymes been secondary to chemotherapy? No one could say for sure. I went to the clinic daily to sit with him, and whenever he curled up in my lap I felt his body relax, and even heard something like a sigh of relief – he was with me, where he belonged. I petted him, staring at the intravenous needle taped to his front left paw with its tube draped over my pant leg. I talked to him and felt his small body relax further. I told him stories so that he could hear my voice, I even read aloud because I wanted to stay at his side; I didn't want to go home.

But his condition did not improve. His eyes seemed glassy, even a bit vacant, and I feared the worst while telling myself it might not happen. I didn't sleep for a week, I lost my appetite. X-rays and ultrasounds were made to determine if Zoli's cancer had spread internally. First I was told he was fine, that there were no tumours, and then the opposite. An operation would be essential to determine the nature of Zoli's problem, including why his pancreatic enzyme levels had not stabilized. What did I want done? *Done?* I wanted to run away with Zoli, get into the car and head anywhere; I wanted the last months to be a bad dream. Instead, I agreed to the surgery and spent the last rainy morning of Zoli's life holding him in my lap and stroking his head. Then I left for an hour to do a few errands, and soon returned to hear that he was scheduled for immediate surgery. He had already been sedated, and as he licked my hand, I thanked him for all of the good times we'd shared.

Time passed slowly during the operation. Here, I think, is one reason why a dog's death has a unique pain associated with it: sometimes we have to make the decision to end our dog's life. "Put to sleep," "put down," whatever euphemism is used, the decision can't always be avoided. The word *euthanasia* derives from the Greek – *eu* for easy and *thanatos* for death – but it's still a chilling decision. An hour into Zoli's operation, a doctor came out to say that it appeared that the cancer had spread. The surgeons could continue to try to save him with an infrequently performed Whipple or Billroth procedure, but if he survived, his remaining life might be a painful one, and one often spent in a veterinary clinic. I felt that the air had been sucked out of the room. Would the surgery give Zoli a few more days, or weeks, or months? No one could say. But whatever time we might gain would be hard on him. Zoli's regular doctor, Richard Medhurst, is a kind man who had promised to tell me when the time came to "let Zoli go" since I didn't want my needs, my ego, to cause him any pain. That grim afternoon, however, Rich was not reachable, so I had to decide alone. Not quite believing my words, I agreed to the impossible, that Zoli would be given a lethal injection – he was already under an anaesthetic and wouldn't be brought back to consciousness. The doctor suggested I might not want to be present since he was, of course, cut open for the surgery. I'll never know if I was wrong to take her well-meaning advice, but I wanted my last image of Zoli to be the moment when I'd patted his head and told him he'd be fine. Later, Rich said I made the only possible decision, and the emergency veterinarians concurred, adding that if I'd requested the surgery, they thought we'd be meeting again in several days to face the tough decision once more.

As I write these words, a two-inch-high pile of his medical records is beside me. When I reread the meticulous, single-spaced, twelve-page report about his last week of life, spent at the emergency clinic, my heart sinks at one line concerning the decline in Zoli's state: "Comes to the front of the kennel to visit but does not wag tail and is not enthusiastic." I'm quoting this report and writing about Zoli in such detail here because in our culture people are somehow supposed to buck up, be realistic, keep a dog's death in perspective, as if the loss is a kind of embarrassment. This is cruel; a dog's death is not a small or insignificant loss. The

American poet Mark Doty recently wrote a memoir, *Dog Years,* about the deaths of his two dogs, a golden retriever and a black retriever. For the past decade Doty has taken the AIDS epidemic as his special subject, and he began *Dog Years* with an imaginary walk through Manhattan after 9/11, asking himself "isn't it arrogance to write about your dogs?" in the face of such tragedy. No, I thought, on reading that question. Doty went on to create a straw dog, so to speak, because he understands that grief about a dog's death is often seen as a kind of self-indulgence: "I know it might seem absurd to place the death of my dog on this page with all these people, vanished parents and children and lovers and friends." He's wrong (and I think he knows it) because one grief, one loss, does not matter more than another; it's like comparing apples and oranges. Perhaps Doty wanted to ward off objections in advance.

Several days after Zoli's death I came across an exceptional book, Wallace Sife's *The Loss of a Pet: A Guide to Coping with the Grieving Process when a Pet Dies.* I've never liked self-help books, but this one should be on the shelf of any dog owner. Sife, who was a human bereavement counsellor, wrote his book after the premature death of his dachshund, only eight years old, and he went on to found the Association for Pet Loss and Bereavement. He offers no program, no simple answers nor grating advice, yet his book is filled with good suggestions and even some exercises, such as keeping a journal where you jot down memories of your dog (this may sound unhelpful, but it is actually wise counsel – it gives you something positive to do). Some people will want to put away the pictures of their dog while others (like me) will prefer to keep them at hand – there's no *right* way to grieve.

The few decisions to be made after a dog's death are unlike those that accompany a human death. Both, of course, require a decision about the body. For some time now I've paid attention to the decisions people make about their dogs' corpses, and I'm often amazed that they show so little concern about them. One friend, from a Greek Orthodox background, buried the body of her toy poodle in a cousin's backyard, knowing that in several years she could return to the spot, dig up the skeleton and place the bones in a special box. And she did. When friends in Los Angeles decided to let their vet send the body of their Cavalier King Charles spaniel Morgan for group cremation, I was particularly saddened. This lovely animal had often spent months of his life – several times, even half a year – in my care, but it was too late to suggest otherwise. I chose to have Zoli cremated alone, and when I brought his ashes home, in a small ceramic urn from the crematorium, I put a photograph of him inside it, with the cremains – what an unpleasant word – and, unlike other friends who can keep the ashes of their dogs on a mantel or bookshelf, I set the jar in the desk, where I feel its presence but don't have to look at it daily, like a familiar bibelot.

Most large cities have support groups for pet bereavement but I wasn't tempted to join one. I was never embarrassed by my grief, and if anyone asked about Zoli I told them what had happened; they would learn a little about cancer and dogs. My neighbourhood is a cliché of impersonal city living. Yet people who'd previously asked why, after surgery, Zoli was wearing a large plastic collar, now asked where he was. My explanation was met with their stories. One man told about a wheaten terrier stolen from his home; a dignified woman in her seventies told of a dog lost, years ago, to divorce; another nodding acquaintance spoke of her own recent cancer diagnosis. A few were surprised to hear that over the past Christmas holiday, when my mother was hospitalized for several weeks, Zoli had accompanied me on our daily visits and slept on the bed beside her as patients, nurses, and even a few doctors stopped to pet him. This says a lot about the emotions below the surface of our alienated society. It's a truism that a dog-owner's blood pressure slows down when he pets a beloved animal. More impressive is that a stranger's dog can have a similar effect on a community.

Not long after Zoli's death, the campus magazine of the university where I teach approached me for an article, and I suggested one about dogs and public space. I wrote about Zoli's life on campus and about his death. In the weeks after it appeared I was amazed at the number of e-mails sent to me by strangers, people who over the years had noticed Zoli and others who just wanted to share an experience of their own. I had admitted that the thought of his death remained painful – I have little use for the language of our culture that speaks of "healing" or "closure." As the American poet and diarist May Sarton wrote of her own dog's death, "there are some losses you can't absorb."

Half a year after Zoli's death, while buying a newspaper, I heard from one of the neighbourhood dog people about a young woman who was at the corner parkette, grieving over a cancer diagnosis for her golden retriever. I stopped to talk with her and even mentioned Sife's book. And I was glad to tell this stranger about my brave companion Zoli, about his surgeries and chemotherapy, and the way he'd spent his days at the vet's office charming the young assistants and befriending a small, gray rabbit. The woman and I smiled tentatively, and she asked about the pug puppy at my side. I introduced Rennie. He will never replace Zoli but he'll be his special self while drawing out new stories from strangers. Dogs may be "beasts of sorrow," as Roger Grenier said, but as they live they teach us about death, if we pay attention. Writing to a close friend twenty-four years her senior, British novelist Virginia Woolf discussed the death of her much-loved spaniel Pinka at her country house in Sussex: "She had a fit and died the day before we came, and here was Percy burying her in her basket and we were both very unhappy – This you'll call sentimental – perhaps – but then a dog somehow represents – no I can't think of the word – the private side of life – the play side." Strange, to imagine the prolific Woolf at a loss for words. Given the emphasis Bloomsbury writers placed on friendship, her term *play side* is a weak one, while *private side* may be closer to the mark. A grief shared is not necessarily lessened by the telling (another myth) but words and stories do acknowledge the isolating nature of loss.

There may be only a few things that a grieving person can learn from someone else's grief, but on reflection we at least have the knowledge that every death, like every life, is unique. Such lessons may be of little help with the next death one faces, but they do make for a community of loss. If any strength is to be found in them, I suspect it comes from the particularities of an individual story. The following belongs to a woman named Marie Bonaparte, a distant niece of the famed Napoleon and also a princess in her own right, married as she was to the prince of Greece and Denmark. But Marie Bonaparte refused the confines of an aristocratic social world. In the 1920s she was psychoanalyzed by none other than Sigmund Freud, and she later became an important French advocate of the growing psychoanalytic movement. She even trained as an analyst herself, translating Freud into French and writing a book about the interior life of Edgar Allan Poe. Her significance regarding dogs comes from her extraordinary book *Topsy: The Story of a Golden-Haired Chow*, and the fact that she introduced Freud to chow dogs, which he came to love and keep at his side during analytic sessions.

Topsy is unique among dog books, a meditation on illness and death that is oddly reassuring. Early in 1935, Bonaparte discovered that her five-year-old chow had a tumour on her lip, one that was diagnosed as a lymphosarcoma. Wellconnected as she was, Bonaparte took the dog to the Curie Institute in Paris for a series of eighteen X-ray treatments. Over the following year she recorded the nature of the experience, and this short memoir became *Topsy*. At the beginning Bonaparte asks a question that might come to the minds of people who aren't dog lovers: "Have we not enough sorrows on earth, which come to us from human beings, from children, without creating others by adopting dogs?" The question is not meant as rhetorical, and neither are those that follow, including one that explains the care Bonaparte sought out for Topsy: "Why this distinction, which even I seem to accept, between a dog and a human being? Topsy, if she can be healed, has as much right to life as I."

Bonaparte spent much of that summer and autumn at her country home with Topsy, at a stage of life when her children were grown and on their own; she was especially aware of the life of her garden and the changing seasons around her, which would continue beyond her own life, and Topsy's. This isolation, which led her to call Topsy "my terrestrial sister," forced Bonaparte to confront – as much as any human can – her own mortality. Although she admits that to love a dog with its short life is "gratuitously to invite Death into one's house," the bond between dog and mistress deepened in "a respite from things human." Bonaparte never regretted her attachment, even as Topsy became emaciated. The ailing dog taught her an important lesson, the only comfort she found – that life must be lived in the present moment. Though her dog was probably cured, the future remained bleak: "For Topsy does not know that there is a country where she and I will go one day, whence no one returns, and that is darker than the darkest of nights. And I bless her for being thus, and for not knowing that which I, alas, do know." What use is this knowledge? It cannot thwart death. Yet Topsy has become "a talisman that conjures away death." The summer passes and Bonaparte concludes with these words about the futility of human endeavour: "That is why Topsy, whose happiness is confined to the narrow limits of each day, is wiser than I, she who simply inhales the scented June air, whilst I strive laboriously to trace vain signs on this paper." *Vain signs?* To read *Topsy* is to disagree.

There is another dimension to this story that should be included. As European political conditions worsened in the late

1930s, it became clear that the Jewish Freud and his family needed to leave Vienna for safe harbour; his sister had already been sent to a concentration camp. Bonaparte was one of the few people who made Freud's rescue a personal mission, and she accomplished it at genuine risk to herself. During the last years of his long battle with cancer, Freud was finally able to leave Austria for London, England, with his family as well as his chow dog. Ironically, Freud's painful cancer – of the mouth and jaw – was reminiscent of Topsy's. And while awaiting his rescue and facing his own death, Freud translated *Topsy* into German, an act of friendship and admiration that must have been at once both consoling and troubling.

Bonaparte's Topsy, like my Zoli, shared with all dogs the ability to "conjure away death," to force us to live, if only momentarily, in the moment – to conjure life. This may go a long way in explaining why we keep dogs at our side, and why we mourn their deaths so deeply.

EMBARRASSMENT

Reviewing an exhibition of dog paintings called "Best in Show" in *The New York Times*, art critic Grace Glueck began by writing, "Dogs. Take them or leave them (as some benighted people do)..." while a week later Henry Fountain, a science writer, followed her in the same pages, asking, "Why were animals front and center for many artists? It boils down to this: animals are a big part of the natural world...." I've never seen an art critic ask why a painter arranged a plate of fruit or set out a vase of flowers as subject matter. And imagine this sentence, "Trees. Take them or leave them...."

The aloof tone of both writers withholds enthusiasm – though they reviewed the exhibition positively – as if any sophisticated soul looking at a painting of a dog must be slightly embarrassed by the subject and at the very least want to explain his interest, if not apologize for it. Such prejudice exists not only in the art world. In her introduction to *Melancholia's Dog: Reflections on Our Animal Kinship*, Alice A. Kuzniar confessed that she found writing about the human/dog relationship in the literary and visual arts "an exercise in mortification." Why? Because her colleagues apparently considered the subject of dogs unsuitable for scholarly study – "it is held to be sentimental, popular, and trivial, both by the academic and by the general lay population. Whenever I had to explain and justify to what I was devoting years of research and writing, I felt embarrassed." Kuzniar, a professor of German and comparative literature at the University of North Carolina, Chapel Hill, has had a very different experience writing about dogs than mine. Perhaps academic colleagues are more willing to accept a man writing a book about dogs than a woman. But I've never felt embarrassed, let alone mortified. In fact, I've been amazed at the continuing number of books and articles devoted to dogs which seem to fascinate the "general lay population," if not university colleagues. The current academic environment in the humanities often places considerable emphasis on issues related to class and gender, and the many reasons behind this – ranging from the increased interest in social history since the 1960s to ideological sympathies – are the subject for another book. Since pet-keeping has been regarded as a bourgeois pastime, anyone interested in dogs must accept the consequences of his or her interests. Embarrassment in this context involves the vagaries of fashion.

Usually thought of as a minor emotion, something even comic, embarrassment has powerful relations in shame and guilt. We're embarrassed when we're caught in an act or situation we want to keep private or enjoy with reservation. In this sense, embarrassment is often associated with pleasure, though unsophisticated or uninhibited or childish. Extremes of emotion such as grief are seldom a source of embarrassment, but sentimental tears might be. Dogs figure into this picture because they tempt us from more worldly pleasures with the quieter ones of a walk around the block or a lively game of fetch; they curl up at our sides with beseeching glances; they make us question our secure place in the civilized world while, ironically, relying on us to supply their own creature comforts. Dogs can be a source of embarrassment precisely because we feel superior to them, which means that they can reveal our deepest fears and inadequacies. Since they communicate without words, they make us recognize the limitations and arbitrariness of language. The warmth of their bodies reminds us that, despite our minds and defences, we're as vulnerable as our dogs. If we pay attention, they strip us of illusions – they embarrass us by exposing our pretensions. In her novel *Bel Ria: Dog of War*, Sheila Burnford included the character of an elderly woman, Alice Tremorne, whose life was transformed by a stray dog. At one point this character remarks, "'I don't think it's we who make fools of dogs.... I am beginning to think that they make fools of us – they show up our needs and weaknesses somehow.'" Why, one might ask, do we want to keep such creatures around? Just because they can penetrate the fragile mask of civilization we wear for each other. Put simply, they give us a-momentary relief from the task of being human while at the same time reinforcing our humanity.

It should come as no surprise that as thoughtful an analyst of human behaviour as Sigmund Freud, generally seen as the father of psychoanalysis if not the study of the unconscious itself, was devoted to dogs; in his case, chows. It's known that he kept a dog at his side in his office during analytic sessions, and he acknowledged the calming effect this had on his patients. One of Freud's most famous case studies, referred to as "The Wolfman," deserves comment here. Based on his analysis of a troubled young Russian aristocrat, Sergei Pankejeff, the study was written shortly after the conclusion of treatment in the winter of 1914–15, during the early years of the First World War. It covers a range of difficult subjects, from masochism, narcissism, sexual seduction, and male passivity to the forgotten memory of a disturbing primal scene – witnessed or imagined by Pankejeff as a child – which psychoanalysis eventually reconstructed through dream analysis. At the core of the account was Pankejeff's unsettling old dream of looking out a window at night onto six or seven white wolves sitting on branches in a nearby walnut tree: "The wolves were white all over and looked more like foxes or sheepdogs because they had big tails like foxes and their ears were pricked up like dogs watching something."

With its echo of fairy tales such as "Little Red Riding Hood," the dream contains curious dog-like wolves, evoking the distant transition from wolf to dog as well as the co-evolution of man and dog. Freud's analysis of the dream revealed, as he called it, "the prehistory of the patient's childhood." Shame and guilt commingled before repressed memories and images that were transformed, in part, into these dog-wolves, as primitive as the primal scene the therapy had uncovered. Whatever you may think of Freud, or of fairy tales for that matter, "The Wolfman" case study shows how deeply embedded wolves and dogs are in the human psyche and how they can serve as emblems of our most painful fears, drives, and instincts. We tend to look away when dogs lick their genitals because, like unpleasant images of ourselves in a distorting mirror, our dogs can sometimes be too close for comfort.

EMOTIONS

Like signs that warn Beware of Dog, there ought to be one proclaiming Beware of Behaviourists, or so I thought when I began my reading about dogs. I did not yet have a dog of my own, but my parents, then in their mid-sixties, had recently brought home the last of their Boston terriers, named Buster as usual, and I fell in love with the puppy. I assured my parents I would take care of him if necessary, and Buster soon made me realize that a dog of my own would likely be in my future. But instead of walking a dog, I read a training manual – I don't recall which one – hence my reservations about behaviourists. By this I mean the mechanistic writers who, when speaking of evolution, refer to dogs only as *parasites* (technically, the correct term). As I eventually learned, not everyone who studies canine behaviour merits a cautionary label, but scientists who never apply the word *emotions* to their subject, preferring only to speak of *instincts*, deserve a pause. (*Intelligence*, discussed elsewhere, is another problematic word, and concept, for such thinkers.) First of all, the word *emotions* carries a lot of human baggage, but there's no good reason to limit its use only to ourselves. Second, the human species also has instincts, and our messy history shows centuries of some very frightening instinctual behaviour alongside more civilized moments. Any desire to reserve the idea of emotions only for humans has, at its core, the kind of assumptions behind the outmoded great chain of being.

In 1995, *When Elephants Weep: The Emotional Lives of Animals*, co-written by Jeffrey Moussaieff Masson and Susan McCarthy, became a bestseller people actually read. Two years later, Masson published *Dogs Never Lie About Love: The Emotional World of Dogs*, my favourite of his animal books. Important here is the way Masson used the word *emotional* in the subtitles of both books;

it was, in fact, a revolutionary thing to do for any serious writer, let alone one with a Harvard Ph.D. in Sanskrit. Linking *emotions* and *dogs* challenged behaviourists who had seemed to own the high road of canine discourse. Looking back, Masson's point is an obvious one: dogs (and animals) have emotions. Beginning with the anecdotal, Masson used his own childhood experiences, as well as encounters with animals during his world travels, as a point of departure, grounding his observations in a broad reading of such books as Charles Darwin's *The Expression of the Emotions in Man and Animals*. (Darwin, as Masson acknowledged, "was unafraid to speculate about areas that seemed to require further investigation.") Masson's time in the Freud Archives, as its projects director, perhaps served him well, since he was unafraid to challenge psychological truisms about animals that saw them essentially as "unfeeling brutes," to repeat one of his chapter titles. The emotions that are generally linked to humans – love, fear, grief, sadness, shame, and joy, to list only a few – are all seen in animals once one surmounts the fear of appearing anthropomorphic. While *Dogs Never Lie About Love* repeats some of Masson's earlier ideas, it builds on the challenge of his first book about animals.

Current writers about dogs rarely dismiss canine emotions, and even a quick look at the indexes of their books will show that they've found something sensible to say about the subject. *Emotions* appears in the indexes of serious writers like Stanley Coren, Vilmos Csányi and Temple Grandin as well as in less scientific work, while a thoughtful writer like Elizabeth Marshall Thomas, in *The Hidden Life of Dogs*, even speaks of the *love* between her two pugs, Bingo and Violet, as a *marriage*, challenging anyone to call it anthropomorphism. This is not just a matter of semantics. Words give humans a kind of ownership of their world, tentative as it may be. Traditions, superstitions and laws all reflect the power of words to harm as well as protect, and most human activity inevitably touches the lives of the dogs around us. If we hesitate to use the word *emotions* for dog behaviour, I suspect it's because we see something of ourselves in dogs that we're afraid to acknowledge. Wanting to feel special, unique, humans are deeply attached to barriers and categories. Since dogs can't object and have to depend on us, we get to luxuriate in our sense of our own superiority when we refuse to share "human" attributes with them.

What, then, are a dog's emotions like? As Temple Grandin bluntly put it, "Mammals and birds have the same core feelings people do." There are many ways to elaborate on this, as various writers have, but it usually comes down to a few essential concerns. Animals have memories, which allow them to have a perception, at the very least, of cause and effect – something at the heart of classical conditioning. This is where the insights of behaviourism become a powerful tool not only in training a dog but in building a trusting bond between a dog and its owner. Behaviourism is a school of psychology founded in the United States by John Watson, although he had significant precursors whose experiments also showed how specific actions and sequences of repeated events can cause predictable emotional reactions. When most people think of emotions, however, they're unwilling to reduce them only to predictable reactions. We like to consider ourselves more mysterious than that. Some dog writers go so far as to conjecture that dogs have pure emotions, or emotions less coloured by shades of feeling. The reasoning appears to be that animals are less complicated than humans so their emotions must also be less complicated. This may, in fact, be true. Grandin suggests that animals aren't ambivalent in their emotions, they don't have "mixed emotions." Like many things written about dogs, this seems to me a partial truth. Some dogs, for example, show an unsettled emotional state while sitting in the waiting room of a veterinary clinic. Is it fear, a rather clear-cut or pure emotion, or anxiety, something more complicated or mixed? The problem here is one of categories. Why should fear in a human exactly resemble fear in a dog? After all, a ten-year-old boy, a twenty-year-old youth, a middle-aged man, and a senior citizen may all feel fear but show it in different ways; even a single individual may manifest fear in different ways over a period of twenty-four hours. Any quest for exact emotional correspondences between humans and dogs seems a foolish one. What is anxiety like for a human being? Books may tell us, as well as direct words from someone suffering it. Canine anxiety, alas, is something we can only observe, or read about secondhand from other human observers. In this sense we move closer to the core of our problem with animal emotions. Put simply, humans often don't trust their own eyes, even if they're genuinely observant. Careless or hurried or self-doubting or curious and analytical, we like to put things into words – and dogs can't.

EXCREMENT

In one of the episodes of his popular TV sitcom, comedian Jerry Seinfeld speculated about what extraterrestrials might have thought when they watched earthlings following their dogs and collecting "it" in small bags; the British writer Stephen Foster, in his memoir, *Walking Ollie,* wrote that "excrement, for the dog owner, is as the tea leaf to the clairvoyant;" and American poet Howard Nemerov, in "Walking the Dog," claimed that excrement was one of the things he shared with his canine pal: "We move along the street inspecting it." Perhaps gossip columnist Liz Smith best summed up this subject in her memoir, *Naturally Blonde,* when she wrote, succinctly, "dog responsibility centers on the alimentary canal."

There's something humbling about picking up after your dog. In our mechanized culture, it may even be a good thing for people to have such a basic, elemental task. Dog-training manuals always devote space to "house-breaking," as the phrase goes, but unlike a human baby, a puppy will never outgrow the need for help. And an older or sick dog may lose control of its bowels and bring its owner face to face with the messier facts of mortality. Dog people accept this but are still embarrassed to be caught in the act. Celebrity gossip writer Dominick Dunne told a story that perfectly illustrates this point. He'd been asked to write a short introduction for a book about Elizabeth Taylor's jewels, published by famed editor Michael Korda in 2002. In his introduction, Dunne recalled his first meeting with Taylor and her then-husband Richard Burton while working on her movie *Ash Wednesday*. On New Year's Eve, Dunne and the film's director came to meet the glamorous couple at the Grand Hotel in Rome: "As we entered the sitting room, Richard was on the floor in a green velvet dinner jacket picking up with a Kleenex dog shit left by their unhousebroken shih tzu, on which Elizabeth doted. Her dogs were never house-trained." It's no surprise that changes to the introduction were requested, though it's not clear who was behind them – Taylor, Korda, or Taylor's publicist. At any rate, Dunne declined to cooperate, and the introduction didn't appear until five years later, in *Vanity Fair*, including alongside it Michael Korda's letter, in point form, with this request up front: "2. Strike reference to RB 'picking up dog shit,' page 2."

If you live in a northern climate as I do, the end of winter is bound to be marked by melting snow that reveals the location and amount of excrement left over the past months by people who refuse to clean up after their dogs. It's not a pretty sight, and the longed-for scent of spring earth mingles with another, more acrid, smell. Not much, it seems, can be done about this, even when No Dumping signs are posted with the threat of municipal fines. In my neighbourhood, the larger the breed, the more likely that it will be sniffing about off lead and making deposits wherever it wishes. I've seen the same pattern from Boston to Los Angeles, which may show something about people who prefer big dogs. A few very civilized European cities, such as Berne, Vienna, and Zurich, and several American cities, too, including West Hollywood, California, have attached metal boxes holding plastic bags for dog waste to utility poles. It's a fine idea, though I've still watched people walk by them, zombie-like, while an unleashed dog did its business on the sidewalk. (The attractive, two-toned gray Viennese bag is printed with a line drawing of a dog and three sketches of how to use the bag itself, as well as this genteel, four-line reminder: *"Hundebesitzer/Innen – Danke für Ihren Beitrag – Nicht für Nahrungsmittel Geeignet! – Nur für Hundekotentsorgung!"* Or, "Dog owners – Thank you for your contribution – Not suitable for foodstuffs! – Only for the disposal of dog excrement!")

The problem of dog waste can, however, seem almost insurmountable. In *The Discovery of France*, Graham Robb's study of the country's historical geography from the Revolution to the First World War, dog waste became a measure of the shift from bygone agricultural life to modern city living. "City dogs today are thought of mainly as an excremental menace," he wrote, with over eight million dogs in France – two hundred thousand in Paris – responsible for eighty tons of excrement each day. Long ago, he suggested, "when manure was gold, this was not a major complaint." Unlike Paris, New York City has passed stringent laws requiring owners to clean up after their pets, and then set out to enforce them. Michael Brandow recounts these efforts, and the ensuing conflicts, in his book *New York's poop scoop law: Dogs, the dirt, and due process.* This study reads like a saga of gang wars for control of the city's sidewalks and other public places. Laboratory science, however, may make such conflicts a thing of the past. In the spring of 2011, the BioPet Vet Lab in Knoxville, Tennessee, was able to identify the dog owners who neglected to clean up after their pets when a system called Poo Prints was used to reveal the DNA of fecal samples registered in their database (registration was a requirement of various apartment and condominium complexes). Similar systems have been used in Canada and Israel, but for now, dogs without registered DNA can bypass them.

Disposing of dog waste has become a civic assignment, usually left to municipal parks departments responsible for the care of parks and playgrounds, as well as a new business opportunity. Stephen J. Dubner and Steven D. Litt, authors of *Freakonomics: A Rogue Economist Explores the Hidden Side of Everything*, have even suggested that neglected dog feces could be tested for fecal DNA against a DNA bank, with individual DNA samples gathered and filed when a dog is licensed, and the offending owners subsequently ticketed. It's not likely to happen soon, though the idea has also been discussed in Europe, in Vienna and Dresden. (Dubner and Litt note that while there were probably at least a million dogs living in New York City in 2003, according to public record only 102,004 were licensed.) Today in many large North American cities individuals unwilling to pick up the dog feces in their own backyards can hire a service for the task. Toronto's entrepreneurial (and aptly named) James Beagle, of Super Scoopers, in business since 1981, has said of his work: "As far as dog poop's concerned, it's repeat business. It never stops." Ahead of Canadians, American scoopers have even formed the Association of Waste Specialists, though membership is not mandatory.

For a while during March 2004, newspapers carried stories about plans emanating, naturally, from "liberal San Francisco" (as the American media sometimes likes to characterize it) about using dog waste as an energy source. Then, just as quickly, such articles vanished. But they gave me an idea, though I feared it was a bad one. I spoke with several owners of local plant nurseries about using dog excrement as a garden fertilizer. Might it be good for the roses? Apparently dog waste, unlike properly treated cow manure, belongs in the garbage, not the garden.

FICTION

In the fall of 1996, after giving a reading at the university where I teach, the short-story writer Mavis Gallant and I were to have dinner. Since I knew she liked champagne, I'd planned to start the evening at my place with some Veuve Cliquot, and hoped that Gallant liked dogs, too, because Zoli, then not quite two years old, greeted guests enthusiastically. Our talk soon turned to dogs, and Gallant asked if I'd started not doing things because of the dog – refusing invitations, not going out. It was coming to that, I admitted, and when she shook her head knowingly, I remembered the closing line from one of her stories, "Luc and His Father": "Whatever happens, don't get your life all mixed up with a dog's." Gallant, who has lived in Paris since the 1950s, could write such a line because she'd once loved a black poodle named Dinah, a dog she'd bought from a Spanish pet shop in 1952 after spotting a forlorn litter of puppies in its window. We spoke, inevitably, of books about dogs like J.R. Ackerley's *My Dog Tulip*. She said, "You can't write about dogs, it always comes out sentimental."

Gallant made a good point – dogs pose a problem for fiction writers. You wouldn't expect this because writers, who often live with dogs, are thought to be introspective, an ideal trait for someone who wants to understand the human/dog bond. Sentimentality is one problem but not the only one. Even the most postmodern works of fiction include plots of some sort, and dogs can too easily become plot contrivances. As well, such dogs often appear as an indication of a human character's personality. The Pomeranian in Chekhov's much-anthologized story "The Lady with the Pet Dog" tells readers about a central character's class and taste, though it has little significance in itself, like the pugs in Gallant's "A Recollection." Picturing the story's eccentric heroine, she described a character with two yappy pugs that wore small, annoying chimes. "She washed them with scented soap and fed them at table, sitting on her lap. They had rashes all over their bodies, and were always throwing up." These dogs are passive figures in the plot – characters live their lives while their pets watch, or not. Of course there's nothing wrong with such fictional dogs, and I like coming across them.

In case it seems that I'm disparaging plot, I want to make a few general remarks. Plot, in essence, is about conflict and change. Conflict comes from what a character wants, what blocks him or her (internally or externally), and how the situation is resolved. If fictional dogs are to be anything more than props, they need to be connected to the conflict at the heart of a story. Too often dogs have been used as role models (in writing for children) or to illustrate a human character's humanity – good characters like dogs, bad characters kick them. It should come as no surprise that the most common event in plots where dogs are not mere decoration is human cruelty, from neglect to outright physical abuse. Only a few fiction writers have been interested in dogs as dogs, attempting to understand how a dog sees and feels about its world. Yet, like the best scientists and social scientists who study dogs, fiction writers can extend our understanding of the human/dog bond and even of dogs themselves.

1. ADVENTURE AND ANIMALS

Writers of genre fiction such as adventure, mysteries, and speculative tales – fiction with unique conventions, written for a specific audience – have often found dogs well-suited to be plot agents. Animal stories are one of the oldest sub-species of adventure fiction, and they thrive on exotic locales and physical action. Novels such as Jack London's *The Call of the Wild* and *White Fang* provided both amply in stories that are now enjoyed for their historical resonance, although at the time of publication

(1903 and 1906 respectively) the Gold Rush was recent history. Dogs had been important workers in the Yukon wilderness, part of human teams, which meant that conflict was built into their daily lives. Jack London, a free-spirited wanderer, had lived the life he wrote about, with the tests of physical strength, psychological trials, daring chase scenes, and close calls that suit adventure yarns. In the case of Buck, his canine hero, the dog had been kidnapped from his comfortable home on a California estate and was challenged by his harsh new environment. From the novel's assured opening lines – "Buck did not read the newspapers, or he would have known that trouble was brewing, not only for himself, but for every tide-water dog, strong of muscle and with warm, long hair, from Puget Sound to San Diego." – it's easy to see why *The Call of the Wild* became an overnight bestseller. Until television and video games won the day, London was also popular with children. I can still recall the first time I read a Jack London novel and was transported from my bedroom to a Yukon blizzard. Few books read as a child can stand up years later to rereading, but *The Call of the Wild* is one of them.

A contemporary of London, and also an American newspaper journalist, Eleanor Atkinson wrote *Greyfriars Bobby* in 1912 for an adult audience, but it soon found a popular niche with children. Set in Edinburgh, Scotland, which Atkinson had never visited, the novel claims to be based on a true story about a Skye terrier who was so devoted to his owner that he suffered just about any imaginable indignity to lie on Auld Jock's grave in the Greyfriars cemetery. (Contemporary Edinburgh and its tourism industry have successfully co-opted Bobby's story in statues, postcards, etc.) With a sharp sense of local dialect – the Penguin Popular Classics edition includes a glossary – Atkinson offered trials, chase scenes, and cliffhangers, but there's nothing mechanical about her tender story, and it can still be read for more than period charm, and without cringing at the evangelical messages that overwhelm other dog classics of the Victorian era, such as *Bob, Son of Battle* (1898) by the British writer Alfred Ollivant. This coming-of-age story about two rival sheepdogs and a young boy who is caught between them became popular with children, even though most of the novel's dialogue was written in the Cumbrian dialect. One last curiosity: *Beautiful Joe* by (Margaret) Marshall Saunders. Published in 1894 and narrated by a dog who identifies himself as "part fox-terrier and part bull-terrier," this still-charming account of a noble dog who, though abused, has remained open-hearted, was also based on a true story, first heard by Saunders when she visited her brother in Meaford, Ontario, on Georgian Bay. (Today a park marks Joe's spot, and there's even a Beautiful Joe Heritage Society.) *Beautiful Joe* is reputed to be the first Canadian book to have sold more than a million copies internationally, proving that didacticism can sometimes be a good traveller.

2. MYSTERIES

Since Sir Arthur Conan Doyle's *The Hound of the Baskervilles* (1902), dogs have pointed towards clues that readers shouldn't miss. Who murdered Sir Charles Baskerville of Baskerville Hall? Was it the ghost of a hound that one of his ancestors killed in 1648? Sherlock Holmes and his sidekick Watson set out to find a less supernatural explanation before another death occurs. And, of course, they did. (The mysterious hound turns out to be a mastiff-bloodhound mixed breed with a salve of gleaming phosphorous around its eyes and mouth.) Inheriting a fine British tradition, Agatha Christie included a wirehaired fox terrier named Bob in one of her Hercule Poirot mysteries, *Dumb Witness* (1937), as both witness to a murder and a suspect. Poirot, who refers to the dog as "Monsieur Bob," inevitably uncovers the identity of the true killer while restoring the dog's good name, once Bob has had enough time to point him in the right direction.

When I spoke with a proprietor of Sleuth of Baker Street, in Toronto – one of the last independent bookstores in North America devoted to mystery and crime writing, and with its own resident dog, a standard poodle named Percy – he referred to the sub-genre of mysteries with helpful dogs as "fluff," saying, "I neither read them nor care to read them." Having ploughed through piles of such books, I understood his viewpoint; a great deal of "cute" writing dominates this popular field, if one can call it that. Following on Conan Doyle and Christie, in recent years Donna Ball, Carol Lea Benjamin, Laurien Berenson, Susan Conant, Lee Charles Kelley, A.J. Orde, Spencer Quinn, Lillian M. Roberts, and David Rosenfelt have let dogs set the plots of their novels in motion by sniffing out a corpse or something of the sort, occasionally in the world of high-stakes dog shows, as in Berenson's *A Pedigree to Die For* and *Underdog*. Unlike purely prop dogs, detective dogs fall into the category of working dogs – they often know things that their human owners have to discover. Just don't expect them to be more than secondary players; it's the humans who restore order by the mystery's end. Lillian M. Roberts, a Palm Springs veterinarian who has written a mystery series with a Palm Springs veterinarian as the quasi-detective, creates a few puzzles of her own. In *Almost Human*, the murder victim owns a Cavalier King Charles spaniel named Frankie, who "looked up at his mistress, wagging his tailless back end happily." What's going on here? Cavaliers are admired for their plume-like tails, and there's even a term for their luxurious paw and tail hair: feathering. Frankie's "tailless back end" makes no sense (was he docked, or born that way?), and when a detail like this appears on page seventeen of any mystery, it's either a clue or an error – in this case, the latter.

One weakness of many contemporary mystery writers, who come up with books almost annually, is that they pad their novels with irrelevant details of their detective's domestic life. Most readers of mystery fiction want puzzling corpses and intricate plots, not romance. Lee Charles Kelley's Jack Field series, about an ex-New York policeman who owns a kennel in Maine, features a smart-aleck hero fascinated by his romantic life. A professional dog trainer, Kelley gives his detective his own theory that a dog pack is a self-emergent system, ending *To Collar a Killer* with a bibliography, but little of this is dramatized. Susan Conant, who has received several Maxwell Awards for fiction writing from the Dog Writers' Association of America, also spends too much time on the personal life of her detective, but those parts can be skimmed. Donna Ball, another dog trainer, is more successful with her Raine Stockton series. The obsession of her dog-training, kennel-owning heroine for her ex-husband can, however, be trying. But Raine's dog, a search-and-rescue yellow Lab, does play a central role in the books. Spencer Quinn's *Dog on It* features a canine narrator named Chet, and manages not to be too coy. The mutt and his master, a private investigator, often misunderstand each other in the most convincing manner. Best of all is Carol Lea Benjamin, another dog trainer-cum-writer who has created Rachel Alexander, a detective heroine (and former dog trainer) who runs a private-investigation agency in Manhattan called "Alexander and Dash," with her pet pitbull Dashiell (named with a nod to Dashiell Hammett of *The Thin Man* fame). Benjamin's best, *This Dog for Hire*, begins with a corpse and a missing basenji who has a date at the upcoming Westminster Kennel Club competition.

Readers who like their canine mysteries blended with the supernatural can turn to Stephen King's *Cujo* or *Pet Sematary*. A two-hundred-pound Saint Bernard, Cujo owes more to the tradition of vampires and werewolves than to real or fictional dogs. King peppers the account of this monster's demise with generalities about dogs that would take pages to unpack. "Dogs," he tells us, "have a sense of self-consciousness that is far out of proportion to their intelligence" – that's just one of many unfavourable asides. When King ties up the mystery by blaming Cujo's behaviour on "possibly destiny, or fate, or only a degenerate nerve disease called rabies. Free will was not a factor," he tries to have his cake and eat it, too. Following *destiny* or *fate*, that dismissive *or only* makes way for a mention of *free will*, a religious concept rarely associated with dogs. In a similar vein, mass-market thrillers like Dean Koontz's *The Darkest Evening of the Year*, with Nickie, an unusual golden retriever, promise preternatural chills. But sketchy, pedestrian writing and cheesey confrontations between Good and Evil leave me cold – and bored. As I said before, the writer of an abecedarian has strong opinions. For mysterious horror *The Hound of the Baskervilles*, though creaky, hasn't been surpassed.

3. POLITICAL ALLEGORIES, SPECULATIVE FICTION, AND SCIENCE FICTION

Eventually the escapist nature of pure adventure loses its edge. For something richer, *The Plague Years* (1978) by Richard Adams is a good place to start. Adams has more at stake than feats of physical survival, although his fine novel, set in the Lake District made famous by Wordsworth and other Romantic poets, has its share of those. Two dogs, a black-and-white fox terrier and a large black mongrel, escape from a laboratory devoted to animal experimentation. Badly injured, they manage to survive against all odds, while the human characters believe that the dogs are carriers of the bubonic plague. I won't spoil the story, except to add that the dogs come off better than the humans.

The adventure genre is flexible enough to accommodate the larger purposes of political allegory. With a distant origin in Aesop's and other animal fables, and also medieval bestiaries, novels such as Mikhail Bulgakov's *The Heart of a Dog* and Tibor Déry's *Niki: The Story of a Dog* belong to the tradition where animals have to stand in for human characters because a political regime makes direct human representation impossible (Bulgakov's novel was published in 1925 in Soviet Russia, and Déry's in 1956 in Soviet-occupied Hungary). George Orwell's *Animal Farm* (1945) may be the most famous novel using the animal-fable genre. Dogs are enough like us, whether anthropomorphically so or not, to be good surrogates in a political allegory. Along with its barnyard characters, *Animal Farm* includes three dogs – Bluebell, Jessie, and Pincher – who, as subjects of the animals' Rebellion against Man, must follow the new Seven Commandments, including number four, "No animal shall sleep in a bed." In this parody of the rise of totalitarianism, potentially worthy sentiments ("All animals are equal;" "No animal shall kill any other animal") are soon perverted in the name of the farm, or state. When puppies are born, they're taken from their mothers and raised by Napoleon, a sinister Berkshire boar, only to return to farm life as his private guards, "as fierce-looking as wolves," in a kind of reverse evolution.

The plots of the best political allegories, like Bulgakov's *The Heart of the Dog* and Déry's *Niki: The Story of a Dog*, transcend their sociohistorical conditions. At issue is the human/dog connection, whether it's in Bulgakov's tale of a Russian surgeon who transplants human glands into a dog and turns him into a half-man/half-beast, a threatening creature called the Commissar who wants to eliminate all "vagrant quadrupeds," or Déry's story about the life of a domestic dog and the people she lives with, a gentle married couple who suffer the brutalities of life under a Communist dictatorship, including privation and, for the husband, imprisonment. Niki, of course, cannot understand the exact nature of her family's sufferings or the Communist logic that pet-keeping is a bourgeois preoccupation, but she suffers alongside her masters, her miseries a reflection of their own. Convincingly canine, Niki is both a dog *and* a symbol, which makes her story all the more powerful. When she is allowed to express her nature fully, to explore the countryside as well as her Budapest neighbourhood, and to live harmoniously with her human pack, Niki is as vibrant and endearing as any novel's heroine, while Camille on her deathbed has nothing over the dog's demise. This short novel, which achieved international success in translation after the abortive Hungarian Revolution of 1956, deserves to be known today much more widely than it is and has recently been reissued by New York Review Books.

Perhaps owing a debt to Déry, at the age of seventy the Hungarian writer Magda Szabó published an extraordinary novel, *The Door*, which tells the story of a prominent woman writer's intense and complicated relationship with her larger-than-life housekeeper, Emerence, whose mysterious history is scarred by the tragedies of the twentieth century. The dog in question, a male mongrel named Viola (there's a reason), is owned by the writer but devoted to Emerence, and the tensions between the women are often reflected in the dog's behaviour. Viola manages to bridge two worlds: that of his cosmopolitan mistress, Magdushka, and the life force of Emerence, who communicates with him as if she were the last human on earth to be able to speak with animals. By the end of the novel, the writer/narrator comes to understand that "the more simple a thing was, the less likely it was to be understood," which might serve as a description of the human/dog bond.

Speculative fiction and science fiction, its relative, are also tricky genres, concerned as they are with ideas as well as stories. In several of the best books in this category, books that deserve to be read not only by genre afficionados, the nature of the human/dog bond is central. Kirsten Bakis's *Lives of the Monster Dogs* is one of the most original. Her novel tells the story of a strange pack of dogs who arrive in New York City in 2009 from a town in the Canadian wilderness where they've been bred with artificial voice boxes and prosthetic hands. The dogs, who walk on their hind legs and sport nineteenth-century clothing, carry the secret of a troubled past which is eventually revealed as the dogs, weary of their half-human/half-dog nature, face mortality. This elegiac story, told in both dog and human voices, is unsettling precisely because it takes a dog's experience seriously, and by implication suggests that human knowledge is just as self-serving as the history revealed in the novel. As the principal dog character of the novel writes in his journal, "It is a terrible thing to be a dog and know it." Anyone who has looked into his own dog's eyes, pondering what is knowable about the dog's inner life – and what isn't – will be moved by Bakis's distorting mirror: What exists beyond appearances?

The dogs in Bakis's novel are neither exactly dog nor human but in-between creatures, and this is often the case with "dogs" in science fiction. One of the most unusual canine characters is the Mechanical Hound in Ray Bradbury's dystopian nightmare, *Fahrenheit 451*. Set in a futuristic world where books are banned and burned (hence the title), the novel's firehouses each have a sinister mascot who "slept but did not sleep, lived but did not live in its gently humming, gently vibrating, softly illuminated kennel." The man-made Mechanical Hounds, with nylon-brushed nostrils, eight legs and rubber-padded paws, can do many of the things than ordinary dogs do – they guard and growl and, when pressed, attack; they are also used in late-night games to torture cats, chickens, and rats. As one character reassures another, the creature is only made up of copper wire, batteries, and electricity. Programmed for brutishness, the dog troubles Montag, the novel's hero: "...all we put into it is hunting and finding and killing. What a shame if that's all it can ever know." Montag's remark is one of the first indications that he will come to question his totalitarian world, and a colleague immediately senses the implications of antisocial thought, asking if Montag has a guilty conscience. Even this artificial monstrosity can evoke the ancient human/dog bond. (In an afterword to the novel, Bradbury referred to the Mechanical Hound as his robot clone of Arthur Conan Doyle's Baskerville beast.)

In a genre sometimes referred to as "future histories," two other classics stand out. The British philosopher and novelist Olaf Stapledon's *Sirius* (1944) tells of a man-made dog with extraordinary intelligence. Stapledon acknowledged his debt to J. Herries McCulloch's study *Sheep Dogs and Their Masters*, but not to the inane scientific experiments in Jonathan Swift's *Gulliver's Travels* or to Mary Shelley's *Frankenstein*. Whatever inspired him, Stapledon's portrait of a "super-sheep-dog," an Alsatian named Sirius (after the Dog Star), belongs on a shelf with them. More than a satire on selective breeding programs, *Sirius* is an indictment of human arrogance. Given human nature, the super-dog can only become an outcast. The novel's tragic end ("Dying – is very – cold," the dog seems to say to the one human who truly loved him) has a mythic resonance. A more wickedly optimistic ending has made Harlan Ellison's apocalyptic short story "A Boy and His Dog" a cult classic, along with the 1975 film version starring Don Johnson. In the year 2034 a fifteen-year-old boy, Vic, and his exceptionally smart dog named Blood, a German shepherd-puli mix, adventure through a blasted postwar world. They communicate telepathically and manage to survive by their wits (mainly the dog's), in a reversal of the guardian role humans usually take. If Blood wants to tease Vic, he calls him Albert – "He thought that was pretty damned funny. Payson Terhune: ha ha." When a young woman tries to get between them, and forces a choice on Vic, the story implies that he chooses wisely: desperately hungry, boy and dog end up eating the girl. As Ellison concludes, "A boy loves his dog." This story, however, is not just the sum of its clever conceit, pop-culture references, and snappy style. Ellison shows a deep understanding of the human/dog bond, which grounds his story's antics in the melancholy knowledge that at the end of time the most profound, unselfish love might, ironically, be the bond between a teenage boy and his dog.

The most complex dog characters in speculative fiction embody the tension between the human/dog polarity. In *The Memoirs of a Survivor*, Doris Lessing sketches the apocalypse through the story of an unnamed middle-aged woman who, with little choice, becomes guardian to a twelve-year-old girl and her pet companion Hugo, a curious, yellow, hybrid dog-cat. At a moment of social decay, where people have for the time being agreed not to eat the meat of dogs and cats, the narrator fears for Hugo's life, while he appears to understand his precarious situation as well. Eventually the narrator comes to accept Hugo's presence: "He was not a difficult animal (I nearly said person!) to share a home with. He did not seem to sleep much; he kept watch. I believe this was how he saw his function...."

But Lessing isn't content to stop with the familiar image of dogs as guards. Addressing the interplay of human/dog emotions, she describes Hugo at the window, watching the outside world, his head dodging back and forth to keep out of sight. He's thinking, she argues, and then dismisses any objections about anthropomorphism. We share our emotional lives with animals and "flatter ourselves" that their feelings are less complicated than ours. She even suggests that dogs may feel something like romantic love in their devotion to us, finally going on to dismiss our intellectual achievements as mechanical and materialistic – space exploration, moon walks, and the by-products of petroleum – arising from a world where we live "in the ruins of this variety of intelligence."

Known for her deep attachment to cats, Lessing reminds us that humans fail their pets more often than they fail us. We seem to need slaves and victims, and this is what our pets sometimes become when we train them into those roles: "But not all, not by any means; all the time, through our lives, we are accompanied, everywhere we go, by creatures who judge us, and who behave at times with a nobility which is...we call it human." Lessing might consider it a small leap from selective dog breeding and training to Bradbury's Mechanical Hound. Why not dispense with messy animal traits altogether? Because there is something we call "human" in all animals.

Lessing included another haunting dog character in *The Story of General Dann and Mara's Daughter, Griot and the Snow Dog*, perhaps to remind us that at the end of the world we will keep our dogs close to us, as one of the last reminders of our humanity. As a side note, I want to add that in 2007 she received (and deserved) the Nobel Prize for Literature, a distinction Lessing now shares with several other writers – Thomas Mann, John Steinbeck, and J.M. Coetzee – who have also written passionately about dogs and animal life. And anyone who hasn't read Coetzee's harrowing *Disgrace* should immediately find a copy. The novel, which begins in the world of university sexual politics, descends into a hellish account of life in rural South Africa. A local animal shelter becomes the refuge of the disgraced hero, who finds penance in disposing of the bodies of euthanized dogs in a respectful manner. As Coetzee's protagonist gradually accepts a place in the makeshift operating room, where he assists in a job that "gets harder all the time," the distinctions between human and animal life blur, and death is given some dignity, if not meaning.

The finest example of the human/dog polarity is a French novel about a human baby born with the head of a spaniel, Jean Dutourd's *A Dog's Head*. As Dutourd's protagonist Edmund du Chaillu matures from babyhood to an adult life of shame, he tries to understand the constant pull between both sides of his nature: the urge to fetch a newspaper, smell a dog on the street, bite an offending hand, in contrast with his desire to serve his country and find loving companionship. Fearing his son's "canine predestination," Edmund's father cautions him that one day he will be a man with duties and rights, and even asks if the dog/boy feels proud to be a man. But what Edmund feels is alienation, because the human world has no place for him. After stints in the army and in banking, Edmund makes enough money from the stock market to buy a house with a library that contains a rare edition of Ovid's *Metamorphoses*, a Roman compilation of Greek myths. Edmund understands the sufferings of humans changed into beasts and their "inability to express themselves, regret for the irremediable, and a profound feeling of subjugation, for animals are always slaves." The myths make sense to Edmund because of his "deep conviction that men and beasts are made of the same flesh, animated by the same spirit, capable of uniting with each other. The ancients, close as they were to the birth of the world, knew this truth; but in three thousand years it had grown dim. In those days a dog's head was not a fatal curse. *Today men believe that an impassable wall separates them from animals.*" (Italics mine.)

Rejecting plastic surgery and psychoanalysis, Edmund remains troubled by his dual nature until he travels to Egypt, where he's overcome by a statue of Anubis, a god with a man's body and a jackal's head. But what can he learn from it? Back home he meets Anne, a young woman who loves him desperately, though he soon realizes that she's lunatic enough to believe they're living in a fairy tale. Sending her to a psychiatric clinic costs him his fortune. They marry after her release and he accepts a job as a country gamekeeper, gradually reverting to dog-like ways – instead of reading, he howls at the hares while his wife speaks to him in a semi-canine language. The novel's ominous closing bypasses Edmund, now lost to doghood, for his wife who, covered with fleas, is happily three months pregnant. While some literary critics like to read this wry book as an allegory about marginalization, that's too easy, too pat, and misses the deep sadness of the novel. Edmund's final victory-of-sorts comes when he claims his head, and all that it implies, through his heart, accepting his animal nature and making the fatal choice to cross over that "impassable wall."

4. CONTEMPORARY AND CLASSIC FICTION

Dogs less prone to a dual nature have been featured in secondary roles in many contemporary novels. In Paul Auster's *Timbuktu* and Cathleen Schine's *The New Yorkers*, dogs highlight our modern condition, angst and all. Like Schine's novel, Alison Pace's *Pug Hill* and Leslie Schnur's *The Dog Walker* are the kind of books sometimes called urban fairy tales, not exactly romance fiction but very much concerned with pairing off people who meet through their dogs. In a similar vein, but more acerbic, *The Hidden Life of Humans* by Canadian playwright Erica Ritter conveys romantic travails both through the reflections of its fortyish heroine and the eyes of a mutt named Murphy that she's dogsitting. (Murphy's sections are set off by a small black image of a dog's paw, as well as a different typeface.) While Oprah Winfrey's Book Club promoted David Wroblewski's *The Story of Edgar Sawtelle*, I found its passages about dog breeding far more interesting than the long retelling of the Hamlet story. More original are the stories told entirely from a dog's point of view, whether by a first- or third-person narrator. This voice is hard to do well and the one-step-removed distance of the third-person narrator is often more effective, maintaining a sense of mystery while avoiding the coyness that animals in the first person tend to exhibit. Only a few fiction writers have used this device, most successfully in the short-story form. Some of their best work has been collected in anthologies such as *The Company of Dogs: 21 Stories by Contemporary Masters*, edited by Michael Rosen, and *The Literary Dog: Great Contemporary Dog Stories*, edited by Jeanne Schinto.

On rare occasion, dogs have been at the centre of fiction. Without Oprah Winfrey to make them better known, here are four exceptional books. First, Jill Ciment's *Heroic Measures*. The story of a Manhattan couple who plan to sell their downtown condo just as their aging dachshund needs to be rushed into surgery, *Heroic*

Measures includes passages told from the dog's point of view that are among the most believeable I've read anywhere. This taut novel (which includes a terrorist threat to the city) balances the fragility of the human/dog bond with the anxieties of urban life after 9/11. Turning back in time, Scottish novelist Andrew O'Hagan's *The Life and Opinions of Maf the Dog and of his friend Marilyn Monroe* recreates the late 1950s and early 1960s with such flair and detail that it's almost like being there. Maf, the narrator, a Westie given to Monroe by Frank Sinatra (and named Maf after the phrase "Mafia honey"), ranges far and wide in his account of celebrity shenanigans during the last two painful years of Monroe's life. But the novel is crafted to keep its narrative voice a dog's voice, albeit a wise and clever one. More than a ventriloquist's act, this splendid book belongs on any shelf beside Virginia Woolf's *Flush*. Rebecca Brown's *The Dogs: A Modern Bestiary* takes its form from medieval books about real and mythical animals. The nameless narrator lives in a studio apartment with her pack of Doberman pinschers who may also be angels. Exploding ordinary reality into a space of mystic and fairy tale visions and then settling back into the mundane, *The Dogs* makes the unseen troublingly concrete. (When the narrator remarks of one dog, "She lived inside my life," most dog owners will nod agreement.) Finally, there's Australian writer Eva Hornung's *Dog Boy*, inspired by the true story of a Russian child, Ivan Mishukov, who, after the collapse of the Soviet empire, was raised by feral dogs from the age of four to six. Hornung's portrait of the human/dog bond in the worst possible conditions is horrific. Romochka, the boy-dog, eventually finds himself caught between his dual natures, yet, as he matures, his harsh life with his dog family seems almost more humane than his encounters in Moscow's human world. This is a work of rich moral imagination.

Admirers of classic novels such as *Anna Karenina* may not immediately think of dogs, but Leo Tolstoy created a complete world, not just a love story for his eponymous heroine. When Levin, a stand-in for the author's version of Christian socialism, returns to his country estate – really a working farm – after a failed marriage proposal, he's greeted by simple peasants and, of course, by his dog: "The pointer bitch Laska ran out, almost knocking Kuzma off his feet, and rubbed herself against Levin's knees, stood on her hind legs and wanted but did not dare to put her front paws on his chest." Argos-like, Laska interests me because of Tolstoy's insight into her character: "[she] *wanted but did not dare to put her front paws on his chest.*" This is not anthropomorphism but rather a subtle presentation of character – a pointer bitch's moment of internal conflict. In *Anna Karenina*, first published in Russia in 1878, even a dog knows how to behave with more restraint than many of the human characters.

When Tolstoy's dogs are asked to do a dog's traditional work, they comply eagerly. *War and Peace* includes a fast-paced wolf hunt that runs over four chapters. The principal dogs are borzoi, a breed associated with the Russian aristocracy before the Revolution, when these dogs lost favour. The hunt is a large affair with almost a hundred and thirty dogs, including nearly fifty borzoi. In spite of the crowd every dog knew its name and its master, and care is taken not to harm any of them. As the mist burns off the mid-September morning several chases begin and soon merge into one, with the wolfhounds and bloodhounds becoming a single pack. Natasha, the novel's heroine, is warned to stay out of the way of the pack, and dogs are praised for being "swift-footed" or "a catcher." Eventually the wolf is caught in a passage that makes it hard to believe wolves and dogs were once related: "It was obvious to the hunters, and to the dogs, and to the wolf himself that it was all over now. The beast, his ears laid back fearfully, tried to get up, but the dogs clung to him." The hunt then shifts to the pursuit of a red fox and finally becomes a contest between two dogs over a hare. Often considered the supreme realist, Tolstoy understood the psychology of individual dogs as well as pack behaviour.

If only Colette, who wrote so well about cats and who was a fancier of French bulldogs (with which she was often photographed), had written about them. However, it's worth seeking out Thomas Mann's "A Man and His Dog," Franz Kafka's "Investigations of a Dog," and Ivan Turgenev's "Mumu," a favourite of mine. "Mumu" tells of a clumsy, illiterate serf who adopts a stray spaniel only to find that his autocratic mistress wants the dog for herself. He hides his pet, who is devoted to him, and ultimately drowns it in a heart-wrenching scene before running away from the restrictions of his life, falling into a kind of madness. (Before Mumu's death, she's fed one final, rich tavern meal, a trope that other literary writers have since used – Brad Watson comes to mind, in his story "Bill.") As social commentary this almost prophetic story ranks among the masterpieces of protest literature, while at the same time it has a delicacy and wisdom achieved by only the greatest of the realist writers. And echoing accounts of dogs that have been faithful after their master's death, Vassily Aksyonov's memorable story "Around Dupont," a tale of émigré life that appeared in translation from the Russian in the *New Yorker*, deserves to be known not only by admirers of contemporary Russian literature but also for its splendid Irish setter.

I've saved the best for last – a short story by Chekhov entitled "Kashtanka." There's more to learn about dogs from Chekhov's eighteen pages than from half a dozen recent canine books. The story begins with a deceptively simple paragraph: "A young dog, a reddish mongrel, between a dachshund and a 'yard-dog,' very like a fox in face, was running up and down the pavement looking uneasily from side to side. From time to time she stopped and, whining and lifting first one chilled paw and then another, tried to make up her mind how it could have happened that she was lost." One might expect an adventure yarn à la Jack London, but this Russian master had something far more original in mind – nothing less than an exploration of loneliness and the longing for home, no matter what that home was. Kashtanka, his dog heroine, had in fact been lost by her owner, a harsh carpenter with a brutish son, both of whom often abused the dog, the boy physically, his father verbally. But Kashtanka longs to return to her familiar rooms, which smelled of the carpenter's trade, even when she's rescued by a kindly stranger, taken back to his apartment, treated well, fed well, renamed Auntie, and ultimately trained to join his circus act (he's a clown), along with the man's trained cat, goose, and pig. One night, during a performance, while Kashtanka is charming the audience, two people call out her old name – her former family. She runs to join them, follows them home, and, as expected, the carpenter immediately dismisses her as "a thing of little understanding." Kashtanka, however, "was glad that there had not been a break for a minute in her life," and vaguely remembers the kindly stranger, the delicious dinners and warm room as "a long, tangled, oppressive dream."

My brief account can't do justice to the story, which some critics have labelled "poignant," as if that allows them to be done with it. Chekhov's great sleight of hand is to write a story in which the dog/human bond is presented as the dog might experience it while, at the same time, creating such a fully realized dog heroine that her experience – consistent with everything we now know about animal behaviour – stands for both a dog's psyche and a human's. People commonly prefer a difficult, familiar situation to a better but new one, just as the abused often seek consolation from their abusers, troubling situations that take us into the world of psychoanalytic insight which Chekhov, a medical doctor as well as a writer, anticipates. "Kashtanka" gains its power because the conflict facing its protagonist is both internal and external, and the final choice demands a complex response from the reader.

FOOD

What to feed the dog? Anyone who has brought a new puppy – or an older dog – home, will have asked this question. Breeders naturally like to make suggestions, as do pet-shop staff, family, and friends with dogs, newspaper pet columnists, and your veterinarian. As Eric Knight put it in *Lassie Come-Home*, "From her [Lassie's] first memory, food had never been her responsibility. At stated times it was provided for her. Man put it down before her in a platter. She had been taught carefully that that was her portion, and she must never eat food that lay elsewhere. Year after year, that lesson had been driven into her. Food was not her responsibility. Man provided it." What kind of providers, then, are we?

In the early spring of 2007, news spread about recently poisoned dogs and cats and the recall of canned pet food. At first the lone culprit seemed to be an Ontario-based company, Menu Foods, and rat poison was the suspected ingredient. To complicate matters, Menu Foods was the supplier to dozens of name brands commonly sold across North America. On March 30, the Food and Drug Administration in the United States announced that it had not found rat poison in the recalled food, but a chemical named melamine, used to make plastic cutlery and in fertilizer. The list of recalled food expanded and soon included the first dry food – the high-end Prescription Diet m/d Feline made by Hills Pet Nutrition. According to the F.D.A., the melamine came from wheat gluten imported to the United States from China. (In 2006, American Customs data showed that 13 per cent of wheat gluten in the U.S. came from China; by the way, the F.D.A. inspects only 1 per cent of all imported food.) While officials were quick with the assurance that melamine was not a known toxin, they lacked the data to show if, or why, it was toxic to cats.

Dog owners had no respite as spokespersons from such

diverse places as Cornell University in Ithaca, New York, the Animal Health Laboratory at Canada's University of Guelph, and the Center for Veterinary Medicine at the F.D.A. continued to admit confusion. Meanwhile, the list of recalled products grew, and by early April over twenty-two types of dog biscuits made by Sunshine Mills Ltd. from tainted wheat gluten imported from China had joined the list. At first the Chinese government denied exporting wheat gluten to the United States or Canada, while TV and newspaper commentators reported that human food had not been contaminated. Meanwhile, on April 5 the F.D.A. warned consumers about puppy and dog chews that might be contaminated by salmonella, and more pet foods – now over a hundred brands – had been recalled. The exact number of pets that had died from these tainted products remained controversial and Senator Dick Durbin, a Democrat from Illinois, called for a government hearing to question F.D.A. officials. According to *The New York Times*, he wanted "standardized federal regulations and inspection requirements in pet food" – something everyone had assumed was already in place. Telephone numbers and website addresses for various hot lines were common features in daily newspapers, reminding readers to be vigilant in selecting the right food for their dogs and cats, as if this advice was particularly helpful. None of the articles I read mentioned the possible presence of imported wheat gluten in human foods, perhaps fearing a public panic from a generation of consumers accustomed to – even addicted to – commercially prepared food.

Events were unfolding like the pages of a bio-terrorist thriller. Animals continued to sicken, individual and class-action law suits were filed, there was a ban on gluten exports from China's Xuzhou Anying Biologic Technology Development Company, and Zeng Xing, an official from the press office of China's General Administration of Quality, Supervision, Inspection and Quarantine (what an Orwellian name – and a press official, no less) announced an investigation, but with no details. According to Audra Ang of the Associated Press, "product contamination is a widespread problem in China." At the same time, the Las Vegas-based ChemNutra Inc., which had imported the gluten and sold it to companies making pet food, offered a press release saying that Xuzhou Anying had never reported melamine in its contents analyses, and that none of the contaminated gluten was sold to manufacturers of food for humans. On April 7, the general manager of Xuzhou Anying announced that the allegations were "under investigation." A few government officials even speculated in media interviews that the profit motive may have been involved in adding melamine to wheat gluten. At the Senate's hearing before an appropriations subcommittee on April 12, Dr. Stephen F. Sundlof, Director of the Center for Veterinary Medicine of the F.D.A., announced, "We know that there's not 100 per cent of the product off the shelf." What remained of the tainted food, recalled a month before, and where was it? No one seemed to know. As well, we learned that fewer that one-third of pet-food-manufacturing facilities in the U.S. had been inspected at least once in the last three and a half years. Better communication, everyone agreed, would be a good thing. And the recalls continued, with a new twist. On April 18, the F.D.A. announced that melamine was believed to have contaminated a rice-protein concentrate, again imported from China, used in dry and canned food for dogs and cats.

If anyone had read Ann N. Martin's troubling book *Food Pets Die For: Shocking Facts About Pet Food*, published in 1997, they wouldn't have been surprised. The animal by-products in most commercial pet food alone are enough to make one pause. And I'm just as guilty for buying commercial dog food as anyone else. The convenience of dry pet food itself makes the product attractive, as does its supposed benefit for a dog's healthy teeth. The Hills Prescription Diet products I've fed my dogs – sold through veterinary offices – offer me the illusion that I'm doing the best by my pet. (I used to feed Zoli IAMS until I passed a large billboard outside Buffalo, alongside Interstate 90, warning that "This is Sally. Cruelly used by Iams" with a picture of a sad-eyed, caged beagle.) Since my vet feeds his own dogs Hills products, the choice has seemed a reasonable one.

The North American pet-food industry has grown into a giant in the years since the Second World War, with familiar individual companies now part of large conglomerates. (Hills Pet Nutrition is owned by Colgate Palmolive.) Pal, the male collie who played Lassie in MGM's popular movie series, had a lucrative contract endorsing Red Heart dog food, his picture pasted on every can of it, but the public never knew that Pal thrived on a diet of homemade beef stew and water. Occasionally I come across people over fifty who remember their childhood dogs usually being fed on table scraps – dogs we recall as living to a ripe old age, even though current statistics from veterinarians assure us that canine longevity has increased. My parents' generation rarely offered their dogs anything other than home-made food, sometimes specially cooked for them, and the occasional commercial dog biscuit as a treat. (In the late 1990s, the upscale Restoration Hardware reissued as a nostalgia item metal canisters for Milk-Bone Dog Biscuits, and I bought one with a Boston terrier on it that brought back memories of family dogs as well as the once-small sections of grocery stores devoted to pet food in the 1950s.)

So I have to ask again, what to feed the dog? Anecdotal evidence will not be much help. At an Easter dinner at the nursing home where my mother lived, with Rennie sitting relatively calmly beside my chair, nearly a dozen people discussed the ongoing melamine scare and swapped stories about dog food. Two people insisted that every dog they'd known who was fed a popular and pricey product had died of cancer, but I had to add that Buster, my parents' last Boston terrier, had eaten that food for sixteen years and had died of old age. I've known people with vegan dogs (a bull terrier, in fact, who lived on a farm and was occasionally given the carcass of a freshly slaughtered pig as a treat); friends who cook a nightly hamburger for the dog, and if pressed by time, replace it with a McDonald's burger; and others who buy the cheapest canned brand during their weekly shopping trip. Some of these dogs are fussy eaters and need coaxing, some eat anything they're offered. Pugs like Zoli and Rennie approach a bowl of dried food with gusto – they would be excellent advertisements for their meal.

Cooking for your dog may appear to be one solution to the problem, but it should be done only after consulting a veterinarian. Finding the right balance of foods, vitamins, and minerals is not an easy task. And no dog's diet should be changed abruptly – home-cooked food has to be introduced with care – because a dog's digestive system is a more delicate mechanism than you might suspect. How good – and safe – are the natural ingredients we buy? That's another inevitable question. In an era of free trade and global economics, the pear in your fruit bowl – and much else that we consume – is more likely to have come from Chile or South Africa than from a nearby farm, let alone your own state or province. In their recent book *Feed Your Pet Right: The Authoritative Guide to Feeding Your Dog and Cat*, two professors of nutrition, Marion Nestle and Malden C. Nesheim, survey the various products available – from common brands to organic, holistic, vegetarian, natural, all-meat, gluten-free, high-fibre, and even kosher products, and they conclude that all pet foods, despite packaging, are made from the byproducts of human food production. The main thing to remember is that like much in life, whatever you do about feeding your dog may turn out to be wrong. The best we can hope for is to minimize the odds.

People who care about dog food always manage to share their concern. In the summer of 1995, when Zoli was four months old, I began taking him with me wherever I went, one afternoon to a bookstore signing for actress Janet Leigh, who was in town to promote her memoir about the making of Alfred Hitchcock's *Psycho*. After waiting in the long line, where Zoli had been much admired, we finally arrived before Leigh, who wore a hot-pink suit with high spike heels to match. I hadn't known that she was a dog person, and Zoli caught her attention at once. As we spoke, I could see that the shop's owners were annoyed by the slowdown, but Janet Leigh was busy relating a recipe she used for home-baked dog biscuits, time stopped, and everything else had to wait.

GARDENS

The garden always echoes a paradisal place, harkening back to Eden, though it can be a dangerous place for dogs. Anyone who fancies the flat-nosed breeds knows that the thorny canes of a rosebush are a threat to these bug-eyed canines; the same thorns can also catch a collie's tail. Since I won't dig up the roses, vigilance is essential if the dog is out while I'm working in the garden. And thorny roses are only the beginning.

Most dog people have probably heard that the Christmas poinsettia is poisonous. As well, azaleas, rhododendrons, holly leaves, all parts of the bleeding heart, clematis and chrysanthemums, foxgloves, daffodils, hyacinths (plant and bulb), tulip leaves and bulbs (not the flower, apparently), the leaves of the lily-of-the-valley, and wisteria pods and seeds, to mention just a few flowers and bushes, are toxic to some degree. While I know little about the tropical gardens of Florida or the desert gardens of New Mexico, the list of toxic plants alters regionally and needs to be investigated on a local basis. (Also check the list of dog-toxic plants on the website for the American Society for the Prevention of Cruelty to Animals.) Dogs will be unpredictable and will eat things they shouldn't. The symptoms of illness from poisioning vary and may include vomiting, diarrhea, lethargy, unusual salivation and breathing, and even death; of course, these may be symptoms of other illnesses, too. If you know what your dog has ingested, take a sample of it to your veterinarian, as well as any samples of vomit or fecal matter.

As well as toxic plants, gardens often include the various commercial poisons that some gardeners insist on using – fungicides, flower- and rose-care concentrates that protect against insects and disease, liquid fertilizers, and outdoor insect killers, in addition to plant-grow concoctions and bone meal. Their cans, bags, and boxes carry warning labels, but dogs don't read them. And don't forget that the seemingly insignificant mould on a dead leaf, left from the previous autumn, can cause stomach upset, although a small clump of fresh grass clippings probably isn't harmful unless your lawn is sprayed with one of the industrial pesticides that are supposedly "safe" after they've been applied for twenty-four hours. If in doubt about something a dog has ingested, it's best to telephone your veterinarian for advice, or an emergency animal clinic.

Invariably, male dogs are drawn to new plantings, to that delicate specimen you've struggled to nourish and bring back year after year. A happy dog enjoying his yard will not always remember good manners, and dog urine won't do a thing to improve the roses, not to mention a row of lettuce. I've found that certain garden jobs – transplanting iris, say – require full attention, and it's best to leave the dog in the house. Rennie has a special fascination with my gardening gloves, and I keep reminding myself not to leave them on the lawn unattended. Perhaps he'll outgrow this and learn to curl up in a shaded corner, as Zoli and Buster did. Then I'll only have to worry about fleas in the grass.

Rennie seems to enjoy watching certain garden jobs, particularly weeding, or when I remove small annuals like nicotiana from their flats and set them in the ground, and then I wonder what's going on in his head. At the risk of anthropomorphizing, I've even asked him what he's thinking ("Why can't I eat *that*?" perhaps) but he keeps his attention on the task at hand. At moments like these I think of the dogs who've spent happy hours in this garden since my family bought the house in 1960. As of this writing, I can see Spotty, Max, Buster, Zoli, Morgan, and now Rennie sniffing a favoured spot on the lawn or a plant in the herbaceous border. Gardens inevitably evoke mortality, and it amazes me to think that some of the rosebushes planted in the summer of 1960 still bloom in profusion, alive now for fifty years, so much longer than any of the dogs who knew the garden too briefly.

Perhaps the wealth of things to write about has stopped the best garden writers from speaking of dogs, but none of the classic books even mention them. In close touch with the cycle of seasons and the pattern of birth and rebirth, perhaps garden writers haven't time to tell about the dogs that enjoyed their gardens and spent hours there. This omission seems to me heartless. Most garden writers do, however, mention the flowering dogwood (*Cornus*). Its common name refers indirectly to the quadruped and it comes from England, where people once used a water-based extract made from dogwood bark as a treatment for mange in domestic dogs. And some prominent gardeners may be too busy to write about their work. Dale Haney, horticulturalist to the White House for more than three decades, did, however, admit that he has also minded every presidential dog since Richard Nixon's Irish setter, perhaps sensibly keeping an eye on what they might do to the Rose Garden and other grounds.

What would an ideal garden for dogs be like? Once all poisonous plants and bushes had been uprooted, as well as poisonous insects and snakes, it is only a somewhat restricted place. One horticulturalist, Maureen Gilmer, has suggested planting a tall grass meadow with flowers, ideal for romping, and also a fleabane herb garden with pennyroyal

(*Menta pulegium*), wormwood (*Artemisia absinthum*), and tansy (*Tanacetum vulgare*). Not likely, I say. Penni Stewart, a sociologist and one of my university colleagues, has rethought her garden to accommodate her Newfoundland dog, Oscar. "Tall and tough," are her plant guidelines, from Joe Pye weed to bee balm. Billowing peonies are out of the question, she told me, but day lilies are fine because they easily survive a large dog's tramping. Canine needs differ from human ones, which include diverse aesthetic concerns; safety comes first for dogs – we make our gardens, just as for centuries we've made, or bred, our dogs. Still, fresh air, a warm spot in the sun and an appealing shady corner are essential; some pleasant scents and protection from rain would also matter. Simple pleasures for dogs and humans alike.

"GOD"

There is no mention of a companion dog for Adam in Genesis 20, where the first man finds names for all of the creatures of paradise – a genuine omission, I've always thought, but the Judeo-Christian tradition, like the Middle East in general, isn't exactly dog-friendly. *Bark* magazine addresses the oversight with its motto, Dog is My Co-Pilot, and Shirley MacLaine, actress, author, and spiritual seeker, noted the obvious in her book *Out on a Leash: Exploring the Nature of Reality and Love*, emphasizing that *dog* is *god* spelled backwards.

The sacred books of the world's major religions have not been particularly kind to dogs. While a list of their grim representations may be instructive, believers of all persuasions can ignore it while nonbelievers will have their skepticism confirmed. The historical moments in which these books were written differ greatly from our own time, but many of their assumptions and prejudices linger today. The Judeo-Christian tradition, with its powerful emphasis on sacrifice, includes only a few stories that suggest a benevolent human responsibility for animals for their own sake; the account of Noah's ark is the most notable one. While dogs are occasionally recognized for their work as guards, more negative images dominate. Linked to beggars in the gospels of Luke and Matthew, dogs received this chilling mention in Revelations: "For without are dogs, and sorcerers, and whoremongers, and murderers, and idolaters, and whosoever loveth and marketh a lie."

Since the early Middle Ages, the Roman Catholic Church has claimed that animals – and, of course, this includes dogs – do not have souls. As part of the concept of the great chain of being such doctrines are far-reaching in their impact and haven't helped dogs one bit. While I don't want to get lost in a debate about human and animal souls, there is one sidetrack worth taking here: in the 1940s a unique camera was invented by Seymour Kirlian that could photograph energy fields. The term *aura* is generally used for such fields, which resemble the halos around the heads of saints. Suzanne Hively devoted one of her columns in the *Plain Dealer* to the subject, and even allowed her own dogs, two Japanese chin, to be included in a Kirlian study. Aura photographs show the fields of colour around humans, animals, and plants, and these colours are considered representative of different emotional states. Hively answered questions about her dogs' general behaviour and these were related to the colours in the photographs; both dogs had predominantly green auras, suggesting harmonious feelings and love of their human and animal companions. Is there a relation between such auras, or energy fields, and the entities referred to as souls? It's a legitimate subject for scientific research as well as for theological speculation.

The occasional Catholic saint may be associated with animals – St. Roch, the medieval patron of pilgrims and plague victims, for example – but these are rare. Roch's story is a variation on the beggar theme of Matthew, and it echoes Luke's account of Lazarus and the rich man, in which Lazarus, a beggar covered with sores, lay at the gate of a rich man's home, desperate for food. When several dogs pass by, they lick his sores. The fourteenth-century Roch, born to a wealthy merchant family during the years of the bubonic plague, made his way from Montpellier to Rome in one of those pilgrimages associated with medieval spirituality. He caught the plague in Piacenza, was reputedly fed by a wild or homeless dog, and was miraculously cured. In time a cult grew around him and the popular Roch became a common figure in European painting and sculpture, always presented with a wound (the bubo) on his leg as well as a companion dog who carried a bread roll in its mouth.

A few contemporary Christians have tried to change their history by offering church services and masses that bless their pets and other animals, and one has to acknowledge any gesture towards reconciliation with the animal world. I attended one of these masses some years ago in a suburb of Boston and watched the happy faces of parishioners who felt that their pets – mostly dogs, a few cats – were being valued by their church; I did not bring a dog with me. These blessings often take place in the autumn, around the feast day of St. Francis of Assisi on October 4, and have, in fact, been a minor Roman Catholic tradition since the thirteenth century. However, during a fall visit to Cleveland, Ohio, in 2000, I read about upcoming animal blessings not only at St. Mark's Catholic Church but also at the Archwood United Church of Christ (Protestant) and the Cleveland Buddhist Temple. And, in December 2004, according to *The New York Times*, Mark Nadler, a cabaret singer, arranged for a bar mitzvah for his thirteen-year-old wheaten terrier. The party, with a chopped-liver sculpture in the shape of a large dog bone, concluded with a chanted blessing over the dog from cantor Herb Strauss, who referred to the celebration as "a real bark mitzvah." These events aside, since Thomas Aquinas, theologians have had a lot to answer for; but in recent decades, perhaps as a response to the growing animal rights movement, there have been earnest attempts to address the subject of animals and ethics.

One of the most important books in this new discourse is Stephen H. Webb's *On God and Dogs: A Christian Theology of Compassion for Animals*. A professor of religion and philosophy as well as a Christian, Webb writes that he will attempt to imagine what it would be like to treat animals as a "gift from God." He calls the relationship between humans and animals one of "grace," which he defines "as the inclusive and expansive power of God's love to create and sustain relationships of real mutuality and reciprocity." Webb believes that animals also participate in grace. After tracing what he considers to be a hidden history of vegetarianism in the Old and New Testaments, as well as biblical and early-Christian attitudes towards animals, Webb examines contemporary theological writing about animals and, particularly, pet-keeping. How we speak about animals, and our sense of their otherness, both emerge as central concerns. Webb asks if there is a language we share with animals – especially those that are domesticated – which allows us "to hear what they have to say," even thought they are "speechless." His answer is the mutual giving that allows us, and our dogs, to communicate with each other. Dogs are central to Webb's endeavour because they share an exceptional relationship with humans. He characterizes this as "excess," which he explains as a way of approaching subjects that emphasize aesthetic and religious matters rather than rational and utilitarian calculations. Criticizing the animals rights movement for its emphasis on utilitarian thinking – an oversimplification, I think – Webb argues for a new theology that will reinterpret the eucharist and all aspects of Christian sacrifice.

Webb's theory of "a vegetarian eucharist" – a eucharist that reinterprets the crucifixion as "the demand to end all nonvoluntary sacrifices" – may be the most controversial aspect of his book, but it is crucial to his desire for Christianity to take dogs to heart. He suggests that people resist the animal rights movement because they would have to admit that animals are capable of suffering, and that "it is overwhelming to contemplate the animal holocaust that is occurring daily in our midst." This is strong language. But to Webb, the solution is evident: "...only a God who suffered like an animal, who faced cruelty without resistance or denial, can empower us in our own efforts to acknowledge and challenge that which is truly unspeakable, the suffering of countless victims who cannot themselves speak in their defense." Whatever you may think of Webb's conclusions, it's worth following along as he struggles to find a place for dogs not only in his own religious tradition but also in our Western discourse on ethics; he demands that we rethink our assumptions to their very core.

Anyone who is not religious may still be interested in this story from the British novelist Virginia Woolf, who was given the gift of a golden cocker spaniel by another writer, the aristocratic Vita Sackville-West. The dog was named Pinka, and Woolf wrote to thank her friend on behalf of her husband, Leonard, while also aimiably relating the dog's settling in: "Your puppy has destroyed, by eating holes, my skirt, ate L's proofs, and done such damage as could be done to the carpet – But she is an angel of light. Leonard says seriously she makes him believe in God – and this after she has wetted his floor 8 times in one day." I never expected to see housebreaking linked to a belief in any deity, but there it is. Early in *On God and Dogs* Webb quotes an aphorism attributed to Abraham Lincoln, and I want to include it here as the ideal summation: "I would not give much for that man's religion whose cat and dog are not the better for it." Hard to do better than that.

HISTORY

Dogs, unlike people, are not historians. Creatures of habit and training, they have good memories that let them recall the things that matter most to their survival. This means, of course, that they have some sense of the past, though animal behaviourists would insist it's a very different kind of past than our human construction.

In recent years North American newspapers and popular magazines have reported each new discovery in the evolutionary story of dogs with enthusiasm, as if knowing the precise moment of the emergence of the canine species and its domestication might change the way any individual dog owner treats his or her pet. Perhaps this relates to the increased popularity of genealogy and the number of Internet sites devoted to it. Certainly the genealogical charts that sometimes come with pedigreed puppies are useful to potential breeders, who need to be concerned with bloodlines, but otherwise I've never understood their appeal. In the summer of 1997 a new study, led by evolutionary biologists Dr. Carles Vilà and Dr. Robert K. Wayne, analyzed DNA samples from wolves, coyotes, jackals, and sixty-seven breeds of dog. It suggested that our bond with dogs, which was previously thought to begin roughly 14,000 years ago, might be considerably older, and that dogs may have been domesticated as long as 135,000 years ago. The 14,000-year time line was based on archeological evidence of domesticated dogs – the oldest known dog's remains, a jawbone, came from a Paleolithic grave at Oberkassel, in Germany. While bones of wolves from human settlements date back as far as 400,000 years, it's thought that these belonged to tamed wolves rather than to dogs, who did not exist as *canis familiaris* until humans began a more settled existence 10,000 to 15,000 years ago. The next significant evolutionary stage was thought to occur between 500 B.C.E. to 500 C.E., when the major breed types were developed, and modern breeds as we know them emerged roughly from the thirteenth to fifteenth centuries. Or so it seemed in 1997.

The study, out of the University of California at Los Angeles, also posited that our present-day dogs have been marked by the genetic fingerprinting of a single lineage of female wolf, and that the four modern breeds thought to be the oldest (the dingo, New Guinea singing dog, African basenji, and greyhound) are only four of many breeds descended from the first groups of dogs, which were thought to descend from the wolf. Almost inevitably, such controversial work was greeted with reservations by animal behaviourists as well as archeologists. (Robert K. Wayne, a molecular biologist and part of the study's team, later altered his opinion, suggesting a much shorter period for canine domestication.) I'm not going to try to sort out objections or examine the nature of mitochondrial DNA, both beyond my expertise and interest, but fortunately, others have. In *Dogs: A Startling New Understanding of Canine Origin, Behavior & Evolution*, Raymond Coppinger, a biology professor and behavioural ecologist, and Lorna Coppinger, who writes about dogs, lament the confusion that has been caused by such widespread, unquestioning media coverage. While Raymond Coppinger believes that mtDNA studies are an exciting area of evolutionary research, he has reservations: "Sooner or later they might reveal a breakthrough on dog genealogies and ages, even if so far they have just added to the confusion." He also suggests that "this information about dogs, wolves, and coyotes, as reported and interpreted, has done real harm." Wolf-restoration programs, for example, have been affected by the the confusing and unreliable conclusions of some of the studies.

Still, geneticists have continued to research dogs, and in 2004 another study, directed by Dr. Elaine Ostrander at the Fred Hutchinson Cancer Research Center and University of Washington, demonstrated how genetic variations allowed scientists to distinguish between 85 different breeds (the AKC recognizes 152 breeds). Following a single mutated gene in collies, the study suggested that several breeds of dogs (the Shetland sheepdog, the Australian shepherd, the long-haired whippet, to name several), also shared that gene. This was related to breeding practices before dog shows became popular and more modern, controlled breeding programs, aimed at producing purebred dogs, kept breeds separate. Using four categories (ancient, herding, guarding, and hunting), researchers found some surprising breed linkages – German shepherds, for example, are genetically closer to mastiffs and boxers than to herding dogs, and cocker spaniels to basset hounds and poodles. (The study did confuse a beagle with a mastiff.) The implications of the study are thought to be important for medical research because humans share certain genetic diseases with various breeds of dogs, and new insights on canine disease may shed light on human disease as well. Meanwhile, research – and the story – continue.

For anyone interested in the history of a specific breed, numerous breed books have been published. Beyond a breed's history, the subject of canine evolution – along with recent research – is well covered in Jake Page's readable *Dogs: A Natural History*, as well as by the Coppingers' formidable *Dogs*. The role dogs have played in human history since the Paleolithic era is the subject of Stanley Coren's tale-filled *The Pawprints of History: Dogs and the Course of Human Events*, which will interest not only history buffs but any dog-lover with even the sketchiest historical sense. Such readers may also want copies of these engaging studies: Jan Bondeson's *Amazing Dogs: A Cabinet of Canine Curiosities*, Mark Derr's *A Dog's History of America: How Our Best Friend Explored, Conquered, and Settled a Continent*, and Katherine C. Grier's *Pets in America: A History*.

HUMOUR

If humour is a matter of taste, the current state of humour involving dogs – cartoons, jokes, inspirational stories and the like – suggests that we're going through a rough patch. Several months after the pet-food scare during the spring of 2007, when almost daily announcements were made about dog food contaminated with melamine imported from China, *Vanity Fair* ran its quasi-satiric feature "Then & Now," including this item: under the "Then" column the Socialite's Bane was "Excess Botox in the forehead" while under the "Now" column it was "Excess melamine in Fifi's kibble." This attempt at relevance struck me as a good example of the problem – too much humour about dogs is really about people, and rarely fresh at that. Much contemporary humour is based less on irony than on sarcasm, where the humourist rubs elbows with his or her audience while everyone remains superior to the subject being sneered at or dismissed.

Dog humour generally falls into two camps: about dogs and about us. Mostly the latter camp dominates. The best humour involves sharp observation of its subject, and too many cartoonists and jokesters don't bother to look at dogs closely, but merely attribute human qualities to them for an easy laugh at human foibles once removed. Harmless enough. Humour thrives on inversion and reversal, but once the inversion is made (dog for human, human for dog), something more is required. Occasionally a talented humorist does make a sharp point. Tom Tomorrow (of "This Modern World"), Lars Leetaru (who sometimes illustrated the "Metropolitan Diary" for *The New York Times*, (including one splendid cartoon where a woman carrying bags of groceries was pulling the leash of her French bulldog, who stood at the curb, its paw outstretched to hail a taxi), Ted Rall ("It's Another Episode of Dog Talk For People Who Hate All Human Beings"), the iconic

Charles Schulz and the much loved James Thurber come to mind as people who have looked closely enough at dogs to transcend easy jokes at their expense. Many of the dog cartoons that have appeared in the *New Yorker* are worth a second look, and the best of them have been gathered together in an anthology, *The New Yorker Book of Dog Cartoons.*

Still, I'm left wondering why humorists are rarely successful in coming up with anything original about dogs. One answer may be that humour itself is often topical, but built on variations of eternal tropes. For example, a cartoon by X. Slater appeared in *The New York Times* in 1997 over the heading "Mike Wallace: The Clintons' Lapdog," sketching the happy Clintons walking a large dog with journalist Mike Wallace's head and a collar reading "'Spike' Wallace" past the White House. Today I have no recollection of the event the cartoon was lampooning. One administration later, British Prime Minister Tony Blair was frequently referred to in the press as "Bush's poodle," a variation on the same point, that serving power is dog-like. Thurber reversed the trope in one of his best cartoons: to the left of a woody hillside, five dogs of various breeds are gathered together as they watch a man, a woman, and a small girl marching to the right, towards the edge of the frame. The caption beneath is both elegant and wry: "There go the most intelligent of all animals." Book illustrators are often better than editorial cartoonists at capturing a dog's doginess and making a clever point of it, possibly because they aren't working with the same deadlines. The simple black-and-white drawings of an exuberant pug that Hilary Knight made for Kay Thompson's *Eloise* come to mind at once.

A separate category, but one that can be considered under humour, is made up of books called "inspirational" or "heartwarming," books meant to conjure an easy smile. I've never understood why people buy such books, and in decades of wandering through bookstores have never seen anybody purchase one. But they must sell or publishers would give up on them. Memoir writers can easily succumb to this temptation with humorous accounts of the antics of their pets. But good humour needs tension, sometimes even a bit of a sting – a frisson of discomfort. When Cindy Adams describes the habits of her dog in *The Gift of Jazzy*, for example, she's rarely funny, just predictable, but when she describes the new ring her actress friend Ellen Barkin wore as "a diamond as big as a pot roast," her writing comes to life. Unusual combinations and disjunctions like that one can give almost any subject a kick. Unfortunately, inspirational dog humour often falls into the old trap of anthropomorphism.

Naturally there's the flip side to heartwarming writing: the black humour that avoids anything inspirational. At its best, such writing can offer a glimpse of human fears, or puncture our pretensions by making readers stop and linger for a moment. Anecdotes about dogs in books about other subjects often provide the richest examples of this vein. In his memoir, *Original Story By*, the playwright and screenwriter Arthur Laurents describes a night on the town with famed Algonquin wit Dorothy Parker. On meeting at her hotel for drinks and dinner, he saw that she had already been tippling. Across the marble lobby she appeared with "one of those repellent little dogs that come with ladies who like liquor. The dog stopped to take a long pee. The clerk behind the desk glared. Mrs. Parker glared back, snatched up her dog and said: 'I did it!'" No matter that writer Alexander Woollcott told a similar story about the British actress Mrs. Patrick Campbell. That Laurents shows so little understanding of the bond between Parker and her dog tells almost as much about him as his anecdote reveals about Parker.

Humorous talking dogs, like ventriloquists' dummies, are always projections of their speakers or writers. Whether in books or movies, such dogs either set out to charm us or, turning the tables, lecture us on human failings. Moose, the Jack Russell terrier who played Eddie on the popular TV series *Frasier,* had a book to his credit (*My Life as a Dog,* by Brian Hargrove), as did Millie, a Bush family English springer spaniel, with her "as dictated to" memoir-photo album written by Barbara Bush. As comic personae, these dogs appear to have purely human agendas – to make money, in Eddie's case, or to blend public relations and politics, as Millie did. (One example of Millie's wit should suffice. She overhears the Bushes talking about her, "Some discussion about me keeping a lower profile. The media were reporting that I was getting more publicity than some members of the Cabinet. Considering some of my press, maybe they should be grateful.") Whatever made *Millie's Book* a bestseller eludes me, unless there's a vast public taste for coyness. But compared to Eddie-Moose and his "Moose-isms," like "To bark, or not to bark, that is the question," Millie's a truly sophisticated wit, with a hint of Barbara Bush's allegedly sharp tongue. Dog personae, when written successfully, operate from a dog's frame of reference, not a human perspective. The imaginative act is in creating the former. The French film *Baxter* (1991), about a sarcastic bull terrier who exploits all the humans around him, comes closer to canine truth, though sentimentalists are likely to find it off-putting. We've taught our dogs the preferred ways to manipulate us, with worshipful eyes; if they behave accordingly that doesn't mean that they're natural comedians, with perfect timing and pratfalls to spare. The matter of animal "emotions" here comes to the foreground. We project our own emotions onto the reactions of our pets and do something very similar when responding to canine humour; we can't help being human. I've seen dogs romping gleefully, but never, I think, consciously making a joke or being "in" on one.

This abecedarian would be incomplete without a few words about that curious classic, *The Devil's Dictionary* by Ambrose Bierce, the virtuoso nineteenth-century American journalist. Known for his cultivated misanthropy, Bierce published in various west-coast newspapers, including the San Francisco *Examiner*; he wrote stories about the Civil War (he'd been a volunteer in the Union Army); and in 1913, at the age of seventy-one, he disappeared forever in the Mexican wilderness while covering a revolution. Initial entries for *The Devil's Dictionary* saw newspaper publication in 1881, and it first appeared in book form as *The Cynic's Word Book* in 1906. Irony was Bierce's favoured device, understatement his stance against optimism and human brutality. Following is the entry for "Dog":

> DOG, *n*. A kind of additional or subsidiary Diety designed to catch the overflow and surplus of the world's worship. This Divine Being in some of his smaller and silkier incarnations takes, in the affection of Woman, the place to which there is no human male aspirant. The Dog is a survival – an anachronism. He toils not, neither does he spin, yet Solomon in all his glory never lay upon a door-mat all day long, sun-soaked and fly-fed and fat, while his master worked for the means wherewith to purchase an idle way of the Solomonie tail, seasoned with a look of tolerant recognition.

It's only right to give Bierce the last word on canine humour.

HUNGARIAN DOGS

Since I've written one book about Hungarian culture and ethnicity, and I gave my first pug the Hungarian name Zoli, this book would seem incomplete to me without a nod in the direction of Budapest. Many dogs come with national identities and associations – the Afghan hound, Brussels griffon, French bulldog, Norwegian elkhound, Rhodesian ridgeback, Russian wolfhound, and Tibetan spaniel (and terrier), to name only a few. Hungary has its own unique breeds, including the komondor, the kuvasz, the puli, and the vizsla, all mid-sized to larger dogs who need plenty of exercise and suit country living. Like many Europeans, Hungarians are dog lovers. Their national dogs fall into the AKC category of working dogs: the komondor, with its white, tassel-like cords of hair, is thought to have arrived in the area known today as Hungary over a thousand years ago, with the nomadic Magyars; the kuvasz, an old Hungarian breed of sheepdog with probable Turkish origins – the name comes from the Turkish *kavas*, for armed guard; the mudi, another mid-sized, black herding/guard dog, relatively rare; the puli, a handsome, mid-sized sheep-herding dog covered with shaggy long black or white curls that resemble dreadlocks; the pumi, a cattle-herding cross between the puli and the German spitzen made in the early nineteenth century; and the sleek, red-coated vizsla, a retriever/pointer, about which the *ASPCA Complete Guide to Dogs* notes, "their energy level can be overwhelming," in my mind definitely a good Hungarian trait. These breeds reflect, in part, the country's agrarian past, when Hungary was made up largely of landed gentry and peasantry.

A country with a difficult twentieth-century history, from tragic pro-German alliances during both world wars to almost fifty years of Soviet occupation, Hungary has produced writers who turned to dogs as human stand-ins or surrogates. Tibor Déry's *Niki*, which I've discussed elsewhere, is an example of the way a writer can use animals in political allegory. Here I want to emphasize that the allegory works best if the dogs are believably doggy. Déry's Niki is a mixed-breed fox terrier, suitable for city living and a step removed from the Hungarian hounds whose breed might have made the dog too obviously symbolic. Yet, during the hard time after the abortive revolution of 1956, Niki's terrier identity didn't prevent the author from being arrested for anti-state activity and sentenced to prison for nine years (he was released in 1960, the result of international protest). Although Magda Szabó, author of

The Door, was not imprisoned for her writing, she and the writer heroine of her novel suffered years of official disapproval and neglect. Viola, her dog character, is also a mongrel. Not very pretty, we're told, but people who saw the dog noted "the extraordinary light in its dark eyes," and immediately sensed "its level of intelligence was almost human."

Pet dogs (and puppies) represent a gesture of hope, the notion that one will be able to protect and provide for them, the belief that life is stable enough for a dog to be part of it. In Déry's extraordinary short story "Philemon and Baucis," about the simple birthday supper of an elderly woman set against the background of machine-gun fire and revolutionary street shootings, a pregnant dog begins to give birth just as the protagonist's frightened wife goes out to find help for her wounded husband and is shot herself. Again, the dog's breed is not one of the more aristocratic Hungarian creations – it appears to be a mutt – and the dangerous background is Hungarian detail enough for this painful tale. As it draws to an end, the old man hears his whining dog and becomes her midwife; the human/dog bond makes an ideal counterpoint to human cruelty. Carefully tending the new mother and her puppies, he loses his sense of time, and "a strange sort of joy crept into his heart." He is so preoccupied with the task at hand that he doesn't realize his wife, ominously, hasn't returned, while "the dog's tail stiffened again, and she was in the throes of another spasm of pain." The dog's labour spasm, a portent of the man's soon-to-come grief, is the final ironic twist on the pastoral title of the story, from a place where death once came gently and naturally to an elderly couple. But even at this horrible moment, a man has a dog at his side.

Hungarian breeds, I should add, are not only known in Hungary or by Hungarians. In a 2007 ranking of the top 157 registered breeds in the American Kennel Club, Hungarian dogs placed in this order: vizsla – 42, kuvasz – 130, puli – 141, and komondor –

144. Admired for his books that feature animals, István Fekete's fine novel *Bogáncs* (1957), about a pumi, was translated into English as *Thistle*, and is worth the search. And in the mystery novel *Death and the Dogwalker*, A.J. Orde's Denver-based, detective-cum-antiques-dealer Jason Lynx owns a hundred-pound kuvasz named Bela (spelled without the properly accented Hungarian é, but that's a small matter in a novel where the dog disappears much too early in the story).

IDENTITY

"I am I because my little dog knows me," wrote the American experimental writer Gertrude Stein in "Identity a Poem" and "What are Masterpieces" over half a century ago, echoing an ancient theme about identity that is as old as Homer's *Odyssey*. In the final book of Odysseus's wanderings, he returns home to Ithaca after an absence of twenty years, and no one recognizes him but his faithful dog Argus, who can finally die, content to see his master once more. The scene – a prototype in western literature for all writing about the attachment of dogs to humans – is a heartbreaking one. In an essential way Odysseus exists unchanged though changed (by time, life, and experience) because his dog waited for him. Unfortunately, few dogs live as long as Odysseus's. This link between individual human identity and canine companionship became the subject of one of the many Nazi racial decrees, which set out to rob Germany's Jewish population of their status not only as citizens but as human beings. Beginning in 1933, when Jewish physicians were forbidden to practise, and culminating in September 1942, when Jews were no longer allowed meat, eggs, white bread, fruit, and milk, the prohibitions were a step-by-step program of state-sponsored dehumanization, and the canine prohibition is no less horrific for being one of many. As of February 15, 1942, Jews were forbidden to own pets.

In the Prologue to the Second Part of Miguel de Cervantes's *Don Quixote* (1605; 1615), often regarded as the first modern European novel, there are two curious stories about madmen and dogs. In the initial, briefer anecdote, a madman in Seville torments local dogs by blowing air into them through a tube he has made from a reed. Once the dog expands in size, the madman turns to any onlookers and asks if they think it's an easy job to blow up a dog. Should the point be missed, Cervantes adds, "Now does your grace think it's an easy job to write a book?" In case this story doesn't "please" the reader, Cervantes's narrator includes another, longer one. In Córdoba, there's a madman who carries a slab of marble with him everywhere. When he comes across a dog, he drops the slab on it, and the dog, in a panic, runs up the street barking and howling. When one furious dog owner asks why the madman does this ("You miserable thief, you dog, why did you hurt my hound? Didn't you see, cruel man, that my dog was a hound?"), the madman retreats, only to return with his marble slab and a new strategy. As he approaches any dog, he stares at it and says, "This is a hound: watch out!" Cervantes's narrator again clarifies his metaphor by adding,

> In fact, all the dogs he encountered, even if they were mastiffs or little lapdogs, he called hounds, and so he never dropped a stone on one again. Perhaps something similar may happen to this storyteller, who will not dare ever again to set his great talent loose among books, which, when they are bad, are harder than boulders.

These stories are about the nature of writing and the importance of stories. While the madman from Seville is like an author writing his book (blowing up a dog), with the dog representing his novel, the Córdoba madman is also an author, the marble slab is his book, and the unsuspecting Córdoba dogs stand in for the author's human audience, his readers. In both versions, dogs have human parallels, as they represent human endeavour (books) or ourselves as readers. We are symbolically one with our dogs. Yet there is an element of ambivalence here too, because the Córdoban madman/author is referred to as "you miserable thief, you dog," and dogs are labelled either as *dogs* or as *hounds*, suggesting different status. The fact that Cervantes chose to use dogs in his allegory of the imagination and storytelling affirms the powerful impact the human/dog bond has had on shaping human identity.

Dogs are assumed to be direct, not manipulative or deceptive; they recognize us beyond superficial appearances. In Mary Shelley's Gothic novel *Frankenstein*, the creature, made up of body parts taken from human corpses, is first seen through a thick fog in the icy region of the North Pole. He passes by on a sledge drawn by a team of dogs, guiding them further north. Rejected by humans and his creator, the strange being of "gigantic stature" is not, apparently, shunned by dogs. What do they see in him? Shelley doesn't say. I want to make a considerable leap in time here. Without attempting a short history of the classical Greek philosophy known as Cynicism – an approach to life that rejects all beliefs and practices it deems false before reason – it's worth noting that the word *cynic* relates to the Greek word *kynikos*, "like a dog," and that one of the first philosophers referred to as a Cynic was Diogenes of Sinope, called "the Dog" by Aristotle. Dogs, while not ordinarily associated with reason, have reasons of their own. This ambiguity in the human/dog bond is the basis of a cartoon by Peter Steiner that ran in the *New Yorker* in 1993: a dog sits at the keyboard of a computer terminal, remarking to another dog, "On the Internet, nobody knows you're a dog." Like most humour involving animals, the cartoon has an anthropomorphic heart, but its black edge acknowledges human fears of deception. Interestingly, the talking dog is the larger of the two, and it addresses a smaller, spotted companion that vaguely resembles an affable beagle like Charles Schulz's Snoopy.

ILLUSTRATION

The last century gave us many notable illustrators of dogs – the subject for a book itself – but I want to discuss the finest one, the mysterious Diana Thorne. A notable dog painter and illustrator from the late 1920s through the 1940s, Thorne, who claimed to be born in Winnipeg, had more than thirty books to her credit (many for children). As well, she held solo exhibitions of her oil paintings, pastels, watercolours and etchings in art galleries across North America. Thorne even painted a portrait of Franklin Delano Roosevelt's Scottish terrier Fala, in addition to dogs owned by many celebrities of her time, including Gary Cooper and Katharine Cornell, and her classic *Drawing Dogs* (1940) went through several reprintings. But around 1950 or so she seems to have vanished. Who, then, was Diana Thorne?

Several years ago, while browsing in an antiques mall, I spotted a tattered, oversized book titled *Puppy Stories*, with colour illustrations by Thorne, published in 1934. That summer I was compiling an anthology of dog stories and hoped to find a good cover subject. Flipping through the book I was struck by one of its pastel drawings, and set out to clear permission for its use. A once-prominent children's publisher, the Saalfield Publishing Company of Akron, Ohio, had closed its offices in 1977, and its papers were in a university archives. Nothing there helped, so I began searching for Thorne's birth and death years elsewhere. After contacting many of North America's best public and museum libraries, I found that only a few were able to do more

ILLUSTRATION 117

"Peppy," a pastel drawing, from *Puppy Stories* – the beginning of my search for Diana Thorne.

than check Internet sites. Reference books were also unhelpful; too many reference writers have been content to repeat "facts" from previous studies, perpetuating errors. I also learned that most libraries have discarded old vertical files of clippings from newspapers and magazines, as if the entire world of print has been scanned and digitalized.

Thorne's year and place of birth were always given as 1895 and Winnipeg, Manitoba, but, oddly, none of the sources included a death year. However, her biography on DogsCo.com, which deals with dog art, suggested that she may have been born as Ann Woursell on October 7, 1895, in Odessa, Russia, and this reference to "Ann Woursell" had to be followed. (Frank J. Leskovitz, responsible for the site, did not respond to my queries.) The earliest newspaper reference to Thorne, in *The New York Times*, was an advertisement she ran on July 19, 1925, for "hand-painted" dresses. New York's garment industry has long been associated with Jewish immigrants, and this advertisement appears to be Thorne's only connection to the "rag" trade. She next appeared in the *Times* in an article on March 6, 1928: Dog Quits Modeling To Lead Her Own Life; Pat, Posing Terrier, Jumps Out of Taxicab in Union Square and Disappears. The missing dog belonged to Thorne, whom the article refers to as "the etcher, of 47 West Fifty-second Street." In less than three years she had changed the focus of her endeavours and gained enough status in the arts community to merit a human-interest article.

Fortunately I visited the library of the Cleveland Museum of Art, which has several thick files devoted to Thorne. One item interested me in particular: a copy of the invitation to Thorne's first New York exhibition, in 1929. It wasn't the invitation itself but its brief artist's biography that mattered. Surely Thorne would have approved it, so she must have also supplied Winnipeg as her birthplace. Shortly after that exhibition, Thorne's work was shown by galleries across the United States. Enthusiastic reviews appeared, along with interviews. *Arts Digest*, the *Boston Post*, the *Chicago Tribune*, the *Christian Science Monitor*, the *Detroit News*, *The New York Times*, and Canada's *Saturday Night* all devoted space to her. In most interviews she spoke of her father as "a wealthy Canadian rancher," but something didn't add up. While in some interviews her family consisted of five sisters, in others there were four sisters and a brother. In the *Saturday Night* profile, she spoke of an idyllic childhood: "What did I do in Winnipeg? Oh, I read Shelley and

ILLUSTRATION   119

took rides on horses." She also recalled joining her father on visits to various Alberta ranchers. In a *Chicago Daily Times* interview from 1930, Thorne claimed that after her cattle-ranch childhood she "went to Munich and Berlin to study art, and was caught there during the war and taken for a spy." *Who Was Who in American Art* quotes her as saying that she was "sent to France and Germany, and later to Scotland to study etching." When another interviewer asked how Thorne came to paint animals, she replied: "It probably all began because I had a wonderful Scotsman for a father, and was born on a farm ranch in Winnipeg, Manitoba." As late as 1940, Thorne told the *Detroit News Pictorial* that at an early age she had "to support five younger sisters because of her father's illness." Was Thorne a fantasist? A habitual liar?

Six months after I began my research, my desk was covered with documents related to Thorne and her family, from such sources as the records of Ellis Island; the United Kingdom Incoming Passenger Lists, 1878-1968; the 1906 Census of Manitoba; the 1911 Census of Canada; and the World War II Draft Registration. The Kerlan Collection, an archive devoted to children's books, had a thick file of letters by Thorne, and photocopies were ordered. Meanwhile, persistent queries had located one of Thorne's relatives, a great-niece. That telephone call led to other relatives, and soon the puzzle began to come together. Thorne's father, Chaim Woursell, first visited Winnipeg in 1903, at the age of thirty-three, bringing with him $2,500; he described himself as a "married cattle dealer." Liking the city, which had a growing community of Russian-Jewish immigrants, he returned in 1906 with his family, and $9,500. The family included his wife Rosa, thirty-two, and six children: Anna, eleven; Abraham, nine; Paulina, six; Ida, four; Samuel, two; and Geta, seven months. Ellis Island records note "Hebrew" alongside their names. Over the years, records of the names of the children vary, and Anna is once registered as Emma. As well, the last name is spelled variously in different documents, but mostly as "Woursell." Thorne's last surviving niece recalled that her mother, Paula (Paulina), claimed that her father had attended university in Russia and had taken his patrimony to Canada, along with an attractive wife. The Woursell family was living in Winnipeg by the 1906 census, but for business reasons Chaim soon moved it to Calgary.

Around 1912 Chaim became ill with a serious lung disease and moved the family to Berlin, Germany, where doctors specialized in his condition. The family had a comfortable life until the outbreak of war. Thorne's brother Abraham was interned, and the family moved to England. Chaim was reputed to be a charmer, attractive to the ladies. Here, of course, the story depends on memory, and memories of old retellings. Abraham was eventually released, and in 1920 the Woursells settled in New York City. That year Chaim made three trips between England and the United States, returning alone and then, seemingly, vanishing. Out of this history Thorne fashioned a persona, and like many artists who devote some of their creative powers to self-invention, she played loose with the facts of her life. Various interviewers described her with these phrases: "that bundle of human energy known as Diana Thorne," "casual and dynamic all at the same time," and my favourite, "Her dark eyes seemed to penetrate to the bottom of things at a glance. She had the quick light step of the walker, small wiry hands – and strong – and an engaging smile." Thorne also had a keen awareness of herself as a public figure and told one interviewer, "Like most public persons, I am frequently misquoted."

Drawing on public records, I can conclude that Thorne was born in 1894 (the date on census records), despite her stories. Her brother Abraham was born on April 25, 1896, according to immigration records and the U.S. Draft Registry. Counting backwards, it's unlikely that Thorne's birth date was October 7, 1895, especially in light of that era's medical conditions. Newspaper

ILLUSTRATION 121

Undated photograph of Diana Thorne, c. mid 1930s. A gift to the Frick Art Reference Library from the Milch Gallery, the photograph is stamped "Burke & Koretke Photo, Chicago."

obituaries, if accurate, can also be informative. I was puzzled not to find one for a person of Thorne's renown, but she did appear as "Diana Thorne" in *The New York Times* obituary for her mother in 1954, and several years later, in 1957, as "Ann Woursell North" in its obituary for Abraham – further proof that Diana Thorne and Ann Woursell were one.

"The Inconsolable"   Diana Thorne

"The Inconsolable," an etching from *Real Tales of Real Dogs* by Albert Payson Terhune (1935).

The letters from the Kerlan Collection include a correspondence from 1930 to 1940 between Thorne and Dr. C.C. Young of Lansing, Michigan, the Director of the Division of Laboratories of the Michigan Department of Health. An admirer of Thorne and himself a dog breeder, Young collected examples of her work for an annotated bibliography with the help of his wife and colleague, Minna Crooks Young. If similar letters had covered Thorne's entire life, it would be possible to construct a detailed biography, allowing for the secrets she kept from even those closest to her. Reference books state that she was married to an Arthur North of Philadelphia, and that she made her home there. (No records corroborate this.) It's even been claimed that she took the name Thorne as an anagram of North. Certainly the name has an

ILLUSTRATION 123

Anglophile ring to it that would appear to a woman who called her father "a wonderful Scotsman" when she knew this to be untrue. The casual and often official anti-Semitism of public life during the years Thorne was making her way as an artist can't be ignored. Many immigrants altered their names in an attempt to join the American-WASP mainstream rather than face the prejudice that was commonplace, and Jewish

Drawings of her spaniel Old Queenie, from *Diana Thorne's Dogs: An Album of Drawings (1944)*.

immigrants faced additional animosity.

Several sources suggest that Thorne may have had a second marriage, to Carton Moore-Park (1877–1956), a fellow artist. Her niece believes that her aunt never married, but that she had a long-term relationship with an older married man, and I've come to agree. Often referred to as a Scots-Canadian artist, he settled in New York City around 1910. My suspicion is that North and Moore-Park were one and the same, another fiction that may have been a cover for an illicit relationship. In her letters Thorne often spoke of her sickly husband Arthur. She wrote, in 1930, "Mr. North was at one time one of England's ablest portrait painters – he is now practically retired – never touches a portrait." Thorne also mentioned a young man named Howard, whose identity is unclear. Moore-Park did have a son named Howard, and such a coincidence seems unlikely. (Moore-Park's wife Annette had followed him to America in 1913, with Howard. According to *The New York Times* of May 25, 1923, she was held on bail before a trial for sending harassing letters to a woman – not Thorne – she'd accused of alienating her husband's affections.) Another puzzle: a copy of a photograph dated 1928, from a vertical file in the Boston Public Library, shows "Diana Thorne" sitting between her sister "Kitty" and her "husband" "Carton Moore-Park." Even more curious, shipping records from 1935 note that Thorne and Moore-Park travelled together to England that summer under the names "Ann Woursell" and "Carton Woursell." Both falsely gave Canada as their "last country of permanent residence."

The financial life of all but the most successful artists is precarious – especially so in New York City's competitive art world. Thorne was smart enough to realize that even during the hard years of the Depression, there was a potential clientele with disposable income that could be used to commemorate their purebred pets, for purebred dogs had become one of the favoured luxuries of that era. She needed to travel frequently for work, moving her

ILLUSTRATION   125

studio to different cities – Boston, Chicago, Detroit – to paint her commissions. She told one interviewer, "Artists do not make money by trying to do so. It makes itself for them when they do not seek it. At least, this was my experience." Not exactly, but the right persona mattered. Thorne wrote about her working methods in the *Christian Science Monitor*, in 1936: "Dogs have been shipped to my New York studio from all parts of the country – from Maine and Arizona, from Florida and from California. If for one reason or another I cannot leave the city at the time the commission is placed in my hands, the owners send their dog to me for a week or two. He lives in my studio with me under my personal care and becomes my friend for life. I enjoy the visits; so do the dogs." Certainly she meant these words, but the effect of the Depression on the art market also became a recurring theme in her letters. In a Christmas letter to the Youngs from 1937, she wrote, "If I'd had one 'Famous Americans' annual or famous women or what have you writing me this year for my biography, there have been half a dozen. At the rate my fame is growing one would think I was coining money – but fame and cash have nothing to do with one another it seems."

Throughout the war years Thorne continued to illustrate dog books for children, some with wartime settings. The death of her kind supporter Dr. Young (1887–1944) must have been a shock. Carton Moore-Park died in 1956. Whatever the official status of their relationship, his death had to have been a great loss. I have no idea how Thorne spent her remaining years, and the nature of her subsequent illness is not clear. By the age of seventy or so her mother was living in what was then called an old-age home, and she did not recognize her own children. Alzheimer's? Early dementia? A similar fate was suffered by Thorne's sister Paula. Sometime in September 1962 Thorne was committed to Manhattan's Bellevue Hospital as "mentally ill." According to cremation documents and surrogate court papers, Thorne died, intestate, at the City Hospital

A Boston terrier from Diana Thorne's *Drawing Dogs* (1940).

on Welfare Island (now Roosevelt Island), one of New York City's hospitals for the poor, in July 1963.

Artists who devote their talent to dogs have often been marginalized. Even the few exceptions, like Rosa Bonheur and George Stubbs, do not have the following of many less interesting and skilful painters. Add to this ambivalence the fact that Thorne was a successful illustrator and we might begin to see why her work is no longer known. But strong, lively drawing was the core of Thorne's versatility. Even in simple ink sketches, her dogs are never lifeless taxidermy, but animated individuals. While I don't want to make exaggerated claims about Thorne's art, from her first exhibition on she was praised, especially for the quality of her

ILLUSTRATION 127

technical skills, and even comparted to Daumier and Toulouse-Lautrec (*Chicago Examiner*) and called "the modern Rosa Bonheur" (*Christian Science Monitor*). Thorne collaborated on a book with Albert Payson Terhune, *Real Tales of Real Dogs* (1935), and he described her art as "vibrant with spirit, with mischief, with intelligence." Thorne was serious about her work. In her 1936 article "Look Doggish, If You Please!" for the *Christian Science Monitor*, she described the pressures she felt as a painter: "Each portrait, even after all my years of practice (and I have had a score of them), still presents a new problem and challenges all my powers to their limit of capacity. Will I succeed in capturing a good likeness? And will the thing also be a good piece of painting? These two achievements seldom go hand in hand." Thorne discussed the need for close observation as a requirement of animal art in *Drawing Dogs*: "The *all-important* things to remember are form, bone structure, and individual character." When the variety of dog breeds is considered, the canine skeleton is actually more varied than the human, and any artist attempting to convey not only movement but a particular dog's position during modelling needs to think of its essential form. A distillation of Thorne's experience, *Drawing Dogs* is both a gracefully-written guide and an apologia for an artist's life.

A German shepherd from *Drawing Dogs*.

In the end, what matters most about Thorne is the talent and attention she lavished on dogs. Her work is important in the context of the changing status of dogs in North American society. Following the founding in 1884 of the American Kennel Club, with its emphasis on purebred dogs, a great cultural shift in pet-keeping had begun. No longer valued mainly for their work – for hunting, herding, and other agrarian practices – purebred dogs, and even beloved mutts, now slept indoors, by the fireplace, or on the living-room sofa. Thorne insisted that she did not focus on specific breeds, claiming, "It's not so much the breed but the individual dog which arouses my enthusiasm." But her portraits of wirehaired terriers and Scotties, dachshunds and spaniels, collies and German shepherds belie her words. Thorne's work, for both commercial consumption and private commissions, assisted this cultural shift, making dogs a true part of the modern human family. As a dog lover I can only be grateful to her, whoever she was. What is the truth of any individual's life? One might even ask if it really matters that Thorne changed her place of birth by a continent and her year of birth by twelve months. In the grand scheme of things, probably not. But – and this is a sizeable but – we don't live our lives only in the grand scheme of things. Was Thorne a bohemian artist, a liberated woman, a self-denying Jew? None of these entirely, yet perhaps a little of each. Above all, she was an artist, and that's why I kept trying to follow her story. And in time I understood that my search for Diana Thorne was actually a shadow of her own search for this creature she called Diana Thorne.

INTELLIGENCE

Though it may sound undemocratic, some breeds of dogs appear to be smarter than others. If anyone made such a claim about human beings of different nationalities it would be seen as an ethnic slur. In fact, in recent years controversy about human intelligence tests, which are thought to privilege some classes and individuals over others, have crystalized the nature/nurture debate, with nurture winning the day. Books such as *The Bell Curve: Intelligence and Class Structure in American Life* (1994) by Richard J. Herrnstein and Charles Murray, and *Race, Evolution and Behavior* (1995) by J.P. Rushton, which posited a connection between race and intelligence, were criticized for their methodology as well as for their conclusions. When discussing as sensitive and controversial a subject as intelligence, methodology counts.

Turning from humans to dogs, it's still important to keep methodology in mind. In 1999, Stanley Coren, a professor of psychology at the University of British Columbia, published *The Intelligence of Dogs: Canine Consciousness and Capabilities*, one of half a dozen dog books to come from this thoughtful, prolific writer. The book caused immediate attention because of its "Table 10.1, Ranking Dogs for Obedience and Working Intelligence." People who had no intention of buying Coren's book could be seen in the aisles of bookstores looking up the ranking of a favourite breed – border collies were at the top of the list, and at the bottom, in the seventy-ninth ranking, the Afghan hound. My favourite breeds ranked as follows: Cavalier King Charles spaniels – 44, Boston terriers – 54, and pugs – 57. (A number of breeds shared the same rankings, especially in the middle and lower range. For example, Boston terriers tied with Akitas for the fifty-fourth spot.) Anyone who studied the list needed to remember that it focused on obedience and working intelligence, both specialized facets of general intelligence, and a convenient measure that perhaps privileged some breeds over others – a pug trying to shepherd a herd of sheep would, of course, be ludicrous. And Coren's methodology should also be considered. He made up a detailed questionnaire for judges of American and Canadian kennel clubs and received responses from 208 of them (nearly half of the judges approached), along with many letters that included additional remarks.

While the questionnaires became the basis of Coren's statistical data, he did acknowledge that the rankings could not allow for a dog's individual personality (some of the obedience judges had also noted variations within a specific breed). Still, anyone looking for a placid family pet, for example, shouldn't come home with a border collie. Even a poodle (ranking second) may require a kind of keen attention many dog owners aren't ready or able to provide. Coren also wrote about "instinctive" intelligence (programmed by humans in an animal's genetic code, with rewards – for example, barking as guard-dog behaviour) and "adaptive" intelligence (more generalized skills and knowledge, such as problem solving). If Coren's Table 10.1 is read in the context of the entire book, his observations should help anyone better understand his canine companion and probably improve the dog's life at the same time. (Coren, by the way, has been a fancier of various breeds, including Cavalier King Charles spaniels, to me further proof of his sound judgement or intelligence.)

Intelligence is partly a human construct, based on our attitudes, superstitions, and traditions. Another professor of psychology, Clive D.L. Wynne of the University of Florida, aptly framed the subject in *Do Animals Think?* with an opening chapter titled "What Are Animals?" As Wynne put it, "How can we treat animals appropriately if we don't even know what they are?" It's always useful to step back from a subject and ask ourselves how we're thinking about it, and why. The seventeenth-century French philosopher René Descartes, famous for the dictum "I think, therefore, I am" (*cogito ergo sum*), thought that animals did not think. His compatriot, the mathematician, physicist, and philosopher Blaise Pascal, known for suggesting that religious faith could be seen as a "wager," shared a similar view with

Descartes: "The arithmetical machine produces effects which approach nearer to thought than to the actions of animals. But it does nothing which would enable us to attribute will to it, as to the animals." Though he admitted that animals have will, it has little to do with reason; they act entirely by "instinct," not by "mind." So much for Descartes and Pascal; even great philosophers, like most people, can't see fully beyond the confines of their historical moment.

The sophisticated study of dogs (and animals in general) is a fairly recent phenomenon and still in its early stages. Humans, we tell ourselves, have evolved beyond some of our more superstitious or primitive beliefs – think of the Salem, Massachusetts, witch trials of 1692, where two dogs were hung for witchcraft along with the twenty people who were also killed. How different is this, though, from the reports of an increase in professionalized dog fights during the summer of 2007, culminating in the trial of football superstar Michael Vick? Hanging dogs for witchcraft or training them as "sport" killers both assume that a dog's intelligence – as well as its being, its life – belong to another category of existence than human life. What, indeed, are animals? In *The Hidden Life of Dogs*, Elizabeth Marshall Thomas remarked that we often study dogs "for what they can teach us about ourselves," and then use this knowledge to our own advantage.

Many animal behaviourists avoid the word *intelligence* just as they bypass *emotion*, using them only with quotation marks and preferring instead the term *consciousness*, as if it is more scientifically neutral, or at least less associated with anthropomorphism. Yet why should a perfectly good word like *intelligence* be so coloured by human connections that it's difficult to apply in another context? Derek Bickerton, a professor of linguistics at the University of Hawaii, was also bothered by the way scholarship about animals treats the concept of intelligence. Discussing the various ways in which animal intelligence has been assessed in *Language and Human Behavior*, he suggested that we judge their intelligence by comparing an animal's similarity with ourselves. Contrasting chimpanzes with dogs, he speculated that their body type may influence our assessment of them. Put simply, chimps and humans can manipulate objects, like knives and forks, while dogs can't. "This may not explain all the apparent differences in intelligence between chimps and dogs, but it surely accounts for a lot of them." In other words, even some of our most sophisticated modern science has been shaped by the great chain of being, which we find difficult to escape. Yet a dog's intelligence serves a dog well. It's interesting that as obvious a point as Bickerton's came from a linguist, someone who studies how languages work, and not from an animal specialist concerned with training and its manifestations.

Thinking is related to training and can even be seen as a product of it. Advanced thinking and more abstract thought would be impossible without some basis of training, even the kind of self-training embodied in the trial-and-error experiments of Pavlov's bells. Thought and training ultimately involve language, the most convenient way humans have for measuring intelligence. Coren lists over sixty words that dogs have learned to understand or respond to (from *bad dog* to *come* to *roll over* and *heel*), and every dog owner will add or subtract a few. Somehow Zoli knew just about every word for *food* and its seemingly endless variations, and Rennie is just like him in that respect. In the summer of 2004, newspapers across North America reported on the findings of a recent article from *Science* magazine in which Dr. Julia Fischer, a researcher at the Max Planck Institute for Evolutionary Anthropology in Leipzig, studied the behaviour of a nine-year-old border collie (naturally) named Rico, who had mastered over two hundred words for more than two hundred objects. The dog was discovered on a popular German television game show, and since the age of ten months had been taught by his family to fetch numerous children's toys (*bunny, panda, red ball*, etc.). As Fischer demonstrated, Rico had the ability to continue to learn new words and remember them when tested four weeks later, but she also insisted that without further study it was not reasonable to generalize from Rico to all dogs, or even border collies. Without reducing Rico to a circus act, albeit one that appeared in *Science*, it's fair to say that his story caught public attention because human beings with dogs are constantly trying to understand what their dogs know and how smart they might be. And naturally we also wonder what they think of us. As the Czech author and playwright Karel Čapek put it, "If dogs could talk, perhaps we would find it as hard to get along with them as we do with people."

"IT" AND IMPERSONALITY

The dog chases its tail. The dog chases his tail. The dog chases her tail.

There's a world of difference between *its, his* and *her* in these three sentences, differences of attitude and value worth thinking about. It's not surprising that most of the scientific books about dogs, from anatomical studies to popular behaviourist titles and works in the social sciences, prefer to use *it* and *its* as a pronoun, as if these words confer distance and objectivity. Deprived of gender, a dog as an *it* seems a suitable subject of study, almost an object – inanimate, mechanical, *not* human, *not* us – lower on that great chain of being and definitely not anthropomorphized. The writer/observer is here in control, superior. Language, of course, always contains some bias. I was tempted to include the word *depersonalized* in the previous list of adjectives, but it includes the word *person* and contains an unstated assumption. "Im*person*ality" in the heading above poses a challenge when we begin to think about the structure of the word.

Science writers often prefer *its* over *his* or *her*, as if scientific objectivity requires some distance from animal subjects, and pronouns can play a role in assuring it. When dogs appear in fiction, poems and memoirs, gender is restored or used when it's known, as is subjectivity, intimacy, and emotion, even where anthropomorphism is not an issue. In most literary writing a dog is not an object, a thing, but a being in himself or herself (I was tempted to write *itself*, which flows more easily). For the sake of variation, non-scientific writers sometimes use an ungendered pronoun as a matter of style – I do this myself – without intending the dog or animal in question to sound like a laboratory specimen, a possession or a piece of property, like a CD player. Yet a subtle bias remains, and the unconscious reasoning seems to be that once we know an individual dog's gender, it's unnecessary to keep repeating it over and over. Still, imagine a scene in the novel *Gone with the Wind* where Scarlett O'Hara wants to go back to its home Tara, and you'll see the disjunction, or think you're reading a misprint.

The difference between *his* and *her* is obvious but deserves comment, especially at a time in history when many pet dogs are neutered. What role does sexuality play in gender? What about sexuality apart from procreation? In the 1920s, a gossip columnist coined the term *it* for the mysterious attribute of erotic appeal and then applied the term to a silent-film actress, Clara Bow, who became known as the "It Girl." (Curiously, but typical of the twenties, there was no "It Boy.") "It" suggested heightened sexiness, a quality of raw sensuality, even animality, that made up the actress's power. While it may seem like a big leap from an old-time movie star to any dog's gender, animality is the link. In a human being, *it* conveys the self apart from nurture, before self-consciousness and civilizing. In a neutered pet dog, however, with no possibility for breeding, the matter of *it* and associations with gender and sexuality seems to recede – people who care for their dog's health and well-being rarely give much thought to their dog's sexual satisfaction.

If my dog is an *it*, what am I? An owner? Gendered words like *master* and *mistress* seem old-fashioned, but *owner* has an edge that reinforces a dog's *it*ness – the dog as possession. *Caretaker* and *guardian* seem like forced terms, a feeble attempt to solve the problem, yet something better than *owner* is needed because words shape the ways we see and act. Yes, we do often "buy" dogs, but not as we buy lamps or apples. (While philosopher Blaise Pascal showed no high regard for animal intelligence, he did object to the acquisitive drive in human possessiveness. One example: when children say "This dog is mine," he argued, it marks "the usurpation of all earth.") Albert Payson Terhune confronted this subject in one of his first dog novels, *Lad: A Dog*, as long ago as 1919, when he emphasized the difference between a dog's "owner" and its "master" – the first term implies only purchasing power; the second, a relationship. ("Any body, with price to buy a dog, can be an 'owner,' but all the cash coined won't make a man a dog's 'master' – unless he's that sort of man.") In many ways we're still catching up with Terhune. In 2003, the City Council of San Francisco attempted to address this problem by replacing the terms *owner* and *ownership* with *guardian* and *guardianship* regarding dogs. Several other socially innovative cities, including Berkeley and West Hollywood, California; Boulder, Colorado; and Amherst, Massachusetts had previously passed similar ordinances – all perhaps without much legal standing – but it was San Francisco's that received the most national attention. In subsequent years, new cities have joined the list, including St. Louis, Missouri; Bloomington, Indiana; and Windsor, Ontario.

Ownership and possession have been important issues in the work of eco-feminists like Donna Haraway, whose *Companion Species Manifesto: Dogs, People, and Significant Otherness* speaks to anyone living with a dog, although the book resorts to contemporary academic language that some readers may find esoteric. Early on, Haraway sums up her concern in this simple phrase: "Dogs are not about oneself." It's important to remember that dogs aren't one of our many projections, or our creation; they are a separate species – beings in their own right, in themselves. In other words, a species made up of individuals, like our own, and one with whom we humans have a long and powerful relationship. The world view contained in *it* therefore raises important issues of animal rights, and a dog's legal position in society, which is discussed elsewhere.

JOURNALISM

Many large metropolitan newspapers include weekly columns about pets, and these are frequently written by women. I'm not certain why gender plays a role here, but it does, and women journalists and their canine subjects often seem relegated to the ghetto of "lifestyle" pages, as if neither are, exactly, serious. Such columns generally cover local and regional animal shows, with an emphasis on dogs and cats; new products may be discussed, and sometimes a book by a local author, or a bestselling title. Yet journalism about dogs has a much richer side, along with its own professional group, the Dog Writers' Association of America. Two of the pioneers of the field were Walter Fletcher, who wrote for *The New York Times*, and Max Riddle of the *Cleveland Press* and later the *Plain Dealer*. Founded in 1935, the association was initially the domain of journalists, but it eventually included dog-book authors as well as people who breed and show dogs and write for small, specialized newsletters like the *Corgi Crier*.

One of the best weekly pet columnists was Suzanne Hively, who retired from the *Plain Dealer* in 2006, at the age of seventy-five. Her insightful columns ought to be collected in a book, and

I suggested this one afternoon, over lunch, when she told me a part of her story. A trained artist who had worked for several years as a commercial artist, Hively then studied journalism at Indiana University and became a general assignment reporter, working on the copy desk and as an editor, and only writing about animals as a sideline. After reporting for the Fort Wayne *Journal Gazette* and the Sandusky *Register*, she came to the *Plain Dealer* in 1970 and soon began her "About Animals" column that went on to win several Maxwells, the award from the Dog Writers, Association of America named after Max Riddle. I mentioned several columns that I particularly admired (one about war dogs, another about Kirlian photography), and Hively fondly recalled a column about a rescue Maltese who needed specialized surgery – that column raised $25,000 for the dog in just twenty-four hours.

The steady demands of a weekly column can easily turn into a trap, but Hively didn't let this happen. Her writing about dogs, never a mere schedule of upcoming canine events, always emphasized the richness of the human/dog bond. Perhaps she wrote with such informed passion because that's the kind of person she is. But I came to suspect that her personal experience with dogs also shaped her writing – Hively has owned and loved and shown a wide range of breeds, from borzois to Afghans, Chinese cresteds, and, currently, Japanese chins; she now looks after four chins and eight cresteds. When I asked why she preferred one breed over another, she explained that she'd always been drawn to dogs that weren't popular at the moment. (Borzois, the dogs of her childhood, had in fact been popular in the 1920s and 1930s, but a child wouldn't necessarily know that.) The switch from larger to smaller breeds was explained pragmatically. When her last borzoi, a Russian import, was twelve and a half years old and ill, Hively found it too difficult to lift the dog into the car to take it to the veterinarian, and decided it was time to focus on smaller dogs. Kyio, her Chinese crested who died at the age of fourteen, was for many years the official crested model for cards from American Greetings, and Hively proudly related how Chinese crested fanciers around the world often sent her cards portraying the dog. And the actress and animal activist Betty White, also a friend of Hively's, once found a card picturing another of her Chinese cresteds in a Los Angeles drugstore and mailed it to the dog herself.

Most people of seventy-seven who aren't downsizing are at least careful not to further complicate their lives, but on the afternoon of our first meeting Hively was excited about her plan to acquire a new Chinese crested from a good breeder in Dallas. A vegan since 1986, she paused when I asked if her own dogs had had anything to do with the decision to change her diet. "Subconsciously," she allowed, and went on to discuss the extensive reading she'd done about meat, food in general, and also medical technology, one of her special interests. I didn't add that I thought all of these dogs must have contributed to her lively, open nature, but she probably guessed my thought and may even have agreed. She did note that about 97 per cent of the people in her life have had something to do with dogs, which may also support a life-affirming personality. At seventy-seven, we should all be fortunate enough to contemplate giving a home to a new puppy.

JUDGING DOG SHOWS

After watching the closing night of the 2007 Westminster Kennel Club Dog show, which was broadcast nationally from Madison Square Garden in New York City, a friend immediately phoned me with the question we ask every year: "Why was *that* dog the best in show?" The question is a good one and I know we weren't the only people asking it. The Westminster show is the second-oldest continuous sporting event in the United States – second to the Kentucky Derby – and part of the ritual may be debating the judges' decisions.

Dog shows are a) exhilarating, b) disheartening, or c) big business. Answer: all of these. Easy to satirize, as shown by the splendid 2000 film comedy *Best in Show*, dog shows, like all such contests including Miss America, the Oscars, and the National Book Awards, thrive on objections and quibbles, which are essential forms of attention. We watch to enjoy the dogs, or movie stars, in their moment of televised fame, while considering our favourites. In the days following the Westminster's ascension of a new "best in show," several friends and canine fanatics, who follow all of the televised competitions, including the annual Eukanuba Tournament of Champions and the British Crufts Dog Show (the Animal Planet Network was still re-broadcasting the 2004 show in the summer of 2007), also phoned with their thoughts. When Dr. Robert A. Indeglia, a cardiac surgeon from Rhode Island and former breeder of Norwegian elkhounds, made his selection on that cold February night, I'm certain he was choosing in good faith. Yet his explanation of his choice seemed romantic at best. He said that he'd looked into the eyes of James, the English springer spaniel, and seen an expression that claimed the night. Dr. Indeglia didn't want to interfere with the dog's entitlement.

The problem here is not simple. If any judge can know the standards of all 165 breeds of competing dogs, and have genuine expertise with the seven categories (herding, hound, non-sporting, sporting, terrier, toy, and working), he or she must possess an exceptional mind and experience. Such a judge would also need to be free of preference or prejudice, also difficult to imagine. Granted that these judges do exist, they are still asked to do something inherently impossible and even absurd – decide which is better, an apple, an orange, or a strawberry. It comes down to that. Winners at the dog shows illustrate this observation. Many of the most esoteric breeds (the pulis or komondors or Rhodesian ridgebacks, to name only a few) rarely make "best in show" in their appropriate categories, but the regular choices of popular breeds such as the elaborately coiffed poodles (toy and standard), as in 2007, or dogs that arrive at the show with considerable advance word and good public-relations work, is common. Is there a poodle lobby, or one for the favoured breed de jour?

The idea of "best in show" is itself the core of the problem. It is based on an unstated assumption of a platonic form of a breed, perfectability that we know is ideal – not only of physical appearance and its components, but of intangibles like personality. Performance in the ring, of course, makes an impression on judges and audience. But this short walk, which reveals a dog's gait in relation to the breed's historical function, also demonstrates the way a much-rehearsed dog moves, both bodily and, in relation to its handler, psychologically – a minimal test. Even if one allows that some springer spaniels are closer to the breed ideal than others (set after all by human beings) a rigid notion of appearance predominates. As well, breed standards change over time, and this only suggests that they're human constructs, not inherent canine qualities. Comparing one breed of dog to another just because they both fall into the "toy" category (a pug and a Chihuahua, for example) tells us little about either animal but a great deal about the human need to define, label, and control the world. Even within breed standards, there's room for an individual judge's preferences. Pugs, for example, can be finer- boned or more heavily boned, and breeders will favour one body type over the other. Historically, pugs may have been leaner, with longer legs, than their contemporary descendants (look at the pug in William Hogarth's wonderful self-portrait with his pug, from 1745), who, in the current American fashion, are stockier dogs, sometimes almost pushing the size of the breed out of the toy category itself. Canadian breeders, on the other hand, have

"Self Portrait" (1749), engraved by J. Mollison, from William Hogarth's oil painting *Self-Portrait with His Pug* (1745). Featured as prominently as the artist himself, Hogarth's dog, named Trump, is much leaner than contemporary pugs.

often favoured smaller, finer-boned pugs, which I prefer, dogs of around sixteen pounds, and not the heavier, twenty-pound plus pugs. Suzanne Hively, the dog columnist who has shown a variety of breeds, once described to me how breed standards can change when a prominent breeder has had many wins. In the 1950s, for example, white patches on a boxer were frowned on, but today they're valued. Hively, who no longer shows her Chinese cresteds, explained that the hairless variety were once truly hairless before they became part of the AKC, but now their skins need to be shaved and handlers regularly use hair-removal chemicals and products on their bodies. Since Japanese chin have become more popular in recent years, Hively foresees almost inevitable changes in their standard as well.

Money pre-selects the dogs in any competition. One example: regular advertising in specialized venues like *Dog News* and *Dogs in Review,* as well as in individual breed magazines, is essential for a dog to have a chance at finding a place in the top ten of its breed, and this can quickly run into thousands of dollars. If a celebrity like Bill Cosby chooses to invest in a show dog like Harry, the Dandie Dinmont terrier, or an unknown but equally well-heeled couple wants the ego-gratification of a winning dog, that doesn't mean that their dogs are in any serious way "the best," they're only privileged by the finances and attention of their owners and professional handlers, and selected because of their approximation of that platonic ideal. In this context, can any dog have individuality? And how does that conform to the breed standard? Think for a moment of the elaborately coiffed poodles that circle the show ring in "show cuts," cuts that have been imposed on their bodies to suit or display breed standards. Yes, every year some commentator explains, almost self-consciously, to avoid embarrassment, that the poodle cut has a history and function. In this sense dog shows are deeply conservative affairs. When, I always wonder, will a daring owner/handler show a poodle with the common "lamb" cut, a cut that reveals the dog as more than a contemporary rococo construction.

Judges, hosts, and commentators at dog shows might begin to address this situation by explaining the reasons for their choices. Imagine judging at any of the popular sports competitions such as the Olympics or World Cups without the open particularities of judgeship. Several years ago, when nationalism and politics too often appeared to enter the judging of international ice-skating competitions, new criteria for judging were created to address potential bias. At the very least, judges of canine competitions should explain why they prefer *this* apple to *that* orange, and commentators need more than pleasant emcee voices and affable manners. The AKC has set standards for each breed, and departures from the ideal appear to be faults, but the audience remains in the dark unless this aspect of competing is explained. A newly educated audience would begin to understand the many elements involved in judging and the entire process would appear less subjective and, at times, irrational.

Between the most popular competitions, afficionados without dogs of their own to show or people who just like the drama of the ring, can turn to a number of mystery novels set in the dog-show world. None of these, however, has much to say about a dog's point of view on the subject. For that, turn to Albert Payson Terhune's *Lad: A Dog* (1919). I cite the publication year again because it's important to recall that almost a century ago a writer thought about the stress a dog must go through during an exhibition, and we have yet to catch up with that perception. In a chapter titled "For a Bit of Ribbon," Lad, the collie, is taken to the *ne plus ultra* of American dog shows, the Westminster, to compete in the novice trials, after a friend of the dog's owners – someone "who loved dogs far better than he understood them" – suggested entering Lad. The indignities suffered during preparations for the show, and the anxieties and discomforts that follow, are, according to Terhune, "a form of unremitting torture." Emphasis is placed largely on appearance and gait, or "the effort to breed the perfect physical animal." Dogs that are born and bred to be show dogs aren't exactly dogs, but living manifestations of the human ego. Lad, fine collie that he is, manages to tolerate the indignities, but only barely. He is an old-fashioned dog, unlike "the up-to-date collies – this year's style, at least;" but a wise judge sees beyond fashion and awards Lad the blue ribbon because he was the kind of dog the judge's Scottish "Shepherd ancestors had admitted as an equal, at hearth and board."

Along the way to Lad's win, Terhune offers a portrait of tightly caged dogs being pummelled and plucked, fluffed and brushed, even sandpapered and shaved, carelessly examined by disinterested official veterinarians, pulled about by choke collars, forced to listen to steady yapping and barking in a constant din of noise, and to smell strange, unpleasant smells. This, of course, all took place before airplane travel, a standard part of the lives of today's show dogs and their professional handlers, who spend a great deal of time in transit. As one of Terhune's characters remarks:

Why, just suppose *you* were brought to a strange place like this and chained into a cage and were left there four days and nights while hundreds of other prisoners kept screaming and shouting and crying at the top of their lungs every minute of the time! And suppose about a hundred thousand people kept jostling past your cage night and day, rubbering at you and pointing at you and trying to feel your ears and mouth, and chirping at you to shake hands, would *you* feel very hungry or very chipper? A four-day show is the most fearful thing a high-strung dog can go through – next to vivisection. A little one-day show, for about eight hours, is no special ordeal, especially if the dog's Master stays near him all the time; but a four-day show is – is Sheol! I wonder the S.P.C.A. doesn't do something to make it easier.

Take it or leave it, Terhune was never afraid of being didactic. People who show dogs have told me that today's conditions are improved, but Terhune's words remain in mind.

Anyone more interested in dog shows as entertainment than in a dog's view of them would do well to seek out *The Kennel Murder Case*, a 1933 movie mystery set in a Long Island dog show, with William Powell as detective Philo Vance. Or, better yet, find a copy of Jane and Michael Stern's *Dog Eat Dog: A Very Human Book About Dogs and Dog Shows*, which follows a canine year leading up to the Westminster show. Their rival Afghans, poodles, and spaniels make for a good story as well as a frank inside view that, by its end, left me sorry for all the dogs on display, subject as they are to the whims of their stage parents. While the Sterns have a great deal to tell about competitions, they say only a few words about judging, although they're aware of its problematic state. Though each standard is precise, they admit that "judging dogs is one of the most subjective procedures in the world of sport." They go on to compare dog-show judging with that of gymnastics or a beauty pageant, which at least have panels of experts. Dogs, unfortunately, face judges with absolute power – if you disagree with the decision, "you have no recourse but to wait for the next show and hope for a judge who interprets the standard the way you like." Given all the money spent on dog competitions, and the high stakes that accompany them, it makes little sense that the human competitors (who are also investors) continue to tolerate this situation. My objections didn't stop me from turning on the 135th Westminster, in 2011, and won't for future competitions, but the dogs – *and the audience* – deserve a more informative show.

KITSCH

Kitsch, like beauty, is in the eye of the beholder. Hermès collars imported from Paris, organic gourmet biscuits from the Three Dog

Bakery (I confess to buying a bag of them for Zoli and Morgan during a visit to Kansas City one summer) – doggy stuff will be sold by somebody wherever people gather. From the Hamptons to Beverly Hills, luxury items prevail, but dog people come in all classes and economic backgrounds, which makes dog shopping almost universal, at least in North America. If it can be combined with a holiday, all the better, and this may explain why dog shops often crop up near tourist destinations. Missing your dog, or feeling guilty because you've left him at home? Buy something. There used to be a splendid shop devoted to dog stuff near San Francisco's Fisherman's Wharf, where I once bought Christmas-tree ornaments shaped like pugs, Boston terriers, and Cavalier King Charles spaniels, while one of the best stores devoted to canine tchotchkes, in Fisherman's Village of Punta Gorda, Florida, (where I bought an inexpensive watch with a pug's face) was destroyed by Hurricane Charlie in the fall of 2004; it has, I'm told, since reopened. So I'm as guilty as the next guy. The university I teach at now sells a dog sweater in the school's colours – not as uncommon as you might think – but I've resisted. Hand-painted plates, figurines, dog-shaped lamp bases, the list of items is endless. Some of the objects are made for dogs themselves, others only for dog owners, though occasionally the distinction blurs. According to critic and novelist Daphne Merkin, "We spend more money annually on pet-related supplies and services (an estimated $35 billion last year) than we do on toys for children." Merkin's statistics, from 2004, are already out of date. Of course dogs don't care about luxury or conspicuous consumption, though they do enjoy getting presents and keep an eye on their favourite possessions (bones, balls, and the like).

I've lumped a lot of things under the heading of kitsch, which Webster's defines as "artistic or literary material of low quality." Kitsch may include an element of intentional humour – for example, the pug salt-and-pepper shakers I bought in Boston, with the salt pug sitting at attention and the pepper pug, head down and rump up, ready to play. Kitsch, generally, is less witty than sentimental or "cute." Yet it's possible for someone to see unintended irony in an object and appreciate it for that perceived kitschy wit. Over time, some items almost transcend the status of kitsch and achieve, through associations like nostalgia, a kind of camp. A new rhinestone dog collar is kitsch at best, but an old one from the 1950s, with the patina of age, might, just barely, have an odd kind of flair to it.

There's a bigger distance between mass-produced, K-Mart decorations and genuinely rare bibelots (Staffordshire spaniels or Miessen pugs), though each has its kitschy aspect. Royalty and royal wannabes have always spoiled their dogs, using them as fashion accessories, and the catalogue for Sotheby's 1998 sale of items from the estate of the Duke and Duchess of Windsor was filled with pug paraphernalia, from silver bowls to needlepoint pillows, all sporting the ducal provenance. A dog, however, appreciates none of these distinctions. Aromatherapy, Les Poochs dog perfume from France, selling for $5,000 for two ounces, and custom-made doghouses built by Doggie Mansions, a company based in Palm Beach, Florida, that prices its homes from $10,000 to $100,000, are beyond kitsch, representing a gilded-age mentality; they are especially troubling during an economic downturn, when newspaper articles tell us that many people, unable to feed their pets, have been forced to give them up to animal shelters.

A few kitsch items can soon become a collection, whether it's meant to happen or not. Over the years, friends, family, and former students have bought me puggy gifts, though I've never thought to collect anything but books and CDs. But kitsch you buy for yourself is almost always preferable to kitsch you're given. I have towels and an apron printed with pug faces; at least a dozen stuffed pug toys, including two pug Beanie Babies, a bar of French soap shaped like a pug and called Le Pug, though in France it's actually *le carlin*,

An early twentieth-century postcard of pugs.

pug needlepoint pillows and coasters, a deck of pug playing cards, T-shirts printed with pug faces (as yet unworn) and a silk neck tie with a pug emblem, a rubber stamp shaped like a pug – the list is endless. Most of the items are kept on the top shelf of the linen closet, several I've given away surreptitiously, and a few – like the ceramic pug spoon rest beside my stove, or my favourite mug for morning coffee – are useful. Yet the most beautiful dog tchotchke I own, and also the gift of a friend, is unfortunately not a pug, but a rare Georgian china inkwell in the shape of a whippet.

I'm reminded of a wonderful scene in Magda Szabó's *The Doors*, which I've mentioned before. One day the elderly maid Emerence collects discarded junk from the street and brings a cheap figurine of a nondescript dog with a chipped ear as a gift to the novel's narrator. What to do with the thing? It can't be displayed prominently, if at all, and an argument ensues between the two women, with the explanation that the china dog is kitsch. When Emerence calls for a definition, she's told that "Kitsch is when a thing is in some way false, created to provide trivial, superficial pleasure. Kitsch is something imitative, fake, a substitute for the real thing." Unconvinced, Emerence reminds her tasteful mistress that she owns a number of objects that are incomplete in themselves, and substitutes, like the fragments of a vase dug up in Athens on her desk. Somewhat chastened for her snobbery, the narrator admits that she sounded like a left-wing art critic but still rejects the figurine (and not because it's chipped), as the argument gets horribly out of hand, with dramatic consequences. As I said at the start, kitsch is in the eye of the beholder.

Sentimentality is the last ingredient in kitsch. When Szabó's narrator refers to kitsch as "fake, a substitute for the real thing," she may as well be defining sentimentality itself. In its essence, sentimentality is false or easy sentiment. Most serious artists dread it, leaving the category to popular and commercial work. Or so they think. In the catalogue to a British exhibition of eighteenth, and nineteenth-century dog sculpture, the curators thought to include a final essay by Steve Baker titled "The Refusal of Sentimentality in Postmodern Animal Art." Embracing parody, irony, and satire, the big-name artists whose works were illustrated (Jeff Koons, Robert Rauschenberg, William Wegman) eschewed the beauty of animal forms for cultural commentary. To my mind, the commentary is of a predictable, sophomoric sort, but Baker prefers words like "troubling and uncanny," arguing that "At its most extreme, the travestying of innocence as a defense against sentimentality can take the form of what has memorably been termed 'art bestiality': a lashing out at domesticity and propriety as contemptibly safe and mediocre." Such preoccupations fade when one looks at the extraordinary marble, bronze, and terracotta pieces by Grégoire Giraud, Joseph Gott, Anne Seymour Damer, and Harry Bates – propriety and safety are the last things that come to mind.

The limitations that characterize ideologically weighted visual art are also common to much postmodern literature. Recently, while selecting several dozen short stories to be included in an anthology of Canadian fiction about dogs, it struck me that the older stories by once-prominent writers who are now considered historical, if not dated, showed more interest in dogs – more keen observation of them, more sympathy and affection for them – than the hip contemporary stories I was reading. These latter efforts tended to be full of easy black humour and were often downright nasty. If the dogs in these stories weren't actually harmed or brutalized, and the human characters made to seem bestial, then the dog/human bond appeared as a bleak connection or dark metaphor. This is especially curious because we're living in a time when pet-keeping has become far more common than it was a century ago, and I'm certain that many of these writers (and visual artists) have dogs of their own. But when they sat down at their computers, they seemed to be overtaken by embarrassment. To be cool – and serious – one must not risk showing any positive sentiment about animals. The result is a kind of writing that I'd like to give a name of its own: postmodern kitsch.

LANGUAGE

Our English word for *Canis familiaris* is *dog*, with roots in both Old and Middle English usage. Over the centuries *dog* has been incorporated into a wide range of terms and phrases, many of them contradictory, some literal and some metaphoric. Think of this incomplete list as just a beginning: dogged, dog-eat-dog, dog days, dog-eared, hangdog, dirty dog, mad dog, seeing-eye dog, top dog, doggone, doggie bag, dog fight, dog tired, dog tag (an animal's or a soldier's tag), dog face (slang for a soldier), dog house (a structure and a place of disfavour), dog tooth (a style in Gothic ornamentation), dog rose, also referred to as dog's bramble (a five-petalled, pink wild rose – *R. Canina* – known by this name in England), dog Latin (mock Latin, and also a slang term for Low Latin) and doggerel, a dog's life, sick as a dog, work like a dog, let sleeping dogs lie, the dogs of war, the hair of the dog (a hangover cure), the black dog (depression), the tail wags the dog, gone to the dogs, putting on the dog, and walking the dog (a kind of bidding in bridge and also a yo-yo trick). In a few instances some of these terms can have several applications: as an adjective *dogged* means determined or tenacious, while as a verb it suggests the act of following or worrying, not unrelated concepts. But can someone enjoy *a dog's life*, with the positive connotations of sleeping, eating, and lying around, while being *dog-tired* or *working like a dog*? And don't forget to extend this list to words like *bitch*, when used out of its dog-reference context as an insult, or to individual creative turns of phrase, such as Shakespeare's line "the hearts that spanieled me at heels," from *Antony and Cleopatra*, an example of exuberant Renaissance word play (instead of the plainer *dogged*, or even the direct *followed*), Shakespeare took the gentle image of the spaniel – a noun, sometimes also used as an adjective, as in spaniel dog – and made it into an evocative verb). Consider, also, words that begin with *dog* as the first syllable – *dogma, dogmatic, dogmatist* – which echo *dogged*, or the quality of stubborn persistence. And, finally, there's *puppy love*.

Now imagine a linguistic world of dog/human polarities with some possible opposites for a few of the terms listed above – humaned, people-tired, sick as a person, human days – and the charge that the word *dog* gives them ignites. *Dog* refers, in part, to our ambivalence about being human, about what it constitutes, how we judge ourselves, and what we can expect from each other given our animal nature, and it betrays a casual hierarchical thinking. Except for a few terms or phrases – *bird-brained, eats like a bird*, or *catty* and *cat's ass* – the English language tends to privilege *dog* as a descriptive point of reference and departure. Why? Is this universal? It's not surprising that we think, speak, and write in terms of associations. As children we learn words and more words to name our world, make our desires known, and gradually to discover and live in a world beyond the self. Since dogs have been at the side of humans from almost our earliest days as a species, even if an individual has never known a dog as a pet, dogs are natural points of reference and figures of speech. And the dog/human polarity is imbedded in more languages than English. Contemporary scholars in the humanities rarely like to think in terms of "universals," but I'm glad to say that English is not unique in its use of the dog as a baseline, grounding point, or motif.

In French, phrases incorporating the word for dog – *le chien,* with a masculine article – have both positive and negative associations, though it seems to me there's a slight emphasis on the latter, as in English. A partial list includes: *avoir du chien* (to be charming, distinctive), *temps de chien* (terrible weather), *avoir un caractère de chien* (a difficult or bad-tempered character), *être un chien couchant* (to be like a cowering dog), *être malade comme un chien* (sick as a dog, literally, but usually for a digestive or stomach problem, not a backache), *avoir une vie de chien* (to have a dog's life, but a difficult one), *traiter quelqu'un comme un chien* (to treat someone like a dog), *parler à quelqu'un comme à un chien* (to speak to someone like a dog), *être couché en chien de fusil* (to lie in a fetal position), and *suivre quelqu'un comme un petit chien* (to follow someone like a small dog), and my favourite, *entre chien et loup* (in the twilight or dusk). Of course there are doggy aphorisms as well: *faire un temps à ne pas mettre un chien dehors* (the weather's so bad you wouldn't even put a dog outside), *les chiens aboient, le caravane passe* (literally, "the dogs bark, the caravan passes," or, just ignore what's happening, go on with what you're doing), *quand on veut noyer un chien, on l'accuse de la rage* ("when you want to drown your dog, you blame it on rabies" – a way of saying that someone's looking for any pretext to do something), and *lâcher les chiens sur quelqu'un* (acting aggressively, as if war has been declared). A few of these terms have counterparts in English, and read almost like translations, while others are unique to the French language.

Similar lists can be made for a wide range of languages, and I've spoken with friends and colleagues, collecting examples from Greek, Spanish, and Hebrew, along with lists I've made for German and Hungarian. My friend Lee Rainey, a professor of Chinese philosophy, has given me this short list of Chinese terms, which I'll offer phonetically: *goutou* ("dog's head," a term of abuse between a jerk and an s.o.b.), *gou tuizi* (literally "a dog's leg," actually a hired thug or henchman), *gou qi* ("a dog's temperament," or flattering superiors and bullying inferiors), *gou cai* (dog talent, referring to people with little talent generally), and a range of sayings, including "like a dog trying to catch mice" for sticking your nose into other people's business. (As a side note, the Chinese character *quan*, meaning dog or canine, is the root – called a radical – of many Chinese characters for other animals, including fox, monkey, lion, jackal, and quadrupeds in general.) Whatever you think of dogs, they've helped shape and define our humanity, which also means our languages. Since we can't live without language, and as a species we've often found it better to live with dogs, all children should be taught to appreciate dogs just as they're given the tool of language. Writers of reading primers like *See Spot Run* may not be fully aware of the association they've made between words and dogs, but they're on to something essential.

LOYALTY

The attribute most commonly associated with dogs is loyalty, along with devotion, its variant. Even people who thoroughly understand that dogs are pack animals, with a keen sense of hierarchy, prefer to think of their own pets as loyal beings rather than as creatures programmed by evolution to look at them adoringly when treated well, and sometimes even when handled carelessly.

Dogs can pay a terrible price for their loyalty. Near the end of Charles Dickens's novel *Oliver Twist*, published in 1838 – which shows how old this convention is – the villainous Bill Sikes tries to escape apprehension after murdering his girlfriend Nancy, a prostitute, along with his unnamed dog, who followed "limping and lame from the unaccustomed exercise." After trying to drown the dog so that it would not expose him to anyone in pursuit, the guilt-haunted thug crosses London and meets his end when he loses his balance, tumbles over a building's parapet and accidentally hangs himself, his body swinging "lifeless against the wall." Instead of ending the chapter here, Dickens adds this finale: "A dog, which had lain concealed till now, ran backwards and forwards on the parapet with a dismal howl, and collecting himself for a spring, jumped for the dead man's shoulders. Missing his aim, he fell into the ditch, turning completely over as he went; and striking his head against a stone, dashed out his brains." This gruesome passage is more interesting than one might think on a first reading. While it's true that Dickens often includes macabre moments of black humour in his books, nothing about the death of Sikes, or of his dog, suggests that a bitter laugh was on the novelist's mind. Even as brutal a character as Bill Sikes – who beat Nancy to death in front of his dog and then wiped the blood off its paws to avoid leaving tracks – can be loved by a dog.

Such loyalty poses a moral problem, marking the difference between canine and human moral imagination. It can be troubling to think that dogs pay allegiance to monsters, whether they're fictional creations like Sikes, or actual dictators like Adolf Hitler, who was known to have cared for his dogs, and had that affection returned. Friends of mine who prefer cats to dogs always cite this quirk in canine allegiance. How to answer? Take them or leave them, that's the way dogs work. Perhaps it's easier to ignore the subject, or prettify it. When David Lean made his film version of *Oliver Twist*, released in 1948, he didn't send the dog to its death; Lionel Bart's musical, and the movie based on it, also softened Dickens's vision. I don't think that Dickens meant to suggest anything redemptive in the behaviour – or love or loyalty – of Sikes's dog. But almost any gentle emotion stands out in the harsh world of this novel, where poverty demeans everyone. Consequently, there's an unmistakable irony to the dog's leap. Like Nancy, he loses his life for being more than a brute.

Dickens's version of canine devotion always reminds me of its flip side, Sir Edwin Landseer's famous oil painting *Attachment* (1829), in the St. Louis Art Museum. But here the pictorial, static nature of the dramatic subject – a moment frozen in time – has open-ended ramifications. The painting is based on an actual event, the death of the young artist Charles Gough in 1805, after he set out on a mountain-climbing trek in England's Lake District, with his companion dog. Missing for several months, Gough was eventually found after someone heard his dog barking and discovered the man's corpse, which the dog had been guarding. This story was well-known in its day and retold in poems by William Wordsworth ("Fidelity") and Sir Walter Scott ("Helvellyn"). Landseer's version sets the mountainside tragedy in a sublime, wild landscape with a dark, distant, threatening sky. In the lower right foreground of the canvas, the dead young man lies face up on his back, caught between boulders. We see his head from the top, vulnerable, as if he were asleep. A brown cloak conceals most of his body, except for his lifeless left arm, hanging over a precipice, and his right hand and arm, which lie under the left hind paw of his dog, who rests her body on her master's chest. The large boulder under the dead man's head seems to give off a glow that shines on the skin of his forehead and also on the head of his loyal pet. One art historian, Robert Rosenblum, has written that the bond

Attachment (1829) by Sir Edwin Landseer (1802-1873). Oil on canvas. The image is based on a real event, the tragic death of a young artist, Charles Gough, during his climb on Helvellyn Mountain in England's Lake District.

between man and dog is here "the almost operatic climax of star-crossed lovers." Death-watch scenes like Landseer's might easily slip into kitsch, but they contain a truth about the human/dog bond that dog lovers value, a connection beyond words that's felt to be eternal.

The apotheosis of death-watch loyalty must be Eleanor Atkinson's *Greyfriars Bobby*, and the nadir, for me, is the popular doggerel poem about the bridge to dog heaven that several well-meaning people sent me after Zoli died. I've managed to forget its title and author. By the way, Gough's dog, unlike Bill Sikes's dog, survived the climbing accident. I hope she found a good new home and the opportunity to be happily loyal once more.

LUMPS

If you brush or groom your dog with care, or just pet and hug it affectionately, at some point you may find an unfamiliar lump or growth somewhere on its body. Never dismiss this as insignificant. If you've determined that the lump is not, in fact, a clump of fur or a mud-ball or the like, there are a number of other matters to consider. Bug bites are one possibility, as well as an ingrown hair (resulting in a follicular cyst). Only a veterinarian can tell if that's the source of the concern, and he or she may need to watch the lump over time or even remove it for a biopsy. If you're fortunate, the growth will be a cutaneous papilloma, which is benign and wart-like, or a cutaneous histiocytoma, not uncommon on younger and smaller dogs; the list goes on. But you may also have come across a mast-cell tumour.

I was sitting in the driver's seat of my car on a Saturday afternoon in August, waiting for a cousin to come out from her condo, with Zoli beside me as usual, anticipating company, when I first noticed two lumps. Since he lived his life curled up beside me – and a big part of it in my lap – feeling the lumps was all the more startling. On his right thigh, the first lump appeared to be a bug bite, and pimple-like to the touch. Then, on a similar spot on his left thigh, another lump, but this one larger and flatter, like half of a squashed jelly bean. (As a puppy, Zoli had had a small lump removed for a biopsy from the back of his head, and it turned out to be a benign cutaneous histiocytoma, a fancy name for a type of benign tumour. Since then I'd been careful about checking for further lumps.) Over the weekend I tried unsuccessfully not to worry, and on Monday spoke with Zoli's vet in Toronto – I hadn't planned to return home for several weeks, preoccupied as I was with my mother's increasing dementia. Dr. Medhurst and I decided that Zoli should have the lumps biopsied at once, and since he was due to have his teeth cleaned, I arranged for both procedures with a local veterinary clinic in Cleveland that I'd consulted from time to time.

Waiting for the biopsy report was protracted by the Labour Day weekend, and on the Tuesday morning after it, Dr. Medhurst phoned to ask if I'd been given the news – Zoli had two mast-cell tumours, or malignant cancer, and both were stage one, the least fatal. I made an appointment to see him in two days and meanwhile requested a quick meeting with the Cleveland vet who'd done the surgery. In her late thirties, she was many months pregnant and clearly preoccupied. "What's the problem?" she asked when I explained that I wanted a full report (neither she nor her office had phoned me, only sending a copy of the report from a California lab to Toronto). Stage-one mast-cell tumours weren't "a big deal," she insisted. She'd removed a number of them from dogs who were alive five years later. At the age of eight and a half, Zoli should enjoy a long life.

After the drive back to Toronto, I immediately took Zoli to see Rich Medhurst. While sitting in the waiting room, I saw a handsome middle-aged couple enter the clinic, followed by a teenage girl, all grim-faced. The well-dressed man was crying openly while the stone-faced woman carried their dog. My stomach churned. Sometimes seeing the world as allegorical is an unfortunate side effect of a literary education. Dr. Medhurst examined Zoli and said that if the disease didn't spread, the prognosis could easily be several years. If it spread? Six months. We would be "cautiously optimistic" he concluded, and arranged to contact the California lab for more detailed information, requesting slides of the tumours for second evaluation. (This took weeks to accomplish, as if time had gone backwards to the nineteenth century.) Meanwhile, with a good friend who is also a neurologist, I began to search through veterinary journals and the Internet for information. It turned out that eight and a half was the average age when mast-cell tumours appeared, and the prognosis, after a year, was fifty/fifty. I also learned that 20 per cent of all dogs get mast-cell tumours, and that cancer in young dogs was very much on the rise.

Mast-cell tumours are the most common malignant skin tumours affecting dogs. Mast cells themselves help the body respond to inflamation and allergies by releasing various chemicals such as histamine, heparin, and seratonin. Such tumours are graded from one to three, and generally appear on the trunk of a dog's body - of course, many of the stories I've heard in the years following Zoli's diagnosis belong to the troubling category of "exceptions." Complete excision, theoretically at least, may be curative, if the cancer hasn't spread internally or to the lymph nodes. (The excision around a tumour must have wide enough margins to assure that it was completely removed, but there seems to be some debate about how wide these margins need to be; as well, these margins must be what is referred to as "clean" rather than "dirty.") Chemotherapy or prednisone therapy are the standard treatments.

Dr. Medhurst, who had been Zoli's vet since his puppyhood, promised that he would treat the dog as if he were his own, and that we wouldn't harm him unnecessarily. But we would treat him with the best procedures available. Fortunately the clinic had a resident cancer specialist, Dr. Ian Sandler, and I also consulted prominent oncologists in Cleveland and Boston. Zoli was shaved closely so that we could check for additional tumours. Several were spotted (they resembled tiny benign warts) and these were removed, some under local anaesthetic, others by lumpectomies, and wider margins were made around the original tumours. (I was told that the first vet had done a clean job of cutting.) More small tumours followed, nearly a dozen in total, most stage one, a few perhaps transitional, or stage two-A. These were also removed surgically. The area around the first excision was clear, but at the far margins more mast cells were sited. After the biopsies came back, he was X-rayed to check his internal organs, and all was clear – the best news in some time. His lymph nodes were aspirated and biopsied, and the surrounding tissue appeared clear.

For Zoli's safety, I decided not to take him to campus on the days when I taught, and the vets agreed to board him for those days and check on him as well. Chemotherapy began in mid-October, and Ian decided to use two-thirds of the standard dosage of Lomustine, a pill administered every four weeks (other oncologists concurred because of Zoli's relatively small size of sixteen pounds). Lomustine is also used on humans, although Ian said that dogs often do better with it than humans. Zoli appeared to be himself through all of this, accepting a new diet of special canned food and tolerating the large plastic collar he had to wear for several weeks to prevent him from scratching his wounds. Since he slept beside me at night, I put a fold-out mattress on the floor, where we slept so that he wouldn't fall and be hurt by the collar. Some days I felt numb, others frantic. But Zoli had always enjoyed his visits to the vet, where he was also groomed monthly, and he continued to pull eagerly to enter its front door. A medical regimen followed: tests (blood counts and screens, pre- and post-chemo screens, liver profiles), medicines, chemotherapy, tests, more medicine. The side effects of the chemotherapy were some anaemia and an off-the-chart white-cell count. By early December, Zoli's blood tests showed a spike in his liver function (increased liver enzymes) from the November chemotherapy, and we had to stop it until his liver healed itself. Would holistic medicine help? In addition to other pills, Zoli was allowed some shark cartilage and ginseng. And iron pills. Since he'd had no new tumours, we continued to remain cautiously optimistic. After another liver spike in mid-December, the holistic medicine was cut out and Zoli had to eat a special diet for his liver. I felt sick at heart, and Zoli, who continued to eat well at first, although he'd lost some weight (down from sixteen pounds to fourteen), slept much of the time, or curled up at my side while I worked, keeping an eye on me. What, I often wondered, did he know or think? Each time I felt a new lump, my heart sank, but all of my latest discoveries were checked by the doctors and found to be scar tissue from his lumpectomies.

Cancer doesn't ask permission, it appears and makes demands. Zoli and I spent the long Christmas break in Cleveland, where he was able to have his blood monitored at the emergency clinic. When my mother was hospitalized for several weeks, Zoli was permitted to accompany me to the hospital where he slept on her bed. Nurses fussed over him and I tried to convince myself that his listless moments were balanced by his continued interest in what the day offered. His white-cell count, still off the chart, was decreasing – a good sign. Prednisone had been added to his regime.

During those long winter months Zoli kept up his good spirits, and at the vet's he befriended a large grey rabbit who'd been abandoned. Vitamin E was added to his diet and his liver count started to go down. But he now refused the special canned food for his liver (not unusual, I was told, and it did smell awful), so I fed him a mixture of chicken, cooked carrots and sweet potato, with some of his dry food. Of course he loved the chicken. But I had to admit that he was more lethargic. At the end of an evening of visiting friends, Zoli often remained on the sofa rather than coming to the door as they left, a notable change. In February, there were several bad bouts of diarrhea on the dining-room oriental rug, but X-rays showed no internal tumours, and Zoli rode along with me to the rug cleaner. I never went out in the evenings, I didn't want to; we were holed up together, proverbial orphans in the storm. I hoped he'd be able to tolerate another dose of chemotherapy by the spring. I tried not to think with words like *cautious* or *optimistic* – I tried not to think at all as I watched the mounting vet bills. And I hated myself for noticing them. We visited Cleveland again, where I'd found an ideal nursing home for my mother. Zoli appeared to be stable and the aging residents all wanted to play with him.

I've already written in some detail about the ensuing pancreatitis that led to Zoli's last surgery, and to his death a month later. After that surgery I agreed to order further biopsy reports so that we might learn something from his death. I don't know what I expected. Seven months after his initial diagnosis of two mast-cell tumours, I picked up Zoli's ashes and awaited the final biopsy, which showed that the cancer may have taken hold internally, with "widespread noninflammatory hepatocellular necrosis" and that Zoli was "soon going to be facing pancreatic exocrine insufficiency." Was his last problem related to the chemotherapy? I can't know. I do know that the last six days of his life had been hard ones for him. He knew that he wasn't well, and that we were separated, but I trust I hadn't made him suffer unduly. His veterinarians assured me that I'd done the right thing for Zoli. But to this day I still feel like a failure – I wasn't able to save my dear friend when he most needed my help.

MAGAZINES

Dog Fancy, founded in 1969, may be the grandaddy of American magazines about dogs, but it's no longer the only one devoted to this passion. It now competes nationally with *Bark* (published bi-monthly), *Dog World, Modern Dog, Dogs in Canada*, and for a smaller niche market within a niche, *Whole Dog Journal: A Monthly Guide of Natural Dog Care and Training*, and *Fido Friendly: The Travel Magazine for You & Your Dog*. Along with more general pet magazines such as *Healthy Pet*, individual cities and regions also have their own dog magazines, as well as newsletters from various organizations, including the *New York Dog Magazine*, the *Pet Gazette* (Boston), the *Cleveland Canine, Dogs, Dogs, Dogs* (Toronto), and publications from the various chapters of the Society for the Prevention of Cruelty to Animals and the Humane Society. And such magazines are not only a North American phenomenon. French dog lovers read *Atout chien,* and *Special chiens*; Spaniards have *Todo perros*; the British follow *Dogs Today,* and *Your Dog*; Germans read *Der Hund*; Austrians, *Wuff* (pronounced phonetically with a *v* for the *w*, as *vuff*); the Dutch, *Onze Hond*; the Hungarians, *Kutya Szövetség*; and for the Chinese, there's *Dog*, published out of Taiwan. Glossy North American magazines differ from their European counterparts in the large number of pages devoted to advertising; otherwise, similar story lines appear.

For dog lovers, these magazines bring a pleasure comparable to the delight that dedicated gardeners share in the worst winter months, when spring and summer catalogues arrive in the mail, tempting and informative. But there's a significant difference. Unlike the readers of niche magazines about gardening or interior decoration or travel or food – with their pages of sumptuous photographs sometimes referred to as "gastro-porn" – readers of dog magazines aren't constantly buying new dogs. Dog magazines need to satisfy more than a steady appetite for something new, from recipes to decorating tips, which other niche periodicals can rely on. (While photographs in dog magazines have been referred to as "pooch-porn," the comparison fails.) Of course, dog owners are just as susceptible to clever or aggressive marketing as anyone else, but the items that catch the eye have to do with accessories and are secondary purchases, although many dog owners will happily read (and buy) just about anything that celebrates a favourite breed.

While dog magazines review new books and products, praise individual breeds, offer tips on a host of subjects from grooming to travel, and on occasion treat common illnesses, it's rare to see an article about cancer in dogs. I know this because I've looked carefully and found no substantial articles about mast-cell tumours, one of the most common cancers, in the back issues of several magazines I've been buying for years. Consequently, when Zoli was diagnosed with cancer, we had to turn elsewhere.

MEMOIRS

In his novel *The End of the Affair*, Graham Greene satirized this solitary character in a men's club: "He was a man in a long grey beard and a soup-stained waistcoat, who looked like a Victorian poet but in fact wrote little sad reminiscences of the dogs he had once known. (*Forever Fido* had been a great success in 1912.)" Despite Greene's warning, there are two kinds of dog memoirs: those worth reading, and those to skip. First, though, it's important to keep in mind the distinction between a memoir and an autobiography. Memoirs tend to cover an aspect of the writer's life while autobiographies offer a bigger picture of it. Good examples of either require candour, self-awareness, and a strong memory – settling scores and self-aggrandizement are common, to be expected, and sometimes even interesting. Writers of dog memoirs need to recognize that, since most dogs' lives have a more limited scope of activity than humans would consider tolerable, any dog memoirist has to surmount potential drawbacks to storytelling. Coyness and glibness are ready temptations, along with the dread anthropomorphism.

Best-seller lists often include dog memoirs by celebrities or non-literary writers. Many of the books in this category are for light reading – they're bulked-up, humorous magazines pieces. A prototype is Jacqueline Susann's *Every Night, Josephine!* (1963). Remembered today for her controversial novel *The Valley of the Dolls*, Susann used the memoir form to tell the story of her life with a black miniature poodle purchased from a Manhattan pet shop in 1954, nurtured through some serious puppyhood illnesses, and, in time, transformed into a local TV personality who had a lifelong battle with weight, fed as she was with carryout from some of the city's swankiest nightspots. Indulged by celebrities of the day (Greta Garbo, Richard Burton, Zsa Zsa Gabor), Josephine lived to sixteen – a miracle considering her diet. Susann's humour runs from coy to self-deprecating and back – she's clearly the precursor of Cindy Adams and her Jazzy books – but her story, aglow with namedropping, is now a historical curiosity, evoking a showbiz lifestyle from the fast-fading past. Other bestsellers share a Norman Rockwellish vision of life and a power-of-positive-thinking attitude. Take, for example, *My Dog Skip* by Willie Morris, a celebration of small-town virtues. Using heavy doses of nostalgia to evoke an early 1940s southern boyhood, the book is devoted to heartwarming banality. A close kin to Andy and Opie of Mayberry, when child Willie falls asleep at night beside Skip, a smooth-haired fox terrier, they hear "lambent whispers of the pecan trees in the breeze." Nothing much happens, and insights are few, but such books provided a fantasy place to escape to. Of course, Morris includes a chapter about dogs and baseball.

On the other hand, Peter Mayle's *A Dog's Life* lacks any hint of nostalgia. A memoir about Boy, of mixed breed heritage, it's told in the first person by the dog himself. Mayle made his reputation writing travel memoirs about life in Provence, and this book is only a slight departure for him. But using a dog narrator raises issues that any first-year creative writing student should understand. The dog ought to have a dog's interests, share its frame of reference, sound dog-like. Instead, Boy, who has read Proust and Voltaire, talks about postnatal depression and group therapy, and drops sitcom one-liners on every page. Anthropomorphised out of existence, Boy is a ventriloquist's dummy too cute by half. There's little plot, or true wit. Of course Mayle includes a chapter about playing ball – tennis here – and one ball inevitably ends up in a bowl of tapenade. This is the kind of dog book that gives books about dogs a bad name. To see how the first-person dog memoir can be handled with flair, find a copy of the long out-of-print *The Diary of a Freeman* by "Black Knight" (a.k.a. Sir Alfred Munnings), a black Pekingese who records life among the British aristocracy in the 1940s and early 1950s. The actual dog was owned by Lady Violet Munnings, and carried by her – in special handbags, including black satin and velvet for evening affairs – to the important events of the day, including Princess Elizabeth's marriage in 1947 and a Guildhall dinner, attend by Lord Mountbatten, where the dog was made an honorary Freeman of London. Keeping to the world of British politics, *Buster's Diaries: The True Story of a Dog and His Man*, claims to have been dictated to Roy Hattersley, a former Deputy Leader of the Labour Party, after he brought the dog home from the Animal Rescue in 1995. The short diary seeks to be endearing, and it's actually cleverly written (Hattersley is an award-winning journalist). Black Knight's book and Buster's and Mayle's also belong to the category of fiction borrowing the memoir genre. The peke's book, published in 1953 – and by far the best of them – creates a vanishing world through a dog's voice that respects a dog's psychology.

Though they may not make the best-seller lists, dog memoirs with a more complex story to tell are not simply niche-market books. Margo Kaufman's *Clara, The Early Years: The Story of the Pug who Ruled My Life* offers a dual story about Clara, the black pug, and her life with the author, and Kaufman and her husband's attempts to adopt a child, first from Russia, then China. Clara can't fill the void in a childless marriage, she is after all, a dog, though one with considerable personality. Kaufman presents her in all her dogginess: affectionate, needy, messy, a character in her own right. Cindy Adams, a gossip columnist for the *New York Post*, is celebrity enough to have appeared on Larry King's show to hawk her most recent dog memoir – she's written three – but *The Gift of Jazzy*, like Kaufman's book, is enriched by a dual story: the long illness and death of Adams's husband Joey, the popular comedian, and the arrival of Jazzy, a Yorkshire terrier. This is an upscale, Park Avenue story, with plenty of fancy cameos, including Barbara Walters, Donald Trump, and even Hillary Clinton; a breezy style and the kind of wisecracks that quickly pall ("A brand-new puppy in your house is like a brand-new marriage to a sex addict. Crazy and exciting – for about two weeks."). But when she isn't giving in to hyperbole, suggesting that Jazzy was "so delicious" she could almost put mayonnaise on the dog and eat him, a story of grief underpins her dog's antics, although Jazzy often gets lost in the glitz.

Niche audiences, when they're big enough, can make or break a book. John Grogan's *Marley & Me: Life and Love with the World's Worst Dog* is a perfect example. In an age where North Americans are devoted to gigantism in all forms (from supersized meals to SUVs), ill-behaved big dogs are the rage. Grogan has tapped into this mind-set with a book that manages to be both successful and unappealing, like a canine episode of Jerry Springer. As if that isn't enough, there's an edge of pride to his confession; Grogan seems to believe there's something endearing about a dog out of control and its dysfunctional family. A similar problem runs through Judith Summers's *My Life with George: What I Learned about Joy from One Neurotic (and Very Expensive) Dog*. George is a Cavalier King Charles spaniel, one of the gentlest breeds, and while reading about Summers's travails, I couldn't help but think that George's biggest problem was his human. Like the Lone Ranger to the rescue, Cesar Millan, in *Cesar's Way*, rides in to train the untrainable dogs – especially when they're owned by Oprah Winfrey or Will Smith. While the book's subtitle is *The Natural, Everyday Guide to Understanding & Correcting Common Dog Problems*, it is a memoir as well, a saga of an illegal Mexican immigrant who made good as a dog trainer to the stars. Exactly who wrote what isn't clear, since the cover and title page add "with Melissa Jo Peltier," and the jacket's short bio of Petlier notes that she's an executive producer of Millan's television program *The Dog Whisperer* and a writer with an Emmy and "more than fifty other awards." Millan appears to be a brand as well as a human being. While he's not formally trained (he does admit to watching episodes of *Lassie* and *Rin Tin Tin* as a child in Mexico, and to having been influenced by Deepak Chopra), Millan advocates firm behaviourist principles common to many training guides. His timely personal story and celebrity connections seem to have been enough for the National Geographic Channel to give him his own TV show. This is the triumph of marketing that suggests the gullibility of our culture: people don't know where to look for good information, there's so much stuff around. Like Millan, the Animal Channel's Sonia Fitzpatrick is another pop celebrity who has written a book, *The Pet Psychic: What Animals Tell Me*. But Fitzpatrick's story – more entertaining than Millan's – has a flaky charm and won't prevent anyone from buying a better training guide.

It would be almost impossible to speak of psychic matters without mentioning Shirley MacLaine. When I picked up her dog memoir *Out On a Leash*, its subtitle, *Exploring the Nature of Reality and Love*, sounded a warning. MacLaine and her past lives are an easy mark, but she's smarter than Mayle and Morris and

Millan, and she writes with genuine feeling and an appreciation that a dog isn't just a conceit on which to hang a book. Her Jack Russell terrier Terry naturally has had some distinguished past lives (as the Egyptian animal god Anubis), but that's to be expected in any book by MacLaine. Still, she pays close attention to Terry, and her observations about the life they share on an 8,000-acre ranch outside Santa Fe are more than talk of karma, though that's there, too. MacLaine presents Terry as her teacher (a common trope in dog memoirs), and the book is written as "a conversation" or dialogue between Shirley and Terry. While the terrier's thoughts appear in conventional English (but in italics), MacLaine writes that she hears them in a language she calls "humanimal," a recognition that human language distorts the animals it represents. A spiritual seeker after truth and meaning, MacLaine luxuriates in the lessons her dog offers, a dog who may exist as a messenger from God: "Perhaps in her warm little body and soul lies all I need to know of life and death and spirit." Terry, MacLaine suggests, may even be a cosmic joke: "Perhaps the TRUTH is my dog Terry, and the joke is that dog spelled backward is God."

Beyond these celebrity titles, which get most of the media's attention, their publishers' advertising dollars, and bookstore space, there are some splendid, if lesser-known, dog memoirs. I'll mention several which are still in print. Donald McCaig's *Eminent Dogs, Dangerous Men: Searching Through Scotland for a Border Collie*, tells the story of a Virginia sheep farmer who decides to find his ideal herding dog. It's difficult to read this book without an image of Lassie in mind, even though she wasn't a border collie. Unlike Millan or Morris, McCaig shows the self-awareness needed by the best memoirists, and he recognizes the way his role as writer effects his story: "I have a writer's concentration, intense but flickering. This concentration is useful writing about dogs; less so when training them. Going blank for ten seconds won't wreck an essay, but is disastrous with sheep coming on like the express..." From the start of his book, McCaig is a trustworthy narrator. This can also be said of Elizabeth Marshall Thomas and her tale, *The Hidden Life of Dogs*. An anthropologist, Marshall Thomas is comfortable watching group dynamics, and a memoir of life with her "dog community," as she calls it – eight dogs, including an Australian shepherd, a shepherd-Lab cross, two pugs, huskies, and even a dingo – lets her record a range of behaviour in answer to a question that sooner or later most dog lovers ask, "Do dogs have thoughts and feelings?" (Of course, she concludes.) The activities she studies, from doggy street-life in Cambridge, Massachusetts, where Misha the husky seems to own the town, to pack life in the Virginia countryside, with forays to Baffin Island, cause Marshall Thomas to conclude, simply, "What do dogs want? They want each other." Not everyone has land and money and time enough for a demanding dog community, but Marshall Thomas's love of her dogs will make anyone with a single pet wonder if he's doing a disservice to that solitary dog companion.

George Pitcher's *The Dogs Who Came to Stay* is the story of two Princeton professors (one of philosophy, the other of music) and the wild, pregnant, black-and-tan mixed-breed bitch Lupa (perhaps a Doberman/Rottweiler cross) who came to live on their two acres, gave birth under their toolshed, and nearly took over their lives. Academics like Marshall Thomas, they have the opportunity to devote themselves to their pets. At first an outdoor dog, Lupa soon learns to trust Pitcher, and instead of running off with other wild dogs ends up making a home for herself and her male offspring Remus in the brick Victorian. The dogs even accompany Pitcher and his partner on a year's sabbatical in Provence (everyone travels on the *Queen Elizabeth* II because Lupa's nerves would be "shattered" by the long flight). The last chapters of this book, an account of how the dogs age and die – Lupa at perhaps seventeen and Remus, several years later, at sixteen – are heartfelt. Anyone who has watched a beloved dog die will know these emotions. With the teacher trope that MacLaine also used, Pitcher writes of Lupa, "She taught me not to resent a beloved person for dying but rather to cherish her all the more. She taught me how to say farewell. And she taught me, at least, how to grieve." For an otherwise moving book, this seems too pat, too easy – just a rhetorical crescendo.

Academics are known for writing convoluted prose full of jargon, yet Marshall Thomas and Pitcher aren't the only exceptions to this commonplace. Vilmos Csányi's *If Dogs Could Talk: Exploring the Canine Mind*, though a translation from Hungarian, reads with more depth of feeling than most dog books written in English, and manages at the same time to make science accessible. A professor in the department of ethology in a Budapest university, Csányi combines observations from his own life with his dogs – Flip, a fuzzy mixed breed, and Jerry, a part-pumi mixed breed – with his professional experience. Unlike Marshall Thomas, Csányi has conducted enough detailed studies to conclude that dogs want people too, and not just other dogs ("With well-designed experiments we can even show that puppies are attracted more powerfully to humans than to their own species"). Alexandra Horowitz teaches psychology at Barnard College, and *Inside of a Dog: What Dogs See, Smell, and Know*, like Csányi's work, combines personal dog stories with a scientific approach to canine cognition. Its rich observations, and clear, eloquent writing will make any dog owner a wiser, more understanding, dog guardian. Both titles are good places to begin reading about dogs.

Any book that opens with a sentence like the one to follow will win me over from the start: "I would like, to begin with, to say that though parents, husbands, children, lovers and friends are all very well, they are not dogs." This marvel comes from Elizabeth von Arnim's *All the Dogs of My Life*, first published in 1936. The memoir traces von Arnim's slow acceptance of her solitary temperament through her relations with dogs; from her early years in Australia to her life in England, her first marriage to a German Count and their home in Germany, and after his death her subsequent homes in England again and then in Switzerland, dog companions always at her side, along with a brood of children and numerous servants. A once-popular novelist, von Arnim brings a fiction writer's sense of detail to her confessions, a subtle irony, and, most important in a book where dogs are at the centre, a keen observing eye. We come to know fourteen memorable dogs who have either died or left von Arnim's story for other reasons, but in the last pages she's ready to attach her life to a fifteenth. When Alice A. Kuzniar discusses von Arnim's story in *Melancholia's Dog* as a narrative of women's isolation, contrasting it to Eric Knight's *Lassie Come-Home* as a male narrative of maturation, she overlooks the sheer busy-ness of von Arnim's life. Anyone who managed the demanding family and domestic responsibilities she faced while writing twenty-one books is less melancholy than exhausted. Of course, von Arnim could say, "I for one am unable to imagine how anybody who lives with an intelligent and devoted dog can ever be lonely" – she barely had time to catch her breath.

When a book has been around a while it occasionally gains a readership and even cult status. Such is J.R. Ackerley's *My Dog Tulip*. Originally published in 1956, Ackerley's memoir of life with a devoted yet high-strung female German shepherd has been acclaimed one of the finest animal books of all time. It is a notable curiosity. Unlike Shirley MacLaine, when Ackerley compares his dog to Anubis, he is only being metaphorical, and a wry humour and elegant style (Ackerley was the literary editor of the BBC magazine *The Listener*) are part of the book's distinction. He devotes an entire chapter to "liquids and solids," and any dog keeper, who has naturally to be concerned with bodily functions and cleaning up, will find it familiar and true.

(When Tulip squats, her expression is "business-like, as though she were signing a check.") Loving his dog almost passionately, Ackerley wants her to enjoy all of life, and the bulk of *My Dog Tulip* is an account of his efforts to find a stud/mate for her, so that she can enjoy the pleasures of sexuality and motherhood. This may seem strange to readers who've been taught that part of being a good dog owner is neutering your pet. Writing half a century ago, when pet-caring styles differed, Ackerley saw another way of acting as his dog's trustee, and his memoir is eloquent about the way people rob their dogs of dignity. With great sympathy he recognizes that dogs lead anxious, strained lives, "So emotionally involved in the world of men, whose affections they strive endlessly to secure, whose authority they are expected unquestioningly to obey, and whose mind they never can do more than imperfectly reach and comprehend." (In 2010, an animated movie version of *My Dog Tulip* opened to enthusiastic reviews. I'm not much interested in film animation, but admirers of Ackerley may find this adaptation – though cleverly drawn – on the sweet side.)

Nearly five decades later, Lars Eighner, a homeless novelist facing a streak of bad financial luck, wrote *Travels with Lizbeth: Three Years on the Road and on the Streets*, an equally fine portrait of the way a dog can keep the human spirit alive. Though Eighner confesses "I must admit the romantic and timeless aspects of a man and a dog seeking their sustenance together...was not lost on me," his version of homeless life in Los Angeles, Austin, and Tucson, may begin with backpacks and bedrolls but it soon descends into a hell of dumpsters, stolen property, alcoholism and HIV infection. Although Cesar Millan has written that the dogs of America's homeless men and women are the luckiest dogs, the danger of their lives, as Eighner records it, is anything but a Frank Capra movie. A half-Labrador retriever mixed breed, Lizbeth keeps her master warm at night and forces him to care for something other than himself. She is young enough to cause few problems, but vulnerable to all the threats (environmental and human) that face her master daily, even when she seems to be unaware of them. There is little reassuring in this book, except that Eighner survived to write it.

Only a few well-known literary writers have tried their hand at a dog memoir, perhaps as a break from more "serious" work. At the end of the First World War in Europe, the German novelist Thomas Mann, then forty-four, published *Bashan and I.* The memoir tells of Bashan, a German shorthaired pointer, and his life (mostly in the country) with the Mann family, although the dog's deepest bond is with the author. Little happens, but looming behind each day is the war's threat to civilization and survival. As Bashan matures from puppyhood, he gives Mann a feeling of independence: "A sense of gaiety and sympathy fills my bosom, as always when I am abandoned to him and to his idea of things." Together they explore the woods beyond Munich, and Mann interrupts his story with a fifty-six-page section called "The Hunting Grounds," a curious entr'acte that evokes the natural world he and Bashan escape to in a pastoral dream of almost mystical longing. Mann notes that "Bashan is no toy spaniel; he is the veritable woodsman and pathfinder, such as figure heroically in books." In a diminished world, the dog's "gallant poise" stands as rebuke to human stupidity. When Bashan sickens, Mann finds the right clinic for him, and some readers may recall *The Magic Mountain*'s sanitarium. Throughout, Mann closely observes his dog's attention to language, his sense of identity, and his logic and dependency, but Mann's occasional remarks about physically disciplining his dog remain unpleasantly in mind.

I'm often curious about once-famous writers whose books are no longer read, because some of their work speaks powerfully of another time and sensibility. Louis Bromfield was a popular American novelist from the 1920s through the 1940s, and his books were often made into movies (his good friend Humphrey Bogart married Lauren Bacall at Bromfield's Malabar Farm, a notable experiment in scientific farming in the Ohio Valley, in 1945), and he also wrote movingly of his love of dogs. In *Animals and Other People* he describes, with special sympathy, a boxer named Rex, who came to Bromfield while he was living in Senlis, France, before the Second World War. Bromfield considered boxers a child-friendly breed – "Boxers are ferocious in appearance, but they have the hearts of big babies" – and his passages about Rex and his offspring Prince stirred up some old preschool memories of my own about the boxer Sandy, whose head had seemed to my four-year-old self such a formidable thing. (Incidentally, Bromfield's wedding gift to his Hollywood friends was one of Prince's pups.) In Canada, the prolific novelist Mazo de la Roche, an international best-selling author for her Jalna series about an old Ontario family, was drawn to Scotties. She wrote a tender autobiographical novel, *Portrait of a Dog*, based on her own dog, Bunty. Using the second person *you* as a direct address to the dog, de la Roche portrays the loss of her family home, her father's death, and the influenza epidemic of 1919 as a muted background to the dog's life. When she asks, "What is it in some people that makes it necessary that they have a dog beside them?" de la Roche poses a question most dog people have pondered, and I like her choice of the word *necessary* for the relationship. Bunty's struggle with blindness and her spirited triumph over it, can't fail to engage anyone who has cared for a dog, and this long out-of-print book is a classic waiting to be discovered by a new generation of readers. In a letter to a friend from 1930, de la Roche confided that her American publisher wanted another Jalna story, not a dog book, which they considered "a waste of my time." Fortunately for her, *Portrait of a Dog* sold well, and her publisher later admitted to an error in judgement.

In the fall of 1960, John Steinbeck and his standard poodle

set out on a three-month road trip in a new truck he nicknamed
Rocinante, with a nod to Don Quixote's horse. The result was
Travels with Charley in Search of America. Steinbeck calls Charley
"an ambassador," a go-between with strangers, and as they drive
from New England west to the Pacific, and back east through the
segregated south, Charley becomes a kind of narrative touchstone.
Steinbeck's love for Charley is all the more noteworthy because
the dogs in his fiction often suffer grievously at human hands – in
Of Mice and Men, for example, an old dog is shot because it smells,
in *Cannery Row*, a character named Doc supplies a commercial
laboratory with the corpses of dogs and cats that may have been
petnapped, and the family dog in *The Grapes of Wrath* is run
over in a particularly gruesome passage. Like Shirley MacLaine,
Steinbeck includes imaginary conversations with his dog (though
italics aren't used), and like Cindy Adams, he sometimes forgets
his dog and concentrates on social commentary. Whenever
Charley returns to the book, there's an increase in energy, and the
poodle's antics – and personality – are often more interesting that
Steinbeck's observations of the road. During a short trip into the
Grand Canyon, for instance, the normally placid Charley appears
to discover his inner wolf, and wildly attacks the windows of the
truck when he sees a bear approach. Puzzled by this behaviour,
though he'd been warned that some dogs go berserk at the sight of
a bear, Steinbeck has to change routes and plans, leaving the park
unseen in order to calm his companion. It's in moments like this
that Charley becomes more than a literary convention and takes
over the book.

I've saved the best for last. Unlike Thomas Mann's Bashan,
Virginia Woolf's Flush *is* a toy spaniel, although *Flush* is not
a personal memoir. I include it here because it is unique in
literature, and a dog's life is the central matter. Woolf tells the
story of Elizabeth Barrett Browning's spaniel, transcending her
source material (letters, memoirs, biographies) in an imaginative

act that produced one of the best dog books ever written. I'll admit from the start that I'm not a Woolf worshipper – she often seems ubiquitous for extraliterary reasons – but she is a very fine writer. Her interest in spaniels was not only literary and historical: she had two cocker spaniels of her own, first Pinker, a gift from Vita Sackville-West, and then Sally, and Woolf wrote about both of them in her diaries. Woolf chooses a third-person narrative over first-person narration, and keeps her account of Flush to the matters a dog values – scents, tastes, and other sensations, and places of comfort, and the people who offer it. The dog "moaned piteously all night because he was not allowed to sleep on her [Barrett's] bed – when he refused to eat unless she fed him," and his initial distrust of Robert Browning, the poet who courted and married his mistress, inevitably ended in a bite. Whether Flush is adventuring in Victorian London or following the splendid smells of Florence, Italy, where he moves with his family, Woolf emphasizes his olfactory communion with the world through remarkable attention to detail. "The human nose is practically non-existent," she comments. "The greatest poets in the world have smelt nothing but roses on the one hand, and dung on the other." But Flush is more than a nose on a leash – he is a great observer who knows every shift in his mistress's moods, "he could read signs that nobody else could even see." The care Woolf takes in creating a moment in historical time and, what was to her, a recently vanished culture, is part of the originality of *Flush*, but its appeal comes from the dog's portrait at the core of the book. Quentin Bell, in his two-volume biography of his aunt, wrote, "*Flush* is not so much a book by a dog lover as a book by someone who would love to be a dog." This is not as strange a summation as it might at first seem. Woolf, with her difficult psyche, escaped so fully into the dog's persona that any reader can see her feat not only as an act of imagination but also as one of envy.

MOVIES

In the mid 1920s, twelve thousand fan letters arrived each week for a star who earned $6,000 monthly, was insured for $100,000, and had his own valet, chef, and personal secretary. No, not Rudolph Valentino – this star was Rinty, also known as Rin Tin Tin, a German shepherd with a history as inventive as one of his movie's plots. On a September morning in 1918, during the last months of the First World War, an American soldier, Corporal Lee Duncan, discovered a litter of puppies in an abandoned German war-dog station. Eventually he brought two of the dogs back home to New York, and after the death of the female pup, trained the survivor for the movies. Like all success stories, Rinty eventually got to the right mogul, in this instance Jack L. Warner, and the rest, as they say, is Hollywood history.

Unlike most contemporary movies featuring dogs, movies aimed principally at children and family audiences, the first dog movies, like those starring Rinty, were made for a general audience. Humour was one approach, as demonstrated by Charlie Chaplin, who performed his Little Tramp routine in *A Dog's Life* (1918), where he and his terrier-mix companion, a poor stray he saves from a dog fight, find a stolen fortune at the end of their slapstick escapades. Of course the dog steals a link of hot dogs from a street vendor, and Chaplin even catches fleas after using the dog's body as a pillow for his head. Just as common was the adventure story, full of perils and heartwarming dog triumphs. Since these early films, a long line of popular dog actors have stared in movies sometimes named after them, or served in supporting roles that were often more memorable than their movies themselves. Dog actors might be a film's central character, as in the numerous Lassie movies, where Lassie usually came to the rescue and, by her gentle – even noble – presence, taught the human characters

From *A Dog's Life* (1918), Charlie Chaplin as the Little Tramp with his mutt companion. The image is reminiscent of Ettore Malanca's photograph of lost Romanian boys and their dog, on page 33

a lesson or two. (Incidentally, Lassie was actually a "he," and not only one dog. From 1940 to 1993, nine different male collies played the role, though Pal, the first and most accomplished, acted in all the MGM movies and in the first two episodes of the CBS series in 1954.) Movies with such wholesome messages now seem old-fashioned, if not creaky, and it may be hard to believe that they once played to large adult audiences. The best of them, such as *Call of the Wild* (1935), based on Jack London's novel, combined adventure, romance, and popular performers – in this case, Clark Gable and Loretta Young – with well-written scripts. (Naturally the dog Buck's story was downplayed.) Entertainment was the key, but it was genial entertainment, without the sharp edge that often marks today's movies. Many of these films are still enjoyable, not only by nostalgia buffs or as period creations.

Start with *Hills of Home* (1948), one of the best in the Lassie series. Lacking frenetic quick cuts and a roaring soundtrack, *Hills of Home* manages to combine an elegiac tone with a hint of late-forties, post-war optimism, no mean feat. Apart from the would-be young lovers played by a fresh-faced Janet Leigh, later of *Psycho* fame but then only twenty, and Tom Drake, there are no child actors spewing cuteness, and all of the principal players are at least fifty years old, if not sixty. Set in the 1870s, in a small Scottish town where the aging local doctor (Edmund Gwynn) tries to keep up his practice, choose a successor, and train his new collie Lassie, who has a terrible fear of water, *Hills of Home* is that rare movie that looks at aging with a clear eye, not evasion or ridicule. Gwynn's character is central to the story, and Lassie's true partner in life. Of course, there's a rescue scene involving a wintry night, a broken bridge, and rushing water, or this wouldn't be a Lassie movie, but the film's depiction of the growing bond between the doctor and his sometimes problematic dog has a great deal to say about love and caring.

Movie dogs have also served as creatures that put the human plot in motion. One of the best examples of this approach is the classic screwball comedy *The Awful Truth* (1937), starring Cary Grant and Irene Dunne, in which a married couple facing divorce battle over an insurmountable problem: who gets custody of the dog? The solution? Stay together. An appealing British romantic comedy, *Storm in a Teacup* (1937) with Vivien Leigh and Rex Harrison, satirizes political ineptitude when the Provost of a Scottish town orders the execution of a dog without a license. The extended scene in which nearly a hundred dogs ambush his mansion during a formal dinner party is well worth the price of the DVD. Dramas and melodramas have used the dog-as-plot convention as well. Think of the old cocker spaniel, Jasper, in Alfred Hitchcock's film of Daphne du Maurier's *Rebecca* (1939), who led the new bride, Joan Fontaine, to an abandoned beach cottage that held dangerous secrets about her husband and his haunting first wife. Staying with Hitchcock, there's also a small yapper in his voyeuristic mystery *Rear Window* (1954), and its diggings in an apartment garden ultimately lead to the dog's death and the puzzle's resolution.

Not all movie dogs have such significant roles. Some are used as props in walk-ons, or to show an audience that along with its white picket fence, a movie family belongs to Hollywood's idealized version of middle America, or simply as a background fixture. In the classic Katharine Hepburn/Spencer Tracy comedy *Adam's Rib* (1949), for example, a character soon to be shot by his wife walks home along a Manhattan street whistling contentedly to himself while a dachshund standing at the curb, with its owner, turns to follow the source of the whistle. If you're not attuned to dogs, you might miss the dachshund altogether, but its presence gives the scene some of the texture of big-city living. Other movie dogs help establish an actor's character, even if they have small roles. One of my favourite moments appears in the 1932 melodrama *Grand Hotel*, where suave John Barrymore plays a character called the Baron, a charming jewel thief and loner who, before attempting to steal some rare pearls from Greta Garbo's melancholy Russian ballerina, has a nuzzle with his pet dog while reclining on the floor. Since the movie takes place in Berlin, the dog is, naturally, a dachshund. The Baron – and only an actor as fine as Barrymore could pull off this scene – draws the dog to his side and says, "This is a very peculiar thing for one gentleman to say to another, but as a matter of fact, you're the one thing in the world I really love." He has yet to meet Garbo.

Almost every movie genre has found a place for a dog, from suspense and thrillers to westerns to horror, though science fiction has generally avoided dogs – except for the curious *Men in Black* (1997), and its sequel, where a pug plays an extraterrestrial visitor. A few films stand out, such as the haunting French study in horror, *Eyes without a Face* (*Les Yeux sans Visage*, 1960), directed by Georges Franju. Unlike most of Hollywood's horror-genre excesses, Franju's ominous movie explores the boundaries between medicine, ethics, and madness as a prominent plastic surgeon struggles to find a new face for his daughter, Christiane, who was disfigured by an automobile accident. The pack of frantic dogs kept at the doctor's estate, oddly resembling his daughter in their despair, are one of the most disturbing features of a movie that eschews cheap tricks to dramatize an obsession gone berserk. Another haunting French film, *Red* (*Rouge*, 1994), from the Polish director Krzysztof Kieslowski, tells of a young woman, an attractive model, who becomes involved with a reclusive, aging former judge after her car hits and wounds his German shepherd. Saving the dog and finding its owner gives her life direction. In one mysterious scene the dog runs into a Catholic church during mass and circles around the congregation, as if in its dogginess the animal has a connection to a spiritual power that humans lack. Among the many questions posed by this intense drama about chance and destiny are: what are we responsible for and why? When the old judge finally tends his dog's litter of puppies, an element of hope enters the film like a miracle. For me, *Red* is essential viewing.

In our new century, independent film makers have already produced several exceptional dark adult comedies, such as *Best in Show* (2000), a smart satire on the dog-show industry, and *Year of the Dog* (2007), starring Molly Shannon, known for her skits on *Saturday Night Live*, as a confused secretary who, after the death of her beloved beagle, finds a mission in life as an animal-rights activist. Yet both movies have much more to say about human foibles than they do about dogs. The best recent independent film to examine the human/dog bond is *Wendy and Lucy* (2008), directed by Kelly Reichardt. The film, a variant on the road-movie genre, presents a homeless young woman travelling the Northwest in search of a job and a new life with her dog, Lucy. The plot is heart-tugging without being sentimental, and the decision that Wendy makes at the film's end is both troubling and right. There are echoes here of a great Italian film – Vittorio De Sica's *Umberto*

An iconic image of canine loyalty, Lassie and Roddy McDowall in *Lassie Come Home* (1943). Lassie was played by Pal, a male collie – the first of many trained for the role.

D (1952) – and this neo-realist classic, as well as the European tradition of auteur filmmaking, probably influenced Reichardt. Also a study of poverty and unemployment, in the years after the Second World War, De Sica's masterpiece insists on the mutuality at the core of the human/dog bond. At the film's end, when Umberto D's terrier Flike jumps from his elderly master's arms to avoid the suicide – before a moving train – that his desperate owner has chosen for both of them, it's as if the dog's life force takes over the screen, and death and suffering are banished for the moment, if not denied. The scene leaves the spectator breathless for it's clear that the small Flike has rescued his master – who has previously rescued him from being euthanized in a dog pound – in the heroic tradition of rescue dogs. (A French adaptation in 2008, *Un homme et son chien*, disappointed some viewers because its star, Jean-Paul Belmondo, appears as an old man and not the young hunk of legend. But the film is an unsettling evocation of a man's aging with only canine companionship, and it deserves an audience.)

Some of the more recent American dog movies – *Sleeping Dogs Lie* (2006), about a young man who is upset to learn that his fiancée enjoyed performing oral sex on her dog, and *Firehouse Dog* (2007), filled with gross-out jokes about bodily functions – suggest that a quality of gentleness has gone out of our culture and movie producers are only too happy to reflect this. Still, in 2006, another collie made a new movie version of *Lassie*, directed by Charles Sturridge (admired for his handsome BBC/PBS series *Brideshead Revisited*), in a meticulous version of Eric Knight's 1940 novel, *Lassie Come-Home*. Despite enthusiastic reviews, the movie soon vanished. Public taste has changed radically since Lassie's earlier incarnations. Children are now accustomed to racy entertainment with special effects, and only the audience for *Masterpiece Theatre* cared for the new *Lassie*. Yet I hope that both children and adults can still enjoy a film like *The Adventures of Milo and Otis* (1989), a movie that almost defies classification – is it a nature film, an action movie, or a pseudo-documentary? It presents the simple story of Milo, a kitten, and Otis, a pug puppy, and their barnyard and countryside pursuits, but with a simplicity that is very sophisticated. Initially made for Japanese television, *Milo and Otis* took four years to shoot and left me wondering how anyone managed to get the animal actors to cooperate so convincingly. More typical of current taste is Disney's *Beverly Hills Chihuahua*, a hit movie from the autumn of 2008. One afternoon I was almost tempted, but instead took Rennie for a walk. Naturally there's a sequel.

From Asta, the wirehaired fox terrier of the 1930's *The Thin Man* series, and Terry, the cairn terrier who played Toto in *The Wizard of Oz* (1939), to Lassie after Lassie, then Benji and Beethoven, Hollywood's acting dogs proved an old adage to be true – most human actors preferred not to work with those natural scene-stealers, children and dogs. Of the two, dogs were often seen as the trickier. Is it fair to call these dogs "actors"? Jack Warner did when he first saw Rin Tin Tin, as have numerous movie critics since then, although sometimes with tongue in cheek. In her autobiography *There Really Was a Hollywood*, Janet Leigh recalled filming *Hills of Home*, her third movie: "Who can compete with the soulful, wise eyes of Lassie gazing lovingly at her master!" The movie's director apparently had less time for Leigh than for Lassie, an enthusiastic swimmer who gave a touching performance as a dog terrified of water. But Leigh did go on to add, "I was surrounded by excellent, well-seasoned, helpful thespians (including Lassie); so I managed to squeak by without making a fool of myself." Some actors do more than "squeak by" and even become attached to their canine costars. Although the leading credits for *Call of the Wild* belong to Clark Gable, Loretta Young, and Jack Oakie, Gable said that a St. Bernard dog named Buck was the actual star of the movie, and by the end of filming he wanted to adopt the dog, even offering $2,000 for him (remember, this was 1935) but the trainer refused. Other actors had only praise for their canine colleagues. When Myrna Loy reminisced about making the *Thin Man* movies, she told her friend Leo Lerman: "We never did know Asta. He was a professional dog. A nice dog,

From *The Call of the Wild* (1935), the Saint Bernard Buck, with Loretta Young and Clark Gable.

but he did his job [in *The Thin Man*] the way his master told him and didn't pay any attention to us." Considering Asta's scene-stealing antics, Loy was indeed generous.

Like their human counterparts, though usually more compliant, movie dogs have been sent on press junkets and promotion tours, and made lucrative contracts for product endorsement. But that's just the start of it. In a famous article published in the *New Yorker* in 1947 and entitled "Come in Lassie," Lillian Ross wrote about the House Un-American Activities Committee, also known as HUAC, and the post-war, anti-Communist "red-scare" as it touched Hollywood. As one film executive told Ross, at that time Lassie was crucial to his studio's financial life: "We like Lassie. We're sure of Lassie...Katharine Hepburn goes out and makes a speech for Henry Wallace. Bang! We're in trouble. Lassie doesn't make speeches. Not Lassie, thank God." Despite the expense of elaborate professional training, and the constant supervision accompanying it, dog actors have always been money-makers in the right films, and the grosses of the most popular canine films offset many tonier flops.

And movie dogs have even created fashions in dog breeds – movie-goers want to live with the dogs they've come to love on the silver screen. A quick look at shifts in the most popular breeds over the last century will show that certain breeds peak in popularity when a movie dog has brought a specific breed to everyone's attention. One example: whenever the Disney empire rereleases the animated *One Hundred and One Dalmatians* (1961), dalmation breeders will notice an upsurge of interest and veterinarians may be asked to help find new homes for "difficult" pets that don't act like cartoon dogs. Here I ought to confess. As a university student in the 1960s, I was part of the generation that fell in love with old movie classics in repertory houses. After watching the glamorous *Thin Man*, I had to have a wirehaired terrier like Asta, and Max, who became more of a family dog, entered my life. Back then I drove a white Volkswagen, and I can still see Max in the front seat beside me, standing dapperly on his hind legs with his front paws on the dashboard, as he looked out the front window with as much aplomb as the finest movie dog. (Today I would never let a dog take this risky position.)

Eventually television inherited the tradition of dog actors, but that's another subject. Anyone with a cable-TV provider offering the Turner Classic Movie channel will have no problem catching up on unusual and even obscure dog movies, many of which are unavailable on VHS or DVD. One April, for example, this treasure-trove station broadcast the rare Rin Tin Tin silent movie *Clash of the Wolves* (1925) as well as *Hills of Home* (1948) and the popular feature *Benji* (1974). A keen eye would also have spotted the peppy 1951 mystery *Behave Yourself!* with Shelley Winters, Farley Granger, and Archie, a scruffy terrier; the classic *The Thin Man* (1934), which introduced Asta along with the husband-and-wife detective team of William Powell and Myrna Loy; as well as several curiosities such as *The Rookie Cop* (1939), about police dogs; *The*

Asta, the wirehaired fox terrier, contemplates a midnight snack in *After the Thin Man* (1946), with William Powell and Myrna Loy.

Adventures of Rusty (1945), about a young boy who rehabilitates a Nazi-trained police dog; *A Dog of Flanders* (1959), wherein an admirable dog helps his master become an artist; and *A Dog's Best Friend* (1960), about the redemptive power of love for a wounded German shepherd. And this was an ordinary month. I've never seen a Lassie movie that hasn't made me want to rush out and bring home a collie, but at least I have the sense to stop myself – Turner Classic Movies will have to remain my substitute.

MUSIC

One evening in 1847 – or so the story goes – while the Polish composer and pianist Frédéric Chopin was living in Paris with the French novelist George Sand, she was amused by the way her pet dog chased its tail, and she asked her lover to set the episode to music ("*le valse du petit chien*"). He did, and the result was the D flat waltz (Opus 64, No. 1) now popularly known as the "Minute Waltz," with its "molto vivace" tempo. Before turning to real dogs themselves, I want to add that Chopin was not the only composer to make dogs come alive in music. One of the most famous musical barks occurs in the second movement of the "Spring" concerto of Antonio Vivaldi's *The Four Seasons* (c1725), where the ostinato barking of the violas is meant to suggest the lethargic barking of a goatherd's dog. You can hear this clearly in most recordings of *The Four Seasons* but the famous one by Il Giardino Armonico is particularly doggy. Centuries later, Edward Elgar's *Enigma Variations* (1899) included a tribute, in number 11, to a bulldog named Dan who, having fallen into the River Wye during a walk with the composer, drew himself out and shook off the water in a captivating way. In our time, the American composer George Crumb has made several dog portraits of family pets in *Mundus Canis* (dog world), for guitar and percussion. Their idiom of quasi-mystical, rhythmic thumping, plucking, scratching, and yelping – though quite doggish – may not be for all listeners. In contrast, the late Leonard Bernstein wrote "Rondo for Lifey," a humorous short chamber work for trumpet and piano, after he watched the antics of a neighbour's Skye terrier. You can hear the dog rouse itself into high-energy playfulness. With both we're a long way from Bob Merrill's popular novelty song "How Much Is that Doggie in the Window?" When recorded in 1953 by Patti Page, it became the number-one hit tune in North America for eight weeks. Occasionally it still runs through my head.

Although the nineteenth-century German composer Richard Wagner insisted that his Cavalier King Charles spaniel, named Peps, reacted to the different musical keys of his master's melodies, he didn't write dogs into his operas. After Peps died, however, Wagner bought another Cavalier, Fips, with a similar sensitivity to key changes. Wagner's good friend, the composer Franz Liszt, knew of this deep attachment, and the Hungarian virtuoso sometimes teased Wagner in his letters by taking on the dog's persona and signing the name *Peps* instead of his own. You might think that dogs would play some role in opera, considering the elaborate plots as well as possibilities for inventive staging, but I've yet to hear of an Isolde coming on stage with a pet whippet, suitably medieval, or a Mimi dying with her toy poodle at her side. In her memoir *On Stage, Off Stage*, the great French soprano Régine Crespin did recall performing the role of the Marschallin in Richard Strauss's *Rosenkavalier* at the San Francisco Opera, in a production where her character, a Viennese aristocrat, held a small dog in her lap during the end of the first act – a dog "that regularly made peepee on my costume, to the great delight of the audience." Perhaps that's explanation enough. In Carl Maria von Weber's *Der Freischütz* (1821), though, the heroine Agatha tells her confidante Ännchen about a terrifying dream of her future wedding day, where she is transformed into a dove and shot to death. Ännchen, a sensible dream analyst in this "*Romantische Oper*" as Weber called it, with its folktale-like plot, explains that dreams rarely come true, illustrating her point in a long aria about a cousin who once dreamt of a mysterious beast – a monster with eyes of fire and clanking chains – that moaned beside her bed, until she woke to see that the creature was not a ghost but only Nero, the family's watchdog. (The music is atmospheric, first foreboding, with an agitated orchestra and its cellos in their darkest aspect, then reassuringly sweet.)

Like composers, performers are sometimes associated with dogs. The concert life of a musician can be very isolating, and a few travel with their pets. The Russian cellist Mstislav Rostropovich regularly toured with his miniature long-haired dachshund, and pianist John Browning brought his papillon to symphony rehearsals, once taking the dog to a masterclass at Toronto's Royal Conservatory, where it ended up asleep in the lap of one of my friends. In her list of prima-donna necessities, Régine Crespin included fur coats, big hats, "a bullying air," and "dogs to keep us company in our hotel rooms." Other musicians have been photographed with their dogs, as if no mere human could understand the depth of the artistic temperament. Fashion also enters such pictures. In the 1950s and 1960s, operatic prima donnas such as Maria Callas, Hilde Gueden and Renata Tebaldi, to name several, commonly appeared in public with their small poodles, the diva's dog du jour. Musicians also often speak of their dogs in their memoirs. In her second autobiography, the late American soprano Beverly Sills wrote not only about her own family dogs but of a strange encounter with the legendary 1930s singer Rosa Ponselle, who received Sills, then a young woman of twenty-four, while propped up in her lavish bed, which was covered with her poodles. Sills recalled at least a dozen of them, and those that weren't on the bed were running about the room: "The dogs on the bed were yapping and scattering leftovers from Miss Ponselle's breakfast tray all over the place. Rosa seemed oblivious to them, and to me." Ponselle, then fifty-six, wasn't an invalid, just a diva holding court.

Dogs do not appear to respond to recorded music with much interest, whether it's on the radio or a CD. While they may seem comforted by a low-playing radio if they're left at home alone, I suspect almost any soft noise would do the job. In 2002, researchers at Queen's University in Belfast published the results of a study of the effects of recorded music on fifty dogs in a local animal shelter. Almost predictably, the sounds of heavy-metal bands were agitating, popular music (and human conversation) caused no different behaviour than silence did, and classical music was seen to be calming. Psychologist Deborah Wells, who headed the study, suggested that "dogs may be as discerning as humans when it comes to musical preference." I wouldn't want to go that far – "discerning" is a loaded word. In order for sounds to be perceived as music, there needs, I think, to be a conception of something called music, an aesthetic category, and not just a neurological response to auditory events.

To help clarify my reservations, it's important to remember that dogs have remarkable ears. They hear sounds at low pitches, just as humans do, but for high-pitched sounds their ears truly excel. The frequency of a sound wave – its cycles per second, known as hertz – determines pitch. As Desmond Morris explained, the human upper range, when we're young, is about 30,000 cycles a second, but the range declines: "This sinks to 20,000 by the time we are young adults and to only 12,000 by the time we reach retiring age. Dogs have an upper limit of 35,000 to 40,000 cycles per second...." More recent research suggests higher figures – as high as 65,000 cycles. In other words, dogs can hear sounds that are, to human ears, ultrasonic. One of my friends, the principal flutist with the Toronto Symphony who also teaches at the University of Toronto, once told me that her poodle Bruno enjoys sitting through the private lessons she gives at her home, but when a student plays the piccolo the dog leaves the room. Perhaps his sensitive ears can't tolerate the instrument's high register.

A dog's exceptional hearing allows it to distinguish sounds from long distances and sense particularities of sound that no person can detect. In *Dogs That Know When Their Owners Are Coming Home*, Rupert Sheldrake discussed the almost telepathic phenomenon of his book's title, and left the matter open to question. Even if dogs do hear things from much farther distances than humans can (four times farther is the common figure), that doesn't explain the activity, or signals, from truly great distances that some dog owners have claimed their dogs can perceive. Stanley Coren, on the other hand, discounts ESP as an explanation and, like Morris, emphasizes the particular nature of canine hearing. His chapter "Play Life by Ear" in *How Dogs Think* is a good introduction to this subject.

Hearing is related to intelligence and a way of organizing the sensory world. (Aphasia, a human disorder, occurs when people hear sounds but cannot translate them into meaningful words, or cannot use language to communicate.) The connection between music and language remains a mysterious one open to conjecture and research. That there is a connection, however, is beyond a doubt, as is evidenced by the birdsong around us. Music and language are both about communication, and anyone who has lived with a dog will attest that different barks have different meanings. In *Animals in Translation: Using the Mysteries of Autism to Decode Animal Behavior*, Temple Grandin cited a talk given by Sophie Yin, a researcher at the University of California, Davis, about dog barks. After studying thousands of barks, Yin corroborated what is obvious to most dog people about the wide range of dog barks, or canine communication. As Grandin observed, when dogs bark at strangers, their barks are "rapid and urgent," but when they bark during play, the sounds are slower and, using a term from music, "richer in harmony": "No one knows what those harmonies mean, but the fact that they vary considerably depending on the dog's situation tells me they likely have meaning to another dog." As most people know, dogs are sensitive to tone of voice, which Grandin called the musical part of language. But I'm not willing to jump to her conclusion. Tone of voice is more than the musical part of language, it's an emotive indicator that clearly communicates meaning (such as approval and disapproval) that a dog will immediately understand.

What, then, about people who insist that their dogs "sing" along with them, or join in Christmas carolling? I've been very fortunate to have some gifted classical musicians as close friends, people with active performing careers. All of them confirm my sense that dogs pay little attention to music, including the splendid practice sessions they may overhear with flute, violin, cello, piano, and French horn, except for unusually high pitches. Pitch is the key. Cavaliers are known to be dogs who "sing," and if I forced my voice into a falsetto range, Morgan would occasionally howl along with me. More interesting is something that happened during a recent long car trip. While I played a wonderful CD version of Wagner's *Die Walküre*, Rennie ignored the creamy voice of the first soprano, Régine Crespin, and didn't blink an eye at the lush mezzo, Christa Ludwig, but he leapt to attention when the bright, steely soprano Birgit Nilsson, as the warrior maiden Brünnhilde, let out her first cry of "Hojotoho!" Did she awaken some ancestral memory of a wolf cry in the forest? A pretty thought. I don't think he was being "discerning," or showing a preference for one type of soprano over another.

I'm glad, however, to report that after I recently bought an old Krakauer piano with a rich tone, Rennie has fallen into the habit of curling up underneath it, to the right of my right pedalling foot, where he sometimes dozes through my practice sessions. Only the most loyal companion would tolerate my endless repetitions and rusty efforts. Beverly Sills's corgi was also comfortable at her piano. When he heard her sing, he came to the piano and settled under it. "However," she reminisced, "when I'd hit a very high note, Bumpy's ears would twang like a banjo." And Régine Crespin had this story to relate about rehearsing with her black poodle, Gino. The dog enjoyed her morning vocalizing and sat at her feet watching her, but after five minutes he would throw back his head and howl. One day she accidentally solved the problem by picking Gino up, and he stopped howling, but from that day on she had to keep him in her arms during her exercises. The dog had trained his diva well, but Gino showed a remarkable ear for her voice. Another time, Crespin recalled, she and several friends were listening to the radio when one of her recordings started up. Gino went to the speaker and then turned to Crespin, "obviously amazed to see that my mouth was closed. Finally he jumped into my arms, thinking it was time for my vocalizing." Along with their pack-animal instincts, perhaps Sills's dog and Rennie were drawn to the vibrations coming from the pianos and not to the music alone. Radios have vibrations too, but Gino's behaviour was in a class by itself.

One of the iconic advertising images of the twentieth century relied on an association of voice and canine loyalty to sell recorded music. *His Master's Voice*, a painting (c.1989-99) by the British artist Francis Barraud of his terrier Nipper, showed the white dog with two black ears posed inquisitively before a gramophone, its head cocked slightly forward and to the left. Robert Rosenblum tells the story of this painting in his engaging book *The Dog in Art from Rococo to Post-Modernism*. After copyrighting the image, Barraud attempted to sell it to the Edison Bell Company, which declined (in this early version, Nipper was listening to a "talking machine," an Edison phonograph). The Gramophone Company eventually bought the image, Barraud altered his painting, and the rest we know. While the dog may be listening to a familiar voice, the image itself promises fidelity in recorded sound. As 1950s advertising copy from the Gramophone Company asserted that the picture's appeal related to the well-known fidelity of the dog, "It is appropriate therefore that this quality of fidelity has been the keynote of '*His Master's Voice*' ever since – fidelity in the reproduction of the works of great musical artists – fidelity to the public who have relied upon '*His Master's Voice*' to provide the latest and best in home entertainment." The technology of recorded music has changed greatly in recent decades, and it's been some time since I've seen Nipper's image (which belongs to BMG Music/RCA Records) used in advertising. But plaster and chalk sculptures of this music-attentive terrier, once prominently displayed in record-store windows, occasionally show up in antique shops and are now popular eBay collectibles. In his witty poem "The Victor Dog," the late James Merrill imagined Nipper's classical listening habits: "The little white dog on the Victor label / Listens long and hard as he is able." A thoughtful evocation of the relation of art to life, Merrill's fantasy makes a distinction between hearing and listening – a distinction, with a symbolic dog at its centre, to ponder.

NAMES AND NAMING

Looking back to the Biblical book of Genesis, it's an act of naming that separates humans from their animal companions. The act occurs *before* the creation of Eve, emphasizing Adam's isolation:

So out of the ground the Lord God formed every beast of the field and every bird of the air, and brought them to the man to see what he would call them; and whatever the man called every living creature, that was its name.

Since Adam, we've been preoccupied with finding the "right" names and nicknames for everything from children and pets to new cars. We define our world and ourselves through naming.

Dog trainers often suggest that two syllable names, with different, strong vowels in each syllable, make the best names because they catch a dog's attention. The ten most popular dog names in New York City, based on the number of dog licences issued by the Department of Health in 2005, were: Max, Lucky, Princess, Rocky, Buddy, Coco, Daisy, Lucy, Lady, and Shadow. With the exception of the one-syllable Max, they all come close to the advice, even if they have a predictable, banal aspect. (I named my wirehaired fox terrier Max.) Fashions in dog names change slowly, and five of the names from this Manhattan list appeared on a similar list of registered dogs in Toronto in 1994, with Max the most popular; followed by Buddy, Toby, Sheba, Princess, Brandy, Sam, Rocky, Bear (yes), and Lady. Most of these names also have a contemporary feel to them and would seem unlikely for the names of pets from a century or two ago, when classical names were fashionable, perhaps because people still commonly read the classics. Napoleon's pug Hercules, Queen Victoria's Nero and Hector, and the greyhound Diane, along with Pompée and Eos, are only a few examples of names popular in the eighteenth and nineteenth centuries, names that sometimes appeared in the titles of paintings by artists such as George Stubbs and Francois-André Vincent, though the dogs were most commonly identified by breed.

Today such names might seem too clever by half if not downright pretentious or, when applied to certain breeds, ironic (say a shih tzu named Hercules). Traditional names like Spot and Fido are no longer common, while names taken from popular culture vary according to the passing scene. Lassie long ago gave way to names like Simba, from *The Lion King*. (The Toronto registry also came up with some of the silliest names, including Barfly, Simone du Beagle and a hairless dog named Scarlett Nohara, signs that the namers are, to be kind, not in Adam's league.) Allan Reznik, editor of *Dogs in Canada* magazine, and a breeder of Cavalier King Charles spaniels, has claimed, "I have a theory that dogs live up to their names. So you call one Blockhead and that's what you'll get." I don't like to imagine how anyone who named a dog Blockhead would treat it. Picking a name puts us in line with Adam and demands reflection. But it's the rare person who, like the last Mrs. Astor, wanting to name her new dog after Winston Churchill, politely asked for his permission (socialite philanthropists are a breed in themselves). Andrea Arden, head of Andrea Arden Dog Training in Manhattan, has also suggested: "Wait a month. A name should mean 'look at me,' but when you're cooing it over and over, the puppy will learn to ignore you. Also, waiting allows you to choose a name that's well suited." What exactly does "well suited" mean? The puppy, after all, will grow into a dog, with all of the personality changes this implies, and the dog will shape some of its personality to its human pack leader.

Inevitably we project something of ourselves on the traits we think we see in a new member of the household, and the puppies and breeds we pick often suggest unconscious identification. Names, then, are codes that reveal our values and aspirations. One afternoon some years ago I was walking Zoli around the block when we came across a middle-aged woman with a handsome Cavalier King Charles spaniel, the Blenheim two-colour (ruby and white) which is my favourite, because of Morgan, also a Blenheim. I stopped, petted the dog, and asked its name. "Bramble," the woman replied. "From May Sarton?" I asked, at once knowing something about the dog's owner, perhaps more than she intended. She nodded with a shy smile. The American writer, May Sarton, admired for her journals about the solitary life, often wrote about her companion cats and dog, and Bramble was the name of one of the wild cats she'd tamed in her village home in New Hampshire. The Cavalier Bramble's mistress soon became a new friend. On the other hand, not long ago I ran into a young couple trying to walk a pug puppy that was bounding all over the sidewalk. When I asked its name, they said something that sounded like *bean*. So I repeated "Bean?" quizzically. "Like in lima bean," the man grinned. I wished them well without asking "Why?"

In the matter of timing a new name with puppy training, not all trainers agree with Arden, offering advice that seems just as reasonable, though the opposite. When I settled on the breeder for my first pug, we agreed that she would use my chosen name, Zoli, from the start, and by the time he came to me in his ninth week, Zoli already knew his name and happily responded to it. In fact, I think he made a quicker adjustment to a new home because he brought not only a familiar towel with his mother's scent but a name he recognized at once, a name that meant familiarity and comfort.

NOSES

This morning, as Rennie buried his face in a patch of my neighbour's front lawn, taking a long, satisfactory sniff or following an unfamiliar scent, I waited patiently beside him. Later, when he got onto the front seat of the car, where I'd just placed a plastic bag that contained a box of fancy salted nuts sealed in cellophane and also gift-wrapped, he began to investigate it intently, sniffing away. Did he smell the nuts through all of those layers of wrapping? He rarely showed similar interest with a plastic bag holding a book. That dogs have spectacular noses is common knowledge, and their evolutionary function may be easily explained by the constant need to search out food or prey. Flat-faced (or brachycephalic) dogs like my pug use their noses just as their more generously favoured relatives might, though you have to be careful that in their eagerness to enjoy a tempting whiff of something they don't accidentally scratch an eyeball.

A dog's sense of smell is his lifeline to survival. This may not be easy to appreciate in a culture that spends billions of dollars every year on colognes and perfumes, scented candles, and air fresheners. As we've evolved, humans now rely on scent largely for pleasure. A pot of chili on the stove may direct us to the kitchen and dinner, but even without the food's smell we likely know where to find it, and who did the cooking. This may account for our preference for softer, sweeter scents. (We even use words with different shades of meaning for olfactory sensations: odour, scent, smell.) Dogs, on the other hand, like strong scents of all kinds. But unlike wolves, as Vilmos Csányi has suggested, "dogs are probably inferior to their ancestors in eyesight, hearing, and smell, since there was no steady pressure through natural selection for these often lifesaving senses to be maximally developed." Still, a dog's near obsession with scent can be discomforting, if not embarrassing. It's not particularly appealing to watch your beloved pet sniff out another on the street, or run up to a pile of old dog droppings like a scientist with a promising find. So we tell ourselves, rightly, that our dogs are greeting each other in the traditional doggy fashion, and try for the moment to look away.

A dog's nose can be seen as a masterwork of architecture. It contains around 220 million scent-sensitive cells, unlike the five million cells in the human nose. (The human retina, on the other hand, is built for a wider range of colour vision than the retinas of dogs.) With such a refined nose for information, dogs have almost left humans at a loss for words, and we've sometimes resorted to anthropomorphic comparisons. In her mystery novel *Fall Guy*, Carol Lea Benjamin used one of the most common metaphors – that of reading – in a passage about walking Dashiell through the streets of Greenwich Village: "While I thought my own thoughts, silently, he read the evening news found on trees, mailboxes, hydrants, radial tires and garbage bags left at the curb to be collected in the morning, and filed his own report in each place." Dog trainers involved in scent work need to learn humility when faced with a dog's superior olfactory sensitivities. Donna Ball dramatizes this in her mystery novel *Smoky Mountain Tracks*, where a young working dog is seen, incorrectly, as unreliable, because the dog's human coworker has, in fact, missed the point of the dog's behaviour, or tracking. As Vicki Hearne has written, scent discrimination begins when a trainer has a dog look for an object the trainer has hidden. "So in scent work it becomes possible to give *advice*, and to give advice about something we are mostly ignorant of (scent)." Up to a point, as Hearne admits. It may be difficult to admit that a tracking dog needs not only to be followed but also to be trusted. Working dogs have been successfully trained to sniff out everything from potential bombs and missing humans to cocaine and truffles. All dogs – whether they're trained workers or not – take in information through their noses, information that eludes us not only for its subtleties but because of human physical limitations and evolutionary history.

Anyone with a flat-faced dog has probably seen it licking its nose, that result of generations of specialized breeding. A dog's tongue is like sandpaper – not the coarsest grade but rough enough to cause damage. In the summer after Rennie turned four, I had to take away his favourite chew toy, a Nylabone, because he'd scratched his lower lip while working the chew so enthusiastically that a small abrasion had developed. Advertised as a "flexible pooch pacifier," the Nylabone was not at fault. After breakfast and dinner, Rennie was accustomed to settling down for a few minutes of vigorous chewing, like someone who enjoyed a cigarette after a meal. Of course he missed his bones and searched the house for them. Once a few days had passed, he seemed to have forgotten his old pleasure. However, he developed a new habit – licking his nose repeatedly. I knew that excessive licking can be a sign of various problems, from boredom or stress to dental trouble. While licking is also a method of self-grooming, anything that looks obsessive should be watched. After consulting Rennie's veterinarian, I decided to use his "chewing" time to take him for a walk. Excessive licking can lead to a condition known as "lick dermatitis," when a dog repeatedly licks the same spot, usually on a front paw or leg, eventually creating an open sore. This can become serious and result in infection. A friend of mine once adopted a seven-year-old golden retriever who came to her wearing socks over his forepaws. She soon learned that the dog, named Hector, had a history of incessant licking. He even licked through his socks and bandages, and the ensuing years were a continuous battle with infection. (In *The Dog Bible: Everything Your Dog Wants You to Know*, Tracie Hotchner notes that it's the large breeds like golden retrievers, Labrador retrievers, and Dobermans that seem especially prone to lick dermatitis.)

Dogs belonging to the flat-faced breeds may have eye problems that are related to the nose, and are even caused by the nose folds. Such conditions are referred to as B.O.S., short for Brachycephalic Ocular Syndrome. In the fall of 2009 we were travelling for a week when I noticed that Rennie was often squinting. A worrier by nature, I took him to a local veterinarian who did several eye tests, called Rennie's condition conjunctivitis (or pink eye), and treated the problem with a triple antibiotic cream and atropine, or numbing drops for pain. This appeared to be reasonable. When I returned to Toronto five days later, I immediately took him to Rich Medhurst, his regular doctor, who saw that the problem was far more serious and made an appointment for us with two of Canada's foremost veterinary eye-care clinicians, Doctors Lionel Goldstein and Richard Klys. In order to save Rennie's eye, which had a deep ulcer in the cornea, they performed emergency surgery the next morning, and our odyssey into canine eyes began.

I offer this story in some detail because eye problems and injuries are very serious, and too often dog owners allow a solvable problem to progress needlessly, or are satisfied with an inadequate diagnosis from a well-meaning veterinary generalist. Flat-nosed dogs – pugs, French bulldogs, bulldogs, King Charles spaniels – often don't blink properly, or don't properly wet their corneas with tears. But that's only the beginning. Rennie's corneal ulcer had two causes: entropion and distichiasis. These are only two of the conditions that brachycephalic breeds can face. Distichia occurs when a second row of eyelashes grows out of the glands that help produce the fatty part of tears, and sometimes these lashes grow under the eyelid and stick into the cornea, with the weight of the lid upon them. (Humans can also have this condition.) In Rennie's case the medial nasal entropion – or turned-in eyelid from the nasal fold – caused the irritation, and the distichia pushed it over the edge. This condition can ultimately lead to blindness.

Here is where the good fortune of catching the problem early enough made all the difference. Lonny Goldstein is a doctor of the old school, who has a rapport with animals that is amazing to watch. With a longstanding special interest is in both animal and human ophthalmology, he has helped with Toronto's Metro Zoo's eye cases, and has even repaired a squint in one of their gorillas. Richard Klys came to train under Lonny twenty-one years ago. He is one of the most calmly focused people I know, which may relate to the fact that he meditates regularly, has a sixth-level red sash in Kung Fu, and periodically goes off to China for teaching. Rennie's eye was saved; he has, however, since developed pigmentary keratitis, another eye condition that requires vigilance. Along with daily eye drops and other medicines, Rennie now sees his doctors at least monthly – he runs into greet them, his tail wagging, as if it's a social call. The list of potential canine eye problems is considerable, and anyone who wants a scare might find a copy of Charles L. Martin's *Ophthalmic Disease in Veterinary Medicine*. More important, if your dog has any change in habit other than normal blinking, tearing, or squinting – any discolouration to the eye, or rubbing and scratching – get help at once.

There's one bit of dog/nose lore I'm loathe to include, but it would be irresponsible to overlook it. Stanley Coren has written that dogs with longer, more wolf-like noses have longer lives than flat-nosed dogs like bulldogs and pugs. I hated reading that. Coren didn't explain the reasons for his observation, and perhaps one day I'll ask him to elaborate on it. But there are some things I don't care to know if I can't do anything to change them.

OBEDIENCE CLASSES

Almost any kind of obedience-class training is a good start – especially for a dog's owner, who needs to understand that he or she is where many behaviour problems begin and end. This may seem harsh, but that doesn't make it less true. One October evening a few years ago I was walking Rennie around the block when an unleashed German shepherd ran towards us, barking. I scooped Rennie up since he'd already been attacked by another unleashed shepherd, and the dog instead grabbed onto my pant leg. His owner, a woman in her early thirties, called softly, "Stop it, sweetie." Sweetie did no such thing. I pulled away, the dog held on, Rennie clung to me, and I said to the woman, "Control your dog." "Sweetie?" she called out again, at a loss. I tried to walk away, her dog still hanging onto my pants, and I said, "Your dog belongs on a leash." "Come on, sweetie," she repeated, to no avail. Increasingly annoyed, I shook my foot – the wrong thing to do – and said, "Your dog needs obedience school." "Fuck off!" she yelled back at me. Fortunately another dog walker with a leashed retriever came along to catch sweetie's attention. The entire episode would have been avoidable if this dog owner had taken the time to train her dog *and* herself.

There are dozens of books about obedience training, from inexpensive paperbacks to pricey tomes illustrated with colour photographs and directional drawings. After deciding which one to buy, a serious matter in itself, most people who purchase them unfortunately don't follow the advice, perhaps because it takes time and patience. If a training book is actually read, other problems may follow, depending on the nature of the advice in its pages. The recent popularity of Cesar Millan's television program *The Dog Whisperer*, and his book *Cesar's Way*, have caused fascinating debate among veterinarians, trainers, and ethologists, with Mark Derr, author of *Dog's Best Friend: Annals of the Dog-Human Relationship*, making some of the best arguments against Millan's quick fixes and simplistic notion that all dogs behave badly when their human fails to be a dominant top dog. Derr, who has called Millan "a charming, one-man wrecking ball directed at 40 years of progress in understanding and shaping dog behavior and in developing nonpunitive, reward-based training programs," speaks for an approach to obedience training based on a more subtle understanding of dog psychology. Deep discounts to bookstores and the National Geographic television network have made the success of *Cesar's Way* possible, but I wish that the same industry forces had backed the fine books by the Monks of New Skete, and especially their *How to Be Your Dog's Best Friend: A Training Manual for Dog Owners*. Anyone who thinks seriously about obedience training without the help of classes ought to purchase and read several books before acquiring a dog, and then think again.

My bias is obvious: take the dog to school. Unless you live in Beverly Hills and insist on a trainer to the stars, most cities have affordable obedience classes, which should be considered a part of the cost of buying a dog. Veterinarians are generally glad to recommend good local trainers and classes, and if your vet can't, chances are he or she doesn't know the local dog community very well, a warning sign in itself. Obedience classes do more than help train dogs, they also help socialize them, an important part of the process. When Zoli was seven months old I took him to his first class in the rented basement of a nearby church, along with a friend who had a young Cavalier King Charles spaniel, Morgan.

Zoli and Morgan often played together and Morgan and I were quite attached. Zoli, an especially friendly and curious dog, always eager to turn the next corner, took to the opening minutes of doggy socializing with enthusiasm, while Morgan jumped onto my lap, giving me that Cavalier look which said, "I'm not really one of those creatures," or something of the sort. But both dogs followed the exercises, practised at home, and completed the ten-week course. Zoli, in fact, won first place in a difficult test: he had to sit at attention, with his eyes on mine, waiting to be released to play, and he kept the eye-to-eye contact longer than any other dog in class, taking home a stuffed toy for his effort. I still smile when I think back on those classes, which were like no other time I shared with my dog.

Over the years I've recommended obedience classes to friends who acquired new dogs, but they've always claimed to be too busy. While obedience classes are a commitment of time, and the exercises learned there need to be practised at home, your dog will thrive on the attention, and since you can't go out for drinks together, or play cards, or equally enjoy a rented DVD, what better way to learn about each other while building trust? Most of the things a dog learns in introductory classes are for its own safety, while the class environment helps make you and your dog work as a team. And that's part of the fun of living with a dog.

PAINTING AND PORTRAITS

There is always something sad about a painting of a dog, even the best of them, by Rosa Bonheur, Sir Edwin Landseer, or George Stubbs. An element of melancholy also shadows portraits of human subjects, though not, for me, in the same degree. Curiously photographs of dogs are another matter. This melancholy perhaps comes from the fact that the often nameless dog subjects are long dead, had very short lives, and left behind only the image in question, a memento mori. You can almost reach out to these animals, but your hand would only touch canvas. Unlike the dogs in great dual portraits, such as Titian's *Federico Gonzaga, Duke of Mantua* (c. 1529-30), of the duke and his adoring white Maltese, or Sir Anthony van Dyke's *James Stuart, 4th Duke of Lennox and 1st Duke of Richmond* (1633), with his hand resting on his greyhound's head, dog portraits are the saddest when the dogs appear alone, isolated from human companionship, the hint of a death mask like an aura to the image.

Thinking about dogs never takes us far from humans beings. The best painters of human portraits catch not only likeness, or realistic correspondences thought of as individuality, but also the uniqueness of the subject rather than an idealization or glamorization of it. In this sense a good portrait is a reading of the subject, even an analysis and interpretation – the artist is expected to *see* something that the ordinary eye, even the camera's lense or eye, overlooks. Too often dog portraits resemble anatomically correct advertisements for a breed's standard, the portrait as a kind of Platonic ideal of the breed itself. Fortunately there are significant exceptions to this generalization. Any dog lover who has spent time ambling through American or European museums will recall the pleasure of spotting a lively spaniel in Velázquez, a winning Pomeranian in Gainsborough or a stately greyhound in Berthe Morisot, especially if the breed is a favoured one. Dogs have served as symbols of fidelity in marriage portraits – Jan van Eyck's *The Arnolfini Marriage* (1434), cuddled with children – Joshua Reynolds's *A Young Girl and her Dog* (c. 1780), and joined in the hunt – Pieter Bruegel the Elder's *Hunters in the Snow* (1565). And they often appear when food is nearby, from religious settings like Titian's *The Last Supper* (n.d.) to more recent domestic scenes, including Pierre Bonnard's *Greyhound and Still Life* (c. 1920–25).

Dogs have even shown up as silent witnesses to art-making in many artists' self-portraits – Rembrandt's *Self-Portrait in Oriental Costume* (1631), William Hogarth's *Self-Portrait with His Pug* (1745), and Gustave Courbet's *Courbet with his Black Dog* (1842), to name only a few. Hogarth's painting (see page 141 for an engraving of this painting) was, for its time, a challenge to current notions of an artist's social status as well as to contemporary ideas of beauty. In 1745 he painted over a more conventional self portrait (with wig and waistcoat), instead presenting himself in his painter's smock, in a framed image that evokes a tradition of statuary busts of famous men. He included his palette to his right side and his pug before him – art and life. The dog, who embodies the natural world, stares out of the larger pictorial space, "bored of sitting so long," as Hogarth's best biographer Jenny Uglow has observed. When the young Courbet painted himself and his black dog almost a century later, with the tradition of European Romanticism well established, he was able to build on associations of the artist as Romantic hero, and dog ownership seemed as natural a part of it as breathing.

While this is not the place for a detailed history of dog paintings, it's important to keep in mind that human representations of animals are as old as the few cave paintings still known to exist. Apart from Greek vases and the pages of illuminated manuscripts from the Middle Ages, and medieval tapestries, dogs most commonly appeared in Western painting in classical, historical, and Biblical scenes where they were part of a crowd and often used as symbols with a range of allegorical meaning, from fidelity and loyalty to animality and lust. Dog portraits as we think of them began in the Renaissance, when wealthy patrons commissioned works that preserved images of their favourite dogs. Yet even here dogs frequently retained some symbolic function, as Edgar Peters Bowron wrote in *Best in Show*, noting the distinctions in royal portraiture: "lapdogs represented as exclusively female companions, large hounds depicted as attributes of male virility." But by the end of the sixteenth century, as Bowron suggested, dogs appeared in paintings "because their masters considered them beloved companions." Representations of dogs then needed to display some degree of individual personality, they had to be more than generic types. By the eighteenth century, which began the great age of dog paintings, dogs were a common feature of middle-class life as well as companions to the aristocracy. Following the advances of Enlightenment science, artists became attuned to scientific and social accuracy in addition to matters of composition and other painterly concerns. Whether their subjects appeared alone, in domestic comfort on plush cushions, in stables, fields and other work environments, or in natural settings like forests, a dog's unique relation to his or her world became part of the finished portrait. Painters who could capture a dog's psychology and bring an individual to life, could command significant commissions, although some, like the masterful George Stubbs (1724-1806), died in debt.

Eventually the Impressionist movement of the mid-nineteenth century changed the way dogs appeared in art, just as it changed all matters of realistic representation. Henceforth, artists had to chose either accuracy of representation or self-expression as their principle aesthetic, which may help explain why dog paintings and portraits are today given little status in the art world and are often relegated to specialized commercial galleries. According to the curators for the "Best in Show" exhibition, European museums have for some time acknowledged the venerable status of the dog in Western painting with important exhibitions, while their American exhibition was the most extensive survey to be mounted on the subject on this side of the Atlantic. Part of the problem seems to be an unstated notion that the dog is not quite a suitable subject for a painting – not quite serious enough – and that dogs belong to the world of sentimentality and kitsch illustration, or to popular culture at best. Despite a few contemporary exceptions, including the Cajun folk-painter George Rodrigue and his popular Blue Dog images, and Stephen Huneck, a printmaker and woodcarver famous for his hand-made Dog Chapel near St. Johnsbury, Vermont, dogs rarely appeal to most artists as subjects. There are a few acclaimed contemporary painters who, though not thought of as dog painters, have included dogs in their work, often repeating a specific breed. Nova Scotia's hyper-realist Alex Colville is admired for his enigmatic black Labradors, the British painter Lucien Freud has boldly combined nude human figures with their canine companions, and British painter David Hockney, for a while a California transplant, is known for his appealing dachshunds. This neglect is curious at a time when dog ownership has increased in popularity, and domestic life is a common subject of art-making. But that popularity itself may account for the dog's lack of legitimate status: dogs may be too ubiquitous to notice.

Except for money. Auction houses like Doyle in New York City have staged an annual "dogs in art auction" to coincide with the Westminster Kennel Club Show, when big wallets hit town, along with the regular art collectors and decorators. In February 2000, Alan Fausel, Doyle's senior vice president in charge of European and American painting, spoke with *The New York Times* about the high prices people are willing to pay for dog paintings: "In a regular sale, they [the paintings] would be lost in the shuffle." He wasn't the only person to appreciate this growing niche market. Commercial galleries like Joan Peck Limited and William Secord Gallery Inc., both of Manhattan, have, over the years, specialized in dog paintings. While prices for unexceptional paintings run in the low thousands, a genuine work of art like George Stubbs's *Portrait of a Newfoundland Dog* (1803) sold at Sotheby's in November 1999 for $3.695 million – an investment rather than a collectible.

Occasionally a single individual will make an exceptional contribution to a subject, and William Secord is such a person. A specialist in eighteenth- and nineteenth-century dog painting, he may be most familiar to dog-art aficionados through half a dozen handsome books about dog painting, but that's only part of his achievement. Founder of the Manhattan gallery that bears his name, Secord was raised on a New Brunswick farm; he told me that his childhood dog was a working border collie who became a pet when the family moved away from the farm. (He also remembered buying, at sixteen, his first painting, a dog portrait, for three dollars.) After studying art history at several Canadian universities, and working at galleries in Toronto and Vancouver, Secord went on to graduate studies in New York while also working for the Museum of American Folk Art. When I asked how he became part of the world of dog painting, he replied without hesitation, "Serendipity." Academically trained in mid-century abstraction, he became the first director of the Dog Museum of America in 1981, and his initial research on the British dog painter Arthur Wardle convinced him that he'd found a rich, unexplored subject that deserved attention. After the Museum of the Dog moved to St. Louis in 1986 (it is now known as the American Kennel Club Museum of the Dog), Secord remained on the east coast and opened his own commercial gallery in 1990. With exhibitions to his credit in the major museums of the world, he has championed famous and unfamiliar artists, and brought respect to a painting tradition that deserved it all along. His current dog is a Dandie Dinmont terrier named Rocky.

The prejudice against dog paintings may also relate to an unstated assumption that they are mere illustrations. But where, exactly, can the line be drawn between a fine artist's rendering in paint or charcoal, or pastel or ink, and a great illustrator's rendering? Canadian painter Emily Carr, admired for her mysterious landscapes of the northwest coast and its looming totem poles, also drew her own sheepdogs. These works are charming though as unlike her "serious" paintings as anything could be. They remind me of Maurice Sendak's drawings for his children's book *Higglety Pigglety Pop! or There Must Be More to Life*. (The cover and title page of the book announce "Story and *Pictures* by Maurice Sendak" – italics mine – bypassing the word *illustrations* generally used in books for children. The dog in question, who searches for identity and belonging, is Sendak's own Sealyham terrier, Jennie. His haunting black-and-white images of her are as memorable as anything he has created.) The twentieth-century modernist movement towards non-representational art, as well as abstraction, may have also contributed to this prejudice. Good or sophisticated art, we're sometimes made to feel, has little to do with verisimilitude. When I mentioned this to William Secord, he remarked that abstract painting can also be good or bad, a distinction worth keeping in mind. Joan Mitchell (1926–1992), one of the greatest painters associated with Abstract Expressionism and the New York School, had a long career accompanied by dogs of many breeds, including poodles, Skye terriers, Brittany spaniels, and German shepherds. She once told a curator, "Music, poems, landscape and dogs make me want to paint. And painting is what allows me to survive." Her first dog, George, a chocolate-brown poodle, is the subject of *George Went Swimming at Barnes Hole, but It Got Too Cold* (1957). An event in itself, the painting proves that slavish representation isn't the only way to approach dogs. Mitchell's large, lush canvas of George's summer-day swim on Long Island presents more than its literal subject, but rather a memory of movement, light, and water associated with her dog.

Magazines about dogs such as *Bark* and *Dog Fancy* usually include a section in the back filled with advertisements that include dog portraits and paintings. In a wide range of styles, from primitive to southwestern to grand-masterish, dog portraits celebrate and memorialize, with images for all tastes and pocket books. Baltimore-based Christine Merill, for example, charges as much as $10,000 for a canvas with one dog as its subject. (Her work, which includes some clever art-historical references, has been

George Went Swimming at Barnes Hole, but It Got Too Cold (1957), by Joan Mitchell. Oil on Canvas.
Mitchell painted the aftermath of her poodle George's afternoon dip on Long Island.

featured in a recent book, *The American Dog at Home*, by Secord.)
Many large cities, however, have less-accomplished dog painters
offering work for considerably less, some advertising in a variety of
venues, from cards in veterinary offices to booths at annual events
like Toronto's Royal Winter Fair. Closer to commercial illustration
than fine painting, most of these commissioned portraits rely on
photographs, which makes the final image a representation several
times removed from its subject. Seldom has the painter known or
even met the dog, and any evocation of its personality can only be
tentative and random, let alone a painterly probing. Are the eyes

set too widely, the ears too close to the head, the nose not quite right? Is the painting, in other words, a good approximation of the photograph? And was the photograph detailed enough from the start? Why not hang a good photograph instead? I wish that some of these artists would search online for an old copy of Diana Thorne's *Drawing Dogs.* Or take a good look at a painting by Sir Edwin Landseer or Jean-Baptiste Oudrey or Albert de Balleroy or Arthur Wardle and see how it has been done. Look closely, and you'll know that a dog is as fine a subject for painting as anything else on earth. The problem is not with dogs but with painters.

PHOTOGRAPHY AND PHOTOGRAPHS

(1.) DOGS AND CELEBRITIES

Two recent British books of photographs – *Women & Dogs* and *Men & Dogs*, both by Judith Watt and Peter Dyer – exemplify the way dogs have been treated in public photography: they are either used as companions to prominent people or photographed alone. The differences that arise from these uses are considerable. When any public figure, from politician to entertainer, appears with his or her dog, the animal always has the quality of a prop, but one that sends a deliberately ambiguous message. The range in meanings depends in part on the breed of the dog, its placement in the image, and its apparent relation to the person who is the actual subject of the photograph. However, certain issues remain constant in all photographs of a single person and his or her dog. At first glance, the image seems to tell us that its human subject is really a person of feeling, of sensitivity, someone who connects to the animal world and by extension deserves our trust and regard. As well, the subject may be just like the viewer – he or she *has* a dog and is willing to show it just for us. In this sense, the photograph appears to be intimate, friendly, almost casual, although we would probably never get to meet the human in question. The photograph is meant to reassure us of the subject's common humanity.

At the same time, though, another message is sent. The human subject exists apart from common humanity and his or her essential uniqueness and isolation or aloneness are illustrated by the companion dog; no other human, the dog seems to imply, is a suitable companion, even if only for the photograph in question. (One quickly thinks of the old political sally, "If you want a friend in Washington, buy a dog.") Look close, the image tells us, and you'll see why you should admire the human subject – and vote for him, or go to her movies, or buy whatever products are being advertised. If you have a dog, the subject implies, you know that you can trust me. Rarely do prominent figures choose to appear in photographs with cats.

The dog as prop needs to suit the message. In the 1990s, when chocolate Labradors were fashionable, President Bill Clinton naturally acquired one, named him Buddy, and appeared with him in many photo ops. In the early 1960s, when opera divas were associated with European glamour, Austrian soprano Hilde Gueden posed for a record album cover with, inevitably, a miniature grey poodle. These photographs aren't included in the books by Watt and Dyer, but many of the images they have compiled will be familiar, and variations of them have been used to stamp certain celebrities with a breed association – the Duke and Duchess of Windsor and their pugs, the French writer Colette and her French bulldogs, Sigmund Freud and his chows.

Contemporary male subjects who want to assert their masculinity (Kevin Costner, Kevin Spacey, Mark Wahlberg, and Sylvester Stallone) appear, respectively, with two yellow Labradors, a black Labrador, a German shepherd, and a briard, in the macho tradition of Ernest Hemingway and Clark Gable, back as far as the silent-screen heart-throb Rudolph Valentino, who were photographed with a German shepherd, an Irish setter, and another German shepherd. Men who are advertising something other than maleness dare to appear with smaller breeds: Frank Sinatra (a West Highland white terrier), Yves Saint Laurent (his French bulldog), Bob Hope (a black miniature poodle), and the iconic photographs of Franklin Delano Roosevelt with his Scottish terrier Fala. When George W. Bush acquired a Scottish terrier he sent several messages – he was man enough to appear with a smaller dog, albeit a dog who would help illustrate his credentials as the anti-F.D.R. Rarely do the men in these photographs, and the numerous others that regularly appear in newspapers and magazines, make eye contact with their dogs. The pets are there and that's enough. Photographs of women and their dogs more frequently show eye contact or active engagement. The dog is still a prop, but it suggests that the female subject is fully engaged, nurturing actively. Georgia O'Keefe bends over to pet her chow, Grace Kelly pets her Weimaraner, Madonna kisses her Maltese terrier, and Jayne Mansfield stares with a mega-watt smile at her Pekingese, while Gertrude Stein's white standard poodle Basket II adoringly stares at her, as if in awe of genius. The women who look out at the camera, and not at their dogs (writers like Vita Sackville-West and Radclyffe Hall, Jacqueline Kennedy Onassis, and Queen Elizabeth II) claim a more masculine power relationship with the camera and the world.

I'm not suggesting that cynical calculation is the only reason why public figures chose to be photographed with their dogs, even when they're aware of the impact a dog makes. People, after all, thrive on attention, just as dogs do. In December 1930, the young Bette Davis and a wirehaired fox terrier named Boojums arrived in Los Angeles's Union Station on the Twentieth Century Limited. When no one appeared to greet the not-yet-famous actress, Davis telephoned her studio. She was assured that someone from Warner Brothers had been sent, but he saw no one who resembled an actress. "How could he not?" Davis replied. "I was carrying a dog." Davis wasn't insincere about her dog. As pet or prop, she knew its value – and in the 1930s, wirehaired fox terriers were one of the most popular breeds. A lifelong dog lover, Davis in fact went on to become the president of Hollywood's Tailwaggers, an animal welfare organization, in 1938. That she enjoyed several different breeds is proved by Watt and Dyer, who include a 1932 photograph of a platinum-blonde-coiffed Davis cuddling one of two bichon frises. And they note in their caption that in 1935 Davis acquired a Scottish terrier named Tibby, which, after Roosevelt's Fala, "was the most photographed dog in America."

Given the implications of human/dog photographs, there's pleasure in decoding various meanings. Whenever I pick up a new biography, I first flip through the photographs to spot the presence, or absence, of dog companions. Colette and her French bulldogs, Toby-chien and Souci, couldn't take a bad picture, while the sensuous joie de vivre of her prose is suggested by the human/dog interaction in her photographs. In 1957, Douglas David Duncan introduced his German-born dachshund Lump to Pablo Picasso during a spring photo-shoot, and the dog was as taken by Picasso as the artist was by the dog. (*Lump* means rascal in German.) He settled into Picasso's home in the south of France where, over the years, Duncan photographed him while Picasso painted and repainted his image. Nearly half a century later Duncan published *Picasso and Lump: A Dachshund's Odyssey*, with more than one hundred images of the Spanish artist and his unexpected canine inspiration – sharing meals, playing games, and cuddling together. Picasso said of Lump, "He's not a dog, he's not a little man, he's somebody else." *Muse* may be the best word for what he was. It's also worth remembering that dogs are sometimes present in photographs even when they don't show up in the final image. Photographer Richard Avedon liked to tell this story about his attempt to take a candid shot of the Duke and Duchess of Windsor. Frustrated by their carefully posed sittings, while setting up his camera he mentioned that on the way to their appointment he'd seen a pug run over on the street, and as these pug-lovers gasped, he took his much-published, unflattering image.

(2.) Dogs and products

In the late 1990s, Estée Lauder ran an advertisement that pictured a dark-haired male model stretched out on a rope hammock with a small boy, ostensibly his son, sleeping on top of him. The man's right arm was artfully draped over the side of the hammock, his wrist near a blond Labrador retriever that was also enjoying the sun. The ad was selling Pleasures for Men, a new cologne. Estée Lauder, however, wasn't alone in using dogs to sell fragance and human body-care products. This is interesting when you consider the number of chemical sprays on the market to mask doggy odours. We may want to smell like "sliced nectarines and watery green leaves," the top notes of Pleasures for Men, but not like our pets. The message of the Lauder dog – of course, a yellow Lab, one of the most popular breeds in North America – has many facets, from hearth and home to macho sexuality. While the man's face is turned away from the camera so that we see only the back of his well-groomed head, and the boy's face, with closed eyes, rests sweetly on his chest, it's the dog that looks up to the camera, mouth open, pink tongue lolling, as if to taste the warm summer breeze. Perhaps it's really enjoying Pleasures for Men. (The photographer would not release the image for reproduction.) Dogs have a long history in advertisements for a wide range of products, from beer (in a clever series of photographs for *Gourmet* in the 1940s and 50s) to designer jeans (in an advertisement in the current *Vanity Fair*). It may be the metaphoric nature of the dog that has convinced marketing people to use them in

Advertisement for Rheingold Beer. This image appeared in the April 1949 issue of *Gourmet Magazine,* and was one of a series that included young women named "Miss Rheingold" and their dogs.

this fashion, since dogs make us think of loyalty, reliability, and companionability. I don't intend to endorse any product, even inadvertently, so I won't name other examples. But the next time you spot a dog in an advertisement, think about what it's really selling there.

(3.) Dogs alone

Several years ago a longtime neighbour in her late eighties died. On the day that an antiques dealer-cum-jobber arranged for an open house to sell off her possessions, I stood in her bedroom looking at several old, framed black-and-white snapshots of dogs she'd once loved. From her appearance in them, the pictures belonged to the late 1940s. One, of a dog alone, struck me as particularly forlorn. Of course, I didn't know the dog's name. No one would want the picture and I hated to think of it being tossed away as rubbish. Why is it that a dog photographed alone seems particularly vulnerable? And how can the photograph seem to share in this vulnerability? The context of the dog's life was missing, and this brought to mind my neighbour's own history. A cousin of the Canadian diarist and diplomat Charles Ritchie and a relation of famed decorator Elsie De Wolff, she had once loved this nameless-to-me dog, and had been loved in return. Had they known the dog, too?

As long as people have held cameras, dogs have been willing, and not-so-willing, subjects. Such old photographs are splendid repositories of social history, just as dog paintings can be, but they deserve to be enjoyed for themselves. One recent collection, *A Thousand Hounds: The Presence of the Dog in the History of Photography 1839 to Today*, edited by Raymond Merritt and Miles Barth, includes a range of images, from anonymous snapshots to work by well-known figures, including Edward Steichen, Paul Strand, Henri Cartier-Bresson, Sally Mann, and Robert Mapplethorpe. As cameras and film have been improved over the last century, requiring less stationary subjects, dogs have became a popular subject. In recent years, pet photography has become a growing business. Photographers' ads are common in the pages of magazines devoted to dogs just as their cards often wait on the counters of veterinary offices. (In 2005, Cameron Woo, publisher of *Bark* magazine, told *The New York Times* that he has had to turn away much of the advertising from pet photographers so that they won't overwhelm the magazine.) Meanwhile, guides about pet photography are available from a variety of sources, and pet photo contests, including one sponsored by the Humane Society of the United States, are in every community.

Good pet photos happen when the dog is in the mood, or has helped to find it, and when the photographer avoids out-of-focus photos from standing too close or long-distance shots from standing too far away. Backgrounds and props count, as do carefully chosen angles, while red-eye and sudden distractions are always possible. Professional photographers know the pitfalls and charge accordingly. In the September 1997 issue of *House & Garden*, for example, Valerie Shaff of New York City offered pet portrait sessions beginning at $500 – a good image can be almost as expensive as a new puppy. Eight years later, Amanda Jones, of North Adams, Massachusetts, was charging $850, although she travelled to various cities and rented studios there for a working base. (She has also produced several books of dog photographs.)

The dog as luxury object, with pricey studio photographs, belongs to one kind of person. But dog owners of all backgrounds and incomes want to record their companions, who are, as Roger Grenier wrote in *The Difficulty of Being a Dog*, so short-lived, in comparison to the human life span, that "the lack of synchronization between human and animal life is bound to bring sorrow." I think we know this and sometimes take photographs to ward off death, or at least to acknowledge the transitoriness of the present moment. Poor photographs of dogs alone can, unfortunately, make an animal look embalmed, which is certainly not the intention. How, then, to photograph energy and life? Repetition helps, and endless patience. There is always an element of luck – and accident – in a good photograph, though many photographers don't like to admit it. My neighbour's snapshots weren't particularly good ones, they were originally blurred and now discolouring, but they told of love and the passing of time, which is always disquieting. When Zoli was dying, one friend who had welcomed him as a guest in her home, asked if I had many pictures of him. I said that I did, and she suggested that I be sure to have pictures not only of him alone but of the two of us together. She was right.

In the current photography world, the most famous dogs alone are probably William Wegman's portraits of Weimaraners. Gotten up in human clothes and twisted into various un-canine positions, these dogs, and the images of them, are not only charmless but, I think, downright unpleasant. Aggressively coy, Wegman seems to believe that he's making a rich comment about the human/dog connection; some critics have even bought the notion. As a young girl, my sister used to enjoy dressing our fox terrier in her doll's clothes, and he cooperated patiently, although after a decent interval he jumped off the bed, wearing whatever she'd pulled over his head, and went off, still dressed, to more congenial amusement. Look into the eye's of Wegman's subjects – they're *not* having a good time of it, they look coerced. In fact, I'm reminded of the writer Colette, who once described a travelling theatrical company with "actors as melancholy as performing animals." A dog dressed in a printed cotton dress and granny glasses tells us less about Granny than it does about the strange inner life of the photographer. Surrealism has, regrettably, now degenerated into advertising and kitsch. Wegman has found a gimmick and exploited it, and it has brought him fame. Whatever impulse led him to dress his first dog and photograph it, long ago evolved into shtick.

Fortunately there are other approaches to photographing dogs. Early in 2008, the California-based artist Meg Cranston, with an activist aesthetic, approached several animal shelters in Los Angeles and arranged for staff members, who were not professional photographers, to provide her with digital images of dogs for adoption. Most of these were taken of the dogs outside their cages, often outdoors and frequently with seasonal backgrounds – there are a few of the Christmas holidays with artificial poinsettias, many heart-references to Valentine's Day, and also some Easter kitsch in artificial pastel tulips and the like. The resulting exhibition, "Every Dog in the Pound," included 750 images which were projected on the blank gallery wall of Toronto's Mercer Union (where the installation had its premiere) and took forty minutes to watch. As Cranston wrote in the exhibit's brochure, "Because the relative photogeneity of the dogs and the overall quality of the photographs presented to the public impacts the animals' chances for adoption, the department now considers generating a sympathetic photograph of every dog essential to the animal's care and survival."

About 70 per cent of the subjects in "Every Dog in the Pound" were large dogs, many of them older, scarred from fights (perhaps they'd been used in illegal dog fighting), and possibly ill. Of the 750 dogs, there were several pugs, a few spaniels and dachshunds and other small purebred toys, but also a goodly number of Chihuahuas. As one image gave way to another, the overwhelming effect of the installation was deeply unsettling. The dogs looked into the camera without artifice or protection, vulnerable and even desperate. Such images, of course, will never be as popular as Wegman's. Although Cranston wrote about the strong, positive reaction to her show, which she presented in progress in Tel Aviv before its premiere, any enthusiasm for the installation will have little meaning for its subjects, many of whom had already been exterminated by the time of the gallery opening. I left Mercer Union on a suitably bleak March morning with Rennie at my side, drained by the plight Cranston had recorded but admiring her as an artist-witness. That's what true art can do.

POETRY

Poets have often done better by dogs than fiction writers. One reason may be that fiction thrives on event, on story and plot, while poetry doesn't. Stories about dogs who grow through trials and adversity tend to be stories written for children. Even the most introspective of modern fiction rarely does justice to the dogs who pass through its pages.

From the earliest appearance of the dog figure in poetry, albeit an epic, Book XVII of Homer's *Odyssey*, a dog was appreciated for his "faithfulness," one of the most common virtues associated with them. We want our dogs to be loyal, otherwise why keep them around? Of the many fine poems by the most famous poets writing in English, as well as those by writers whose names are unfamiliar outside a small circle of readers, one in particular stands out. This curious elegy by Lord Byron, who helped create the movement of English Romanticism, manages at once to be clever, misanthropic, and loving:

INSCRIPTION ON THE MONUMENT OF A NEWFOUNDLAND DOG

When some proud son of man returns to earth,
Unknown to glory, but upheld by birth,
The sculptor's art exhausts the pomp of woe,
And storied urns record who rest below;
When all is done, upon the tomb is seen,
Not what he was, but what he should have been:
But the poor dog, in life the firmest friend,
The first to welcome, foremost to defend,
Whose honest heart is still his master's own,
Who labours, fights, lives, breathes for him alone,

Unhonour'd falls, unnoticed all his worth,
Denied in heaven the soul he held on earth,
While man, vain insect! Hopes to be forgiven,
And claims himself a sole exclusive heaven.
Oh man! Thou feeble tenant of an hour,
Debased by slavery, or corrupt by power,
Who knows thee well must quit thee with disgust,
Degraded mass of animated dust!
Thy love is lust, thy friendship all a cheat,
Thy smiles hypocrisy, thy words deceit!
By nature vile, ennobled but by name,
Each kindred brute might bed thee blush for shame.
Ye! who perchance behold this simple urn,
Pass on – it honours none you wish to mourn:
To mark a friend's remains these stones arise;
I never knew but one, – and here he lies.

Byron's catalogue of human weaknesses is set against the self-evident virtues of the dog, and may seem familiar to anyone who has also been frustrated by foibles unseen in a canine companion. In his shorter "Epitaph to Boatswain," Byron, then twenty, gave the dates of his dog's brief life, but did not add that Boatswain died of rabies while Byron "cradled him in his arms," as one of his biographers noted.

EPITAPH TO BOATSWAIN

Near this spot
Are deposited the Remains of one
Who possessed Beauty without Vanity,
Strength without Insolence,
Courage without Ferocity,
And all the Virtues of Man without his Vices.
This Praise, which would be unmeaning Flattery

If inscribed over human ashes,
Is but a just tribute to the Memory of
Boatswain,
a Dog ...
Who was born at Newfoundland, May 1803
And died at Newstead Abbey, 18 Nov. 1808.

No one reading these lines – notable for their simplicity – will be surprised to learn that Byron wanted to be buried in the tomb eventually built for Boatswain. (Another of Byron's many biographers, Leslie A. Marchand, claimed that this "Epitaph" was not in fact written by Byron but by his friend John Cam Hobhouse, as a joke. I'll leave the debate to literary historians.)

The association of dogs and death is a common one in literature. Like the character in Mavis Gallant's story who warned his son "Whatever happens, don't get your life all mixed up with a dog's," British poet Rudyard Kipling, also known for his animal stories, struck a similar cautionary note in "The Power of the Dog." This is the poem's first, memorable stanza:

There is sorrow enough in the natural way
From man and women to fill our day;
And when we are certain of sorrow in store,
Why do we always arrange for more?
Brothers and Sisters, I bid you beware
Of giving your heart to a dog to tear.

The best dog poems are often elegies, since dogs are with us for such a short while and poetry benefits from a mix of intense feeling and form. One of the finest is "Good Night" in W.S. Merwin's recent collection *The Shadow of Sirius*, which includes several moving elegies for beloved dogs. But not all dog poems are about death, and readers who enjoy poetry will want to look up

Jonathan Swift's "On Rover, a Lady's Spaniel, Instructions to a Painter," W.H. Auden's "Talking to Dogs," James Dickey's "A Dog Sleeping on My Feet," Philip Larkin's "Dog Poem," James Merrill's "The Victor Dog," and James Wright's "The Old Dog in the Ruins of the Graves at Arles." And if you can find a translation of "To Kachalov's Dog," a much-loved Russian poem by Sergei Esenin, you'll have something special ("Let's go, the two of us, and bark / Up at the moon when Nature's silent"). Beware, however, of poets like Elizabeth Barrett Browning, who has a mind shaped by the chain of being and speaks of her dog's "low" and "lower" nature. Three good anthologies are *The Dog in British Poetry*, edited by R. Maynard Leonard (which includes William Wordsworth's "Fidelity" and Sir Walter Scott's "The Wanderer's Dog," inspired by the subject of Sir Edwin Landseer's painting *Attachment*), *Dog Music: Poetry about Dogs*, edited by Joseph Duemer and Jim Simmerman, and my favourite, *Doggerel: Poems about Dogs*, edited by Carmela Ciuraru. Written entirely in dogs' voices, the poems in *Unleashed: Poems by Writers' Dogs*, co-edited by Amy Hemple and Jim Shephard, give off a whiff of William Wegmanish self-consciousness, but it's worth looking up Maxine Kumin's "Gus Speaks" and Lawrence Raab's "Katie's Words."

There's another side to the subject of dogs and poetry, although I may sound eccentric if not downright nutty: Can dogs enjoy poetry? One winter, when Rennie was a year old, I bought a copy of Alexander Pushkin's long poem (or novel in verse, as it's sometimes called) *Eugene Onegin*, in a much-praised translation by Charles Johnston. The work of translators is often overlooked and in this case it's especially important to acknowledge Johnston's version, with its elaborate rhyming patterns evoking the energy and inventiveness of the Russian classic. One night, while reading in bed with Rennie beside me, I decided to try an experiment. I began reading aloud, from the beginning:

My uncle – high ideals inspire him;
but when past joking he fell sick,
he really forced one to admire him –
and never played a shrewder trick.

Rennie looked up at once and appeared to follow the words. I kept reading and he cocked his head sideways and sat at attention. Was he following the rhymes? (Each fourteen-line stanza is far more elaborate than the few lines I've quoted.) *Onegin* is two hundred pages long, so, after five or six pages I stopped and picked up a novel from the bedside table, flipped to the opening and read half a page of prose aloud. Rennie soon tired of it and put his head down. I went back to *Onegin* and he perked up. The next night I tried a few free-verse poems by Louise Gluck – well-wrought poems but without the rhymes and rhythmic energy of Pushkin, which Johnston has referred to as the poem's "brio." No reaction. Then I took up *Onegin* again and Rennie showed the same curiosity of the previous night. I used a similar tone of voice for all of my readings, though it's hard not to get caught up in Pushkin's verse. This very unscientific experiment left me concluding that dogs – or at least Rennie – can respond to the verbal play and repetitions involved in poetic rhyming. We're often told that dogs have the intelligence of an average two-year-old child, and children of that age certainly do enjoy the sound patterns of nursery rhymes. It would be interesting to devise a proper experiment and test my hypothesis.

PUGS

I came to pugs by accident. Friends of mine had a blind and deaf twelve-year-old dog named Diga, and one summer they left him with me for several weekends when they travelled. At first I felt uncertain about taking care of a dog who, during the best of times, was restless from the cortisone he had to take daily. But in no time I came to admire the dog's bravery (that seems the best word) as he followed me about, slept on a pillow on the floor beside my bed, took his pills willingly and adjusted to a new caregiver. When I showered in the morning, the dog leaned against the side of the tub. By the end of the first weekend, I knew that one day I would have a pug of my own. Books about pugs all say that the breed's Latin motto is *Multum in parvo* (A lot in a little), and they're right.

Pugs have a long, convoluted history, with murky origins several thousand years ago in the monasteries of China and Tibet. The breed's wrinkle-faced, flat-nosed ancestors were probably the foo dog and the Pekingese, and pugs were once considered to be a hunting dog, according to the Zhou dynasty *Book of Rites*, from around 800 B.C.E. (there were three classes of dogs: hunting, water, and edible). Eventually pugs made their way to Europe as part of foreign trade, where they became popular in Holland (as the *mopshund*), in Russia, and eventually across the continent. Pushkin's *Eugene Onegin* includes a scene where a hallway is full of bustling guests, laughing young girls, and the "yap of pugs"; the poem's years of composition (the early 1820s) and its country-house setting both suggest that pugs were by then a common feature of Russian life. That pugs were a pampered part of English country life by the early nineteenth century is evident from Jane Austen's novel *Mansfield Park*, begun in 1811 and published in 1814. Lady Bertram, the mistress of Mansfield Park, spends much of the book sitting on a sofa with her pug, and at the thought of a long visit from her niece – the novel's heroine – she remarks, "I hope she will not tease my poor pug." (She doesn't.) European aristocrats took to the pug's winning ways, as did the growing middle class. Most breed books include lists of famous pug fanciers, from William III and Mary II, who brought their pugs with them from Holland when they ascended the British throne in 1688, to Josephine, wife of Napoleon Bonaparte, whose pug (or *carlin*) named Fortune is reported to have bitten her new husband on the leg on their wedding night, to Queen Victoria, who popularized the breed. Closer to home, pugs were accepted by the American Kennel Club in 1885, when the first one was registered.

Equally interesting is the etymology of the English word *pug*, which first appeared in the *Oxford English Dictionary* in 1566 as a term of endearment for humans, not animals. Word usage evolves and by 1664 *pug* also meant demon, imp, monkey, and sprite, perhaps picking up an association from Puck, the impish fairy from Shakespeare's *A Midsummer Night's Dream*, though the *OED* isn't keen on this theory. It does seem that monkeys were the initial animals to be called *pugs*, although the term had broader usage, and by the 1730s *pug* was also used for dogs, then commonly called *pug dogs*. By this time one standard definition was "a dwarf breed of dog resembling a bull-dog in miniature." However it happened, the name suits a breed whose face resembles a closed fist (*pugnus* is the Latin word for fist, another possible source).

Despite the *OED* definition, pugs are not miniature bulldogs. Exactly what they are is a trickier matter. All purebred dogs are man-made, and pugs can't claim to be the exception. Along with their complicated Asian ancestry, and after their arrival in Europe sometime in the sixteenth century (no one really knows when or how), they have been selectively bred and interbred to create the modern standard. Relatively short-legged, cobby-bodied dogs usually weighing between fourteen to eighteen pounds, and with the characteristic flat face, pugs – who belong to the toy-breed category – are either fawn-coloured with a black face mask (the fawn can tend to either silver or apricot) or totally black. Fawn pugs are generally double-coated (Zoli was), which means they shed more than their single-coated black relatives, but there are some exceptions (like Rennie). Stocky or squarish (*not* fat), pugs have tails that curl tightly back over one hip, right or left; a double curl, like Rennie's, is particularly prized by breeders and competition judges. When a pug is relaxed or asleep, its tail uncurls. Their velvety ears are no longer cropped, as was once a fashion (Queen Victoria helped stop this cruel practice), and in shape are called either "button" or "rose" ear, depending on the way they fall. The handsome pug named Trump in Hogarth's self-portrait, from 1745, lacked the essential black face mask.

In a sense pugs are constantly evolving, although the recent fashion for mixing different breeds – the puggle, for example, a pug-beagle cross – seems arbitrary and wilful. Why anyone would want to breed a pug, a dog with potential breathing problems because of its flat face, with a beagle, a dog known for its hunting – and scenting – skills, is beyond me. Of course, you could ask why pugs have flat faces in the first place. Most breed books avoid the topic, but Jake Page, in *Dogs: A Natural History*, suggested that by 1200 C.E. the Chinese had established something like the pug that "could almost be called a breed." These flat-faced dogs, with pushed-in nostrils, he compared to "the Chinese fetish for binding royal women's feet." Along with the process of selective breeding for their small size, the miniature dogs were "achieved by methods we would deplore, such as starving the puppies, keeping them in cages too small for them to grow, and other rough (and useless) measures...." I'm more than willing to "deplore" this grim history as long as I can keep my pug. Individual dogs belonging to the flat-faced breeds can pay a price in health problems for the human desire to live with one. While I wouldn't breed pugs myself, I am guilty of loving the breed and, because of my purchases, encouraging breeders. A way out of this dilemma may be to adopt a pet from an animal rescue site.

Blame the breed's current popularity on a movie – in this case, *Men in Black* (1997), with its visitors from outer space played by pug dogs. Since then, pugs seem to be everywhere, in commercials, on greeting cards, and with photograph books devoted to them

(Jim Dratfield's *Pug Shots* and *Pugnation*, Beverly West's *Pug Therapy*, and Nancy Levine's *The Tao of Pug*). There are gatherings for "pug runs" in local parks, mass-produced Chinese needlepoint pillows, and even salt-and-pepper shakers. It wasn't always like this, though pugmania has long been an aspect of the breed's history. When I first approached Noreen Talbot, one of Canada's best pug breeders, in the fall of 1994, pugs weren't the ubiquitous creatures they've since become. In April 1995, nine-week-old Zoli was shipped to me by air from Thunder Bay, Ontario (actually carried in the plane's cabin by one of Noreen's friends, who was coming to Toronto), and he captured attention everywhere we went. "I haven't seen one of those in years," people remarked again and again. Pugs were sometimes associated with the Duke and Duchess of Windsor, famously devoted to the breed. (In 1998, diehard royal watchers and nostalgia collectors were able to bid on the Duchess's collection of pug kitsch – needlepoint pillows, silver and china bowls, ceramic figurines – in Sotheby's sale of her estate. A more recent auction devoted solely to Windsor-pedigreed pug memorabilia took place in February 2008, during the 132nd Westminster Kennel Club Dog Show. Three woolen coats made for the Windsor pugs, purchased from the Sotheby's auction, were given an estimated sales figure of $1,500 to $2,500.

The New Pug by Shirley Thomas is the most comprehensive book on the breed, including considerable detail about breeders and kennels as well as common bits of history, breed standards, and sensible advice repeated in most books. For anyone drawn to pugs and romance, Alison Pace has written *Pug Hill* – a novel that belongs to the genre referred to as "chick-lit" – about a young woman who regularly goes to a corner of Central Park near east Seventy-fourth Street, where neighbourhood pugs gather. Naturally she meets Mr. Right and his pug. More interesting is the contemporary Irish poet Nick Laird, who included a poem called "Pug" in a recent collection.

Addressing his own dog, he wrote: "Your weapon of choice is a sneeze." Now that's a man who understands pugs.

QUADRUPEDS

A dog is a quadruped, though we don't often think of them as such, and a quadruped is simply any animal with four feet. Whenever *Homo erectus* stood up for good, some 1 to 1.8 million years ago, we lost our quadruped status, and with it a line of vision and connection to the earth that emphasized scent as much as sight. This is more significant than it might at first seem, and may even account for the tendency of *Homo sapiens* to consider themselves superior to other animals. According to the classical Roman poet Ovid, in his *Metamorphoses*, humans were created looking up, and animals down; he was, we know, wrong. A dog, like other quadrupeds, has four feet technically referred to as "paws," and these feet have "claws" rather than fingernails, though groomers sometimes speak of a dog's nails, and a few nutty types are foolish enough to have them polished. When a human hand is either clumsy or oversized, it's sometimes called a paw, and of course the noun can turn into a verb and suggest a clumsy or inappropriate touch, something not exactly human and reasonable – our language is full of such hierarchical distinctions. We teach our dogs to "shake a paw" or "shake hands," and then reward them for behaviour perceived to be a good human imitation, or at least obedient. Some people buy winter boots for their dogs, to protect them from the cold and also from various calcium chloride blends of ice melter. Generally the word *feet* rather than *paws* appears on the packaging for such boots. My dogs have been unwilling to keep boots on for longer than a minute or two, apparently regarding them as some kind of human indignity not suitable for quadrupeds. This may also indicate a failure in training on my part.

RESCUE MISSIONS

We begin in Paris, Kentucky, with Daisy, a white toy poodle, age six, weighing 10.4 pounds. Sometime in June 2008, after the death of her elderly owner-guardian, Daisy was taken by disinterested relations to what is known as a "high-kill" pound (as opposed to a "no-kill" shelter), where unwanted dogs are "put down" quickly, without ceremony. But in 2008, Daisy didn't automatically face extermination. Soon she was released to a rescue team, along with a lone boxer, and driven north to another shelter, in Englewood, New Jersey, which functioned almost like a safe house in a time of civil war. This comparison may at first seem disarming, but it's important to suggest the amount of serious activity and energy that goes into giving dogs a second chance. Daisy, unlike the Kentucky boxer, did not remain in Englewood, to be placed in a new home there, but was next driven further north, to New Hampshire, where she found temporary refuge in a foster home belonging to a woman associated with Puppy Angels, someone who rescued poodles, kept an eye out for them, and remained in contact with an elaborate network of other committed dog rescuers. In a sense, Daisy just happened to be on her run.

Telephone calls were made – if this is beginning to sound like an espionage thriller, well, there is an element of melodrama to the endeavour of rescuing dogs; that quality, along with many complex emotions and beliefs, may help fuel the good work of rescue groups. Within days, an old friend of mine, a financial planner now living in Boston, headed to New Hampshire, along with her own twelve-year-old poodle, Cricket, who regards herself as Dowager Empress of the Universe. My friend liked Daisy at once, Cricket didn't bark or object, and another rescue came to a satisfactory conclusion.

The Internet is full of rescue sites, and such organizations have flowered in the last decade, along with the Internet itself. AdoptaPet.com or Petfinder include world-wide directories of animal shelters, and it's easy to spend hours on their websites. Run by volunteers and occasionally receiving financial support from various pet-food companies, these groups, and hundreds of others, have varied goals, standards, and operating procedures. Some even arrange for up-to-date medical treatment (vaccinations, heartworm tests, etc.). Many rescue groups deal only with a specific breed, like Greyhound Lovers, which attempts to find homes for retired racing dogs. According to statistics from 2000, in that year alone nineteen thousand unwanted greyhounds were killed (greyhound racing, by the way, is not legal in Canada). Rescuers from one group regularly talk to those in other associations, and word of mouth counts. My Boston friend learned of Puppy Angels through a colleague; she was approved as a potential home because her work allowed for a fairly flexible schedule. I've known other people who could have provided excellent homes but were turned down for some amazing reasons – one woman, then sixty-five, was told she was too old to adopt a dog.

Not all sagas are as straightforward as Daisy's. And there is, of course, a risk for the rescuer as well. It turned out that Daisy was not six years old but at least eight ("Probably *not* ten," my friend's veterinarian suggested) and in general good health, although she had the beginning of cataracts as well as a small benign tumour that required surgery. Not everyone is willing or able to bring home an older and possibly ill dog with unpredictable medical expenses ahead, but thousands of people have proven up to the challenge and continue to consider rescuing abandoned dogs. (Unfortunately, Daisy died three months later from cancer of the spleen.)

Rescue missions aren't always communal activities, nor are they planned events. And sometimes they fail terribly. There's a thick file of newspaper clippings beside me about people who have unintentionally sacrificed their lives for their dogs. On January 22, 1996, the *Toronto Star* ran this headline – Two die trying to save dog – about a man and his stepson who fell through the ice on Lake Aquitaine (near Toronto) while attempting to rescue a dog that managed to survive on its own. Two years later, on March 30, 1998, the *Toronto Sun* ran this headline in large capital letters: OWNER DROWNS TRYING TO SAVE DOG. The article, reporting how a forty-seven-year-old roofer had jumped into the Humber River and been overcome by its current, was accompanied by a colour photograph of the dog in question, a Rottweiler named Zack, who sat looking forlornly out of the window of a van after swimming back to shore. I might have chosen from any number of similar articles, but the point to be made is that such stories, while not daily occurrences, are kin to the work of rescue groups.

Some humans appear to have an instinct to save the lives of dogs, and the dogs don't necessarily have to be their own. The story of one such man, Randy Grim, is told by Melinda Roth in *The Man Who Talks to Dogs*. In the roughest sections of east St. Louis, Grim took it upon himself to rescue wild street dogs. Roth described him as a well-educated, successful, thirty-five-year-old businessman who was "sardonic, easily stressed, and disillusioned with the human race." Accompanying him through neighbourhoods that resemble Third-World countries in his old, unheated Volkswagen bus, Roth portrayed a man who refuses to be defeated by an indifferent society and conditions that might make anyone turn away in horror. As Grim wrote in the book's epilogue, the life of a stray dog in most major cities is "a death sentence, because there are few well-funded organizations that address the problem, so there is little hope for dogs stuck in the cycle of chaotic torture." Lost, abandoned, or born on the streets, the number of feral dogs is increasing. Roth's description of the dead dogs she and Grim came across – some shot, some run over by cars, others curled up in what seemed to be a natural death from illness – makes for painful reading. Her book, however, is a testament to human courage and stubbornness. Eventually Grim founded Stray Rescue of St. Louis. Every city needs a man like him.

RIGHTS

Too often the image that comes to mind when people speak of animal rights is that of a fanatical protester throwing a can of paint at a well-dressed woman in a fur coat. This cartoon is popular with the media, which likes to simplify complex subjects into sound bites. The popular satiric movie *Year of the Dog*, from 2007, treated its uptight heroine's new sympathy for animals, after the death of her beagle, as a two-hour comedy skit about mourning gone awry (she does destroy her meat-eating sister-in-law's fur coats), while Cathleen Schine's gently satiric novel *The New Yorkers*, from the same year, also included a dotty heroine campaigning to clear her upper-west-side neighbourhood of offending dogs until she inherits her sister's teacup Pomeranian. Laughter aside, the idea of animal rights as a serious matter for public discourse is that rare thing, a historically new idea. Its origin is a single book: Peter Singer's classic philosophical treatise *Animal Liberation*, first published in 1975 and based on an article he wrote for the *New York Review of Books* two years before, which introduced the phrase *animal liberation*. It's humbling to think that a book by one person can help turn an idea into a contemporary movement – an idea that found its moment in time, following the civil rights, women's, and gay liberation movements of the1960s.

Animal worship was common in the ancient world, where some animals were considered sacred. The Egyptian god Anubis, with the body of a man and the head of a jackal (long thought to be one of the proto-dogs in canine evolution) may be the most famous, but he wasn't alone. Alongside animal worship, however, was animal experimentation, especially among the scientifically minded Greeks. The accounts that scientists have left us are often hair-raising, and would cause most readers to turn a sympathetic eye to Peter Singer, the Australian philosopher now teaching at Princeton University. A century before him, however, the American Society for the Prevention of Cruelty to Animals, founded in 1866, was one of the first advocacy organizations to raise consciousness about animals, along with the American Anti-Vivisection Society, founded in 1883. These societies were, in part, a product of the nineteenth-century cultural shift in Europe and North America from an agrarian-based economy to an industrial one, and the revolutionary implications of economic change began to benefit dogs. (It should come as no surprise that modern dog-breeding as we know it also began in the latter half of the nineteenth century.) The Humane Society of the United States, which one might think has had a long history, was only founded in 1954, and today there are a number of organizations devoted to some form of animal rights, including People for the Ethical Treatment of Animals (PETA), the Animal Liberation Front, and the Animal Legal Defense Fund.

What, exactly, is meant by *animal rights*, an umbrella term that covers a large territory? And what might they have to do with dogs? Over four hundred years ago the Renaissance essayist Michel de Montaigne, whom I've quoted elsewhere, expressed his sympathy for animals. While humans owe each other justice, they owe animals not only "respect and duty" but "gentleness and kindness." Between humans and animals, he wrote, "there is some sort of intercourse and a degree of mutual obligation." A position that includes "respect," "duty" and "mutual obligation" is a good beginning. Unfortunately the direction inherent in Montaigne's words was not followed. From Immanuel Kant, who argued that animals have only an indirect moral status, to Nietzsche and Heidegger, the most famous philosophers have generally failed to shed light on the moral status of animals, while many contemporary academic philosophers sometimes get lost in the differences between wild and domestic animals, or in issues like genetic manipulation. Singer, who introduced the term *animal liberation*, pointed out that animals, like humans, can suffer, and therefore, like humans, have rights and interests. On the surface this may seem an obvious point, but the question of whether animals suffer was actually long debated by philosophers. While the moral status of animals has been part of the discourse of Western civilization from the start, its history is not impressive. Notions like the great chain of being are just one example of the way familiar prejudice, under the guise of authoritative theology, bypassed complex ethical thought.

To mark the thirtieth anniversary of animal liberation, Singer surveyed a stack of new books in the field, and succinctly defined the debate. He asked if speciesism – which he defined as "the idea that it is justifiable to give preference to beings simply on the grounds that they are members of the species *Homo sapiens*" – can be defended. If not, he then asked if there are other human characteristics that justify the way humans place "far greater moral significance on what happens to them than on what happens to nonhuman animals." Singer, who naturally opposes speciesism, does not address the issue here in terms of rights, but instead argues persuasively that a difference in species isn't ethical justification for privileging the interests of the human species. As theory, Singer's distinction is a fine corrective to the human-centric tendency of much Western thought.

Practically speaking, lawyers today now regard animal law, an offshoot of animal rights, as a serious and legitimate part of their practices. For the last decade they've been catching up with the growing discipline of animal law, which is currently taught in more than seventy North American law schools, including Harvard and the University of Toronto. Since 2001, and his first gift to Harvard, Bob Barker, the popular host of *The Price Is Right* and an animal-rights advocate, has established endowments of one million dollars each at a number of law schools, including Columbia, Stanford, Duke, and the University of California, Los Angeles. Shortly before his eighty-first birthday, Barker discussed the current state of knowledge about animal rights with *The New York Times*: "The laws are not stringent enough, and unfortunately the laws that we do have are not necessarily enforced.... The most important thing we can do is change legislation involving animals." While Barker is not the only celebrity to speak out about animal rights – Hollywood's Doris Day and France's Brigitte Bardot are two of the most well-known actresses to do so – the scope of his generosity should impress anyone skeptical about celebrities who get attention for themselves through their favourite causes.

In 2004 the American Bar Association formed its first committee on animal rights. Issues ranged from the rights of apartment renters and condo and co-op owners, veterinarian malpractice, and pet trust funds to suits for injury and custody battles. Some of these subjects have been treated for laughs in popular entertainment, such as the clever screwball comedy, *The Awful Truth*, from 1937, with its splendid courtroom scenes between a battling married couple, Cary Grant and Irene Dunne, over their wirehaired terrier. Since divorce is far more common today, the situation may have a different resonance with contemporary moviegoers. Meanwhile, animal rescue groups – some devoted to specific dog breeds – want to be able to deny pets to abusive or unsuitable owners, though the definition of unsuitable may sometimes be open to debate. Naturally, prospective pet adopters dislike home visits and requests for references, but the desire of rescue groups to protect shelter dogs from further distress makes sense. A few movies, however, have been more direct than *The Awful Truth* in raising the general issue of animal rights, even if only as a tangent. In his political thriller *The Stranger* (1946), which Orson Welles directed and starred in with Loretta Young, he dramatized the story of post-war Nazis hiding out in small-town America and included snippets of controversial contemporary footage of liberated concentration camps. But the film also starred a handsome Irish setter as Red, Young's loyal dog, who becomes an important figure in the plot when he is poisoned in the woods by a villain who doesn't want his disguise revealed. After actor Richard Long, as Young's brother, finds the dog's body, he asks, "What does the law say about this kind of murder? Is it the same as killing a man? It ought to be. It's just as bad." While the American Bar Association probably wouldn't go that far, at least it has made a start.

Changes in sensibility often have to precede changes in law. Banned breeds and battles over canine use of public parks are the most commonly reported subjects that touch on animal law, but for dogs they're probably the least significant. Dog rights and human rights are not the same thing, which dog owners (or "dog lobbyists," as some journalists have called them) sometimes forget in their zeal to claim portions of public space for their pets. In 2006, Governor Arnold Schwarzenegger of California signed legislation that put his state in the forefront of animal rights. New laws made it a crime to leave animals untended in vehicles in hot or cold weather, or without adequate ventilation. Police are allowed to break windows to save a dog, and owners face fines and six-month jail sentences. This wasn't the only new California law, either. It is now illegal to leave a dog tethered and untended for more than three hours, another sensible piece of legislation. If a dog's owner refuses to act like a responsible guardian, someone else has to.

Though few states have animal laws as strong as California's, progress is happening across North America. Stories about cruel puppy mills occasionally capture public attention for a few days, but Hurricane Katrina had staying power, with TV images of lone dogs afloat in the wild flood waters. It took less than a year after the disaster for the U.S. Senate to pass, unanimously, a bill that requires emergency agencies to plan for pet evacuation as well as for their shelter and care; a month later the House of Representatives passed the bill, 349 to 24. But 24 votes against the family dog? As if to illustrate Bob Barker's point about inadequate animal legislation, in New York state, for example, any driver involved in a vehicle accident that hurts a dog or cat is obligated to notify the police or try to find the animal's owner. A fine of $100 can be made to someone who disregards the law. While irresponsible pet owners often let their dogs and cats wander about untended – unneutered, too, but that's another matter – the fine is ludicrously low for something that would be labelled a hit-and-run accident if a human were involved. (Although my focus is on dogs, since 1997, New York law has covered cats as well.)

The reverse side of animal rights is human responsibility, which falls to a dog's owner. A few places have gone overboard with legislation about this. Under Ontario's health-protection laws, for example, outdoor restaurant patios are forbidden territory for dogs, even though veterinarians claim that they pose no health hazard. And Ontario isn't alone here, either. More serious are the frequent reports, over the past decade, of out-of-control dogs – usually pitbulls and Rottweilers – which capture public debate whenever a dog has mauled or even killed someone. Although animal-rights activists insist that these breeds can make good pets, the fact remains that they can also make good weapons, and may be genetically programmed to be so through inbreeding. (In 1997, a *New York Times* editorial noted that the city's largest animal shelter claimed that pitbulls made up 40 per cent of the dogs brought in because of attack bites.) Inevitably, legislation regarding pitbulls has been passed, in some instances banning them from an entire city; naturally, confusion results when the family boxer or French bulldog is mistaken for a pitbull – I was once asked if Zoli, a trim little pug, was a pitbull. But some laws regarding risky breeds have been found unconstitutional. In Ohio, a 2004 decision of the state's Supreme Court overturned legislation that required owners of dangerous pets to confine them and acquire liability insurance. (The particular case that led to this reversal involved a German shepherd that had seriously injured a neighbour; the dog, a repeat offender, had previous complaints against it.) As often happens, the reversal was based on a narrow reading of the law – in this instance one that argued the rights of dog owners to dispute the labelling of a dog as "vicious" or "dangerous" by a dog warden. Rarely, however, does anyone ask why a person would want a potentially troublesome pet. Between 1986 and 1994, Rottweilers jumped from being the fifteenth most popular breed in the United States to second place, which says more about American society than it does about the dogs who, historically, have been trained for dog-fighting, now universally outlawed in North America.

The idea of animal rights is important in a multicultural society easily charmed by the temptation of cultural relativism. As global economics slowly change the way people everywhere think about themselves, animals will also be seen in different ways. I'm not going to discuss the Korean practice of eating dog meat, although a former student of mine did give me a graphic description of visiting a "dog restaurant" in southern Korea, where you picked out the caged creature that was to be your meal. I can only shake my head at that *and* at the abysmal way factory farming of animals in North America has developed. This reminds me of the conclusion of Joy Williams's fine article about animal rights in *Harper's* magazine more than a decade ago: "Our treatment of animals and our attitude toward them is crucial not only to any pretensions we have to ethical behaviour but to humankind's intellectual and moral evolution. Which *is* how the human animal is meant to evolve, isn't it?" There is nothing particularly comic about animal rights in themselves, and until we're willing to admit this, we are less than we might be. Unfortunately our dogs suffer the consequences. Anyone in doubt need only read one short book – Singer's *Animal Liberation* – to begin an evolutionary process that might be called human liberation.

ROMANTIC LOVE

The following quotation does not come from a romance novel but rather from Jack London's *The Call of the Wild*:

> Love, genuine passionate love, was his for the first time. This he had never experienced at Judge Miller's down in the sun-kissed Santa Clara Valley. With the Judge's sons, hunting and tramping, it had been a working partnership; with the Judge's grandsons, a sort of pompous guardianship; and with the Judge himself, a stately and dignified friendship. But love that was feverish and burning, that was adoration, that was madness, it had taken John Thornton to arouse.

London's word choices are noteworthy – *feverish, burning, adoration, madness*. This is the language of a torch song gone wrong, yet the writer is not a sentimentalist but tough-guy Jack London, no sucker for love stories. John Thornton, his human hero, has saved Buck's life, and man and dog share a deep communion in the harsh northern land, where "Buck knew no greater joy than that rough embrace and the sound of murmured oaths, and at each jerk back and forth it seemed that his heart would be shaken out of his body so great was the ecstasy." While contemporary ethologists have debated whether the word *love* can even be applied to a dog's emotions, literary writers like London have been less fearful of sharing the term with dogs. Doris Lessing, in fact, made the connection head-on when she suggested that "the emotional devotion" a dog has for for his master or mistress was something like romantic love, "all pining and yearning." Lessing might have been writing about London's Buck. We're happy to think of our dogs in terms of devotion and fidelity, but the idea of romantic love is somehow an embarrassing one when linked to dogs. Romantic love, we tend to forget, is a learned emotion, with its origins in the medieval tradition of courtly love. Humans can learn to have all kinds of emotions, just as dogs can. In Buck's case, however, the "passionate love" he felt, and showed, came directly out of his own experience – London called it "genuine."

Elizabeth Marshall Thomas referred to the bond between her pugs Violet and Bingo as a "marriage," and praised their lifelong devotion; she was not, she insisted, anthropomorphizing them. I've seen something similar – and unusual – in two dogs owned by the writer Suzanne Hively. In 2001, Suzanne purchased a Chinese crested female named Willow, a puppy that promised to grow into a fine show dog. She arrived by plane shortly before 9/11 and was traumatized from the start. Suzanne and her veterinarian Robert Hutchison carefully observed the new puppy, who appeared "catatonic." Because of the disruption to the airlines it was impossible to return Willow, and Suzanne decided to give her a home. Willow acted as if she'd been abused, but that scenario was out of the question. It was decided that Willow was – for want of a better term – mentally retarded. When I met her she sat on Suzanne's lap staring blankly, her tongue lolling out of one side of her mouth. But that's not the end of Willow's story, or the reason for introducing her. Three years later Suzanne acquired a male Japanese chin, also a potential show dog, named Eden. As he grew, Eden's mouth appeared to be deformed, and the exhibition ring was out of the question. But Suzanne kept him because Eden had fallen in love with Willow. Love at first sight, like a thunder clap. Eden followed Willow about, watched her every move, slept on the floor outside of her kennel. (He would rather sleep there than on Suzanne's bed, a true measure of devotion.) During one of my visits, while Willow sat in Suzanne's lap, Eden stood by definitely distressed. Willow, however, seemed oblivious to his devotion. What was going on? Suzanne suggested that perhaps Eden sensed something was wrong with Willow and he may have also felt something was wrong with himself. Her dogs are treated equally – every night she massages each of the dogs for exactly seven minutes, taking precisely one hour and thirty-one minutes to assure her troop of balanced attention – but Eden may have somehow recognized that he wasn't like the other show dogs. His talent was for seemingly unrequited love. Like the troubadors of the courtly love tradition, whose pattern he fits perfectly, Eden has learned to be content with an aloof fair maiden and an all-absorbing passion, whether it's returned or not.

SECOND DOGS

Second dogs, like second children, benefit from your experience. They come into our lives for diverse reasons, with the death of a previous pet the most common. Brochures about grieving pet loss and thoughtful veterinarians will often suggest choosing a different breed for a second dog, to avoid comparison or the misguided notion that a new dog can serve as a quick replacement. Some second pets are acquired when people think that a first dog, who spends the days alone while its humans are away at work, will be happier with a dog companion. Whatever the reason, there are only three choices possible: the same breed, a new breed, or a mutt.

After Zoli died, in March 2004, I knew that I had the summer free from teaching, an ideal time to train a new dog if I could face the prospect. And I feared that if I waited until the following summer, some part of my psyche would harden and I would never have another dog companion. People offered condolences with the same advice: don't get another pug, it will be too painful. I tried to imagine a Boston terrier like Buster or a Cavalier King Charles spaniel like Morgan in my life, I made myself thumb through breed books with glossy photographs, I told myself not to stay rooted in the past. Images of Tibetan spaniels caught my eye, and near the end of April I spoke with several breeders, but I couldn't decide what to do. Instead, I took a plane to Florida to visit a friend, found myself restless, cut the trip short, and returned to a northern spring that reminded me of the April days when I first got Zoli and was housebreaking him on a lawn filled with wild violets. The only question I needed to ask any breeder was whether or not there was a history of mast-cell tumours in their dogs' blood lines.

Eventually a magazine article about a veterinarian who was also a pug breeder led me to another good breeder, Pam Salamone, and we had as many phone talks as I'd once had with Noreen Talbot, who placed Zoli with me. By the end of May I visited Pam, perhaps because she'd taken the time to hear my story of Zoli and had spoken about the grief she still felt over the loss of a favourite pug of her own. My mother, who was then living in a nursing home because of advancing dementia, came along for the drive; although her memory was shot, she was cheerful. One four-month-old pug in the breeder's litter was still available, and he sat quietly in my lap. He was a charming creature and didn't exactly resemble Zoli, which I considered a point in his favour. But I couldn't decide. Two weeks later I drove back, again taking my mother along, and this time the sad-eyed dog seemed a real possibility. But the owner of the puppy's dam had not paid her share of medical bills and there was some confusion about when the dog could be sold legally. This complication oddly caught my fancy. My mother, who sat stroking the puppy, looked up at me while I debated and said,

"He'll remind you of Zoli. It will be like taking care of one of his relatives." When she added, "He needs someone to love him and you can give him a home," I knew she was right – and I was amazed that despite her illness she could make such a connection. She couldn't have told anyone the year, or her age, but she managed to pull her thoughts together in good motherly advice. I agreed to take the puppy once the legal complications were resolved, and set a deadline of mid-June.

At home, I began to have second thoughts, which I now see as part of the process of making a commitment to a second dog. Money hadn't changed hands so I could easily have backed out. Then a prominent breeder of Tibetan spaniels contacted me about an available puppy, born of champions. I'd taken pictures of the pug puppy, but when they were developed I was still uncertain – I couldn't put Zoli out of my mind. Adult pugs vary in size, and I didn't want one of the larger ones (who might hit twenty pounds) since I travel often and always found Zoli, a portable fifteen pounds, the ideal size, easy to carry on daily errands or on vacation, into airports, shops, even department stores and the occasional restaurant. Size was also a consideration because I wanted a dog who could accompany me to campus and not make students and other faculty uncomfortable. People rarely object to a well-behaved fifteen-pounder of any breed, and any dog I've know has quickly figured out that if he doesn't want to stay home alone, he has to behave out of the house.

June was passing, the pug puppy's legal situation had been resolved, and in a state of mixed emotions I brought Rennie home. It was the best thing I could have done. I relate this story in some detail in case you ever have to decide about getting a second dog and debate about its breed. I am apparently that creature known as a pug-person – pugs make sense to me, they're my kind of dog.

And training, the second time around, takes a natural course. As with second children, you know what to expect, what to watch for, what to avoid. Surprises will likely be different and new, since each dog is an individual, but similarities are also significant. Zoli had been quick at housebreaking, as was Rennie. Since he was five months old when I brought him home, Rennie was more than ready to make a bond with one person, but I had to work to overcome his natural shyness about the physical world since he'd traded a large country yard for city life, with curbs and elevators and unfamiliar loud noises. Zoli had taken to the city with his customary enthusiasm – *I'm here, let's go* – but Rennie, at first more timid, need coaxing and reassurance. Given a chance, common sense and persistence usually solve most issues in life. Within a month Rennie was willing to step into an elevator and cross the street without freezing up. My friends welcomed him; his vet later confessed that at first he'd been concerned about the puppy's timidity, and was glad to see that patience had solved any potential problems. This patience I frankly owed to Zoli who, as my true first dog, had taught me what to do.

SHARED DOGS

While many dogs have accustomed themselves to living in human families and dividing their attention and affection, one person will always be top dog. Whoever is responsible for feeding and caretaking usually has that role, although other family members may convince themselves that they're the dog's favourite. And dogs, cleverly enough, know how to play along with our fantasies. Such dogs are not shared dogs but family dogs, where the family replaces the pack. Shared dogs have more divided loyalties and more complicated lives, with humans as the source of their situation. I know this from personal experience, but first I want to relate a story that appeared in newspapers across America from the summer of 2007 through the spring of 2008.

The dog in question was a shih tzu named Puddles – at least that was its first name. Puddles belonged to the Gutierrez-Cavasos family who live in Alice, Texas, next door to the town's mayor, Grace Saenz-Lopez, all good neighbours. Trouble began when the Gutierrez-Cavasos family went on summer vacation and left the ill Puddles in the care of their neighbour. On returning they learned that Puddles had died during their holiday. At the same time, their neighbour, the mayor, had acquired an identical shih tzu of her own, named Panchito. It took some time for the mess to be sorted out in the courts. Grace Saenz-Lopez resigned her job as mayor, Panchito, now Puddles again, was returned to her rightful owners, and, well, the story goes on with criminal charges against the Saenz-Lopez sisters. At the civil trial, Ms Saenz-Lopez explained that she could give the dog better care than her neighbours could, since they were also responsible for four young children. The judge, who knew the ex-mayor and considered her a decent human being, had to return the dog to the owners, but he denied Gutierrez's claim for nearly $10,000 in court costs. I knew exactly how Ms Saenz-Lopez felt. The grim expression on her face in newspaper photographs, as she held Panchito-Puddles up to her cheek, should serve as a warning to anyone who becomes attached to a friend's dog.

During my dinner with the writer Mavis Gallant, which I mentioned earlier, one of the things we discussed was the dilemma of sharing a dog. Her own poodle had spent a great deal of time with friends who lived in the country, and everyone naturally considered their care to be the best for the dog. This is a big part of the problem, but not the whole story. Early one snowy Saturday in January 1995, several months before Zoli came to live with me, I drove close friends to Guelph, Ontario, where a well-regarded breeder of Cavalier King Charles spaniels had a puppy for sale. She explained that the dog was nearly housebroken as he bounded enthusiastically across the linoleum floor, dribbling urine along the way, and it was love at first sight. There's something especially poetic about a Cavalier's face. One of my friends said "yes" immediately, the other "no." Cavaliers were considered to be a good writer's dog, undemanding and patient, and "yes" won out. In the meantime, Morgan and I bonded. In the following weeks he often fell asleep on my chest while my friends continued to argue about housebreaking. By the time Zoli arrived, in mid-April, Morgan had become part of my life. So the two dogs grew up together, Zoli genuinely interested in Morgan's company, big-hearted dog that he was, and Morgan tolerant of him but eager for my attention.

When my friends announced their planned move to the west coast the following year, I dreaded the loss of Morgan. Instead, he spent the first six months of 1996 with me and Zoli. This set a pattern for future years, when Morgan came for three months here and four months there, each time adjusting as if he'd finally come home. At least that's how I saw it. When I visited my friends Morgan slept by my side as usual. It takes a great deal of tact to navigate a situation like this one, and any tensions in a friendship are likely to come to the surface. I always felt that Morgan was left alone too much, while my friends thought me overly solicitous. When Morgan was long overdue to have his teeth cleaned, I arranged for the procedure during one of his visits, and of course considered the abscess that was discovered a sign of neglect. I knew he wasn't neglected but that was beside the point. He became a fixture on campus, along with Zoli, and each time I had to return him I was filled with regret. Meanwhile, I asked myself if Zoli minded sharing my attention during those visits; I still have no answer. Yet if I left the two dogs alone for an evening, when I came home they would be curled up side by side on my bed, leaning against each other and looking out the bedroom door for me.

There is a special bond you can have with one dog that changes with two – it's no longer *us* but *you* and *them*. I wouldn't change my experience but I wouldn't welcome another one like it. After Zoli died, I didn't have the chance to visit my friends right away, so I never saw Morgan again – he died a year later, of the heart troubles that Cavaliers are prone to. If you have a choice about sharing a dog, my advice is, don't. And I hope that Grace Saenz-Lopez now has a dog of her own.

SPACE

The first dog sent into space was named Laika, in a Soviet satellite called Sputnik II that weighed just over 1,120 pounds. Launched on November 3, 1957, during the Cold War years between the Soviet Union and the United States, Laika gave the Soviets a decided advantage – if short-lived – in the space race. (The first Sputnik, weighing only 184 pounds, had been launched into orbit a month earlier.) Would a Russian man soon follow the dog? Today it seems like ancient history.

Laika was a female mixed-breed found on one of Moscow's streets. She was sent into space, in part, to mark the fortieth anniversary of the Bolshevik October Revolution. The first living creature in orbit, Laika did not survive the experiment; she died from extreme heat and lack of air after the satellite was launched. Various sources give her differing survival times – one suggests that she died within hours of takeoff, others say that she was alive for a week. Laika is unexpectedly celebrated in a unique small museum in Culver City, California, founded in 1989 and called the Museum of Jurassic Technology. There are specially commissioned oil portraits of her as well as of the four other Soviet dogs who were sent into orbit after Laika's death: Belka and Strelka, in 1960, who did survive the trip; Zvezdochka, in 1962, and Ugolyok, in 1966, who still holds the canine record for the longest time in orbit, twenty-two days. This museum is the work of David Wilson and was the subject of Lawrence Weschler's book *Mr. Wilson's Cabinet of Wonders*. Wilson's curiosity about Soviet space, however, is shared by others. *My Life as a Dog* (and the 1985 film based on it) by Swedish writer Reidar Jönsson, tells a moving story, set in the late 1950s, of the thirteen-year-old boy Ingemar Johansson and his dog Sickan. From the novel's start readers can guess that the dog is already dead, although Ingemar believes him to be alive somewhere in a kennel. As the health of this boy's gravely ill mother worsens, Ingemar develops a passionate interest in Laika, has frequent visions of her, and comes to identify with the dog, even crawling about on all fours and barking. An extraordinary creation of a childhood crisis, the novel reinforces the deep connection between a boy and his dog through Laika's tragic image.

In a lighter vein, this story was told by the critic Diana Trilling in "A Visit to Camelot," which first appeared in the *New Yorker*. After a dinner at the Kennedy White House in April 1962 (four years after the Americans successfully launched their own rocket, on January 31, 1958), Trilling asked Jackie Kennedy about her recent European trip, where she'd sat next to Russian Premier Nikita Khrushchev during a state banquet in Vienna. Admitting that she'd felt nervous, the First Lady had wondered what to talk about, and settled on animals as a safe subject. "I just love Russian dogs," she told him, and of course he immediately offered to send one to her. The President was naturally annoyed that Khrushchev had so easily gained a "diplomatic advantage." Mrs. Kennedy went on to complete the story, saying that she still had the dog at the White House, but he posed a problem (which most dog owners will find unlikely) because she wanted to mate the dog but she didn't have another Russian dog: "I'd have to mate him with an American dog. I've been working on it, and I've been told that it won't take:

a Russian dog and an American dog won't mate." Trilling doesn't say who gave Mrs. Kennedy this odd advice, but she does note that the anecdote never appeared in newspapers of the day, since it would have been an embarrassment to the President. The story is all the more puzzling because later that year Khrushchev gave the Kennedys a small white Russian mutt named Pushinka – or "fluffy" – daughter of one of the Russian space dogs, and with the Kennedy's Welsh terrier she produced a four-puppy litter, which the President referred to as "pupniks."

Space, of course, doesn't refer only to distant galaxies, but can involve something closer to home, including the use of public space (beaches, parks, streets, playgrounds, hiking and bicycle trails, etc.) contested by many dog owners in events journalists sometimes refer to as "dog wars," an inane term, since it's usually humans who do the fighting. Dog parks, or portions of parks designated for off-leash dogs, are often in the news. Many cities even have websites for such parks. Other cities have built specially enclosed dog runs, like Riverside Park in New York City's Upper West Side. Whenever I took Zoli there, the activity was so fierce that we sat on a nearby park bench; he didn't seem to mind. Dog-friendly spaces for the unleashed are perfect places for your pet to pick up a variety of canine diseases, rarely mentioned in pro articles, and free-runs can allow for canine aggression, especially when a dog's owner hasn't been trained to handle an overly energetic pet or is indifferent to his or her dog's public behaviour. Attack dogs pose a particular problem, whether in dog runs or elsewhere. In 2003, a pair of pitbulls living in New York City's exclusive Turtle Bay mauled several neighbourhood dogs (a standard poodle and a sheepdog, both larger breeds) and severed the head of a fourteen-year-old Chihuahua. Since dog-on-dog violence is not covered by legislation, there's little the police, or the city's Department of Health, can do to stop it.

Inevitably the increased human desire for a green space that unleashed dogs can use has caused municipal legislation across North America while, at the same time, raising issues about animal and human rights. Dog owners have in recent decades become a powerful lobby group with influence and money on their side (a 2000 study from Statistics Canada showed that since 1992 Canadians have spent roughly the same amount on their pets as they did on child care). In Europe, on the other hand, most cities welcome dogs in public places, including some restaurants, although Parisian parks often sport signs warning everyone to stay off the grass. At the designated dog park in Lakewood, Ohio, the city even went so far as to install a dual-purpose water fountain with a waist-high spigot for humans and a ground-level trough for dogs. This did little to calm nearby residents, who complained about the noise of excessive barking. In 2006, city workers were measuring the wind's direction to determine where and how the sound was carried into homes some five hundred feet away, in Rocky River, a neighbouring suburb. Just as perplexing is a story out of Montreal, Quebec, where in 1999 the city built a dog run in Notre Dame de Grace Park, not far from the home of Roland Proulx, an administrator at the University of Montreal. Soon after, Proulx began to complain that he could no longer enjoy his yard, or have an alfresco meal there, because of the offending stench from the park. While dog owners blamed the city for not providing enough dog runs, Proulx expressed his frustration in the *Globe and Mail*, claiming that we have a social problem with dogs: "We've lost control. These dog owners, you know, it's a religion. I've seen some people in cars, how do you say, *necking* with their dogs. Like you would with your girlfriend! Yes, there's a big problem." But not about dogs.

TELEVISION

When television usurped movies as North America's preferred

form of entertainment in the 1950s, it began where the movies left off, with various series based on old films: *The Adventures of Rin Tin Tin* ran from October 1954 to August 1959; *The Thin Man* with Asta from September 1957 to June 1959; *Topper*, with its ghost dog, the St. Bernard, Neil, from October 1953 to October 1956; and *Lassie*, in several manifestations, from September 1954 to September 1971. Gradually, television added its own twist to the tradition, with TV dogs particularly popular on situation comedies about family life. While the first TV families, like the Ricardos of *I Love Lucy*, weren't dog owners, even *Lucy* eventually ran an episode where a puppy was bought for Little Ricky and, as if to prevent objections from their landlords, the boy named him Fred after the crusty neighbour Fred Mertz. Once the Ricardos moved to the Connecticut suburbs in their sixth season (1956–57), a dog was sometimes in residence, mirroring the postwar pattern of suburban life. Still, many television families remained dogless – Donna Reed's, Dick Van Dyke's, Andy Griffin's, even Beaver's. Dogs could always be brought in for an episode by writers who were running low on original ideas that week. Usually such dogs offered a little plot complication, but were quickly written out of the scenario.

It was also during the 1950s that television and politics began to forge their unholy alliance. When California politician Richard M. Nixon received the 1952 Republican vice-presidential nomination, his finances came under public scrutiny. On the evening of Tuesday, September 23, after *The Milton Berle Show*, he gave what is now known as the Checkers speech, explaining his financial situation, including gifts from powerful backers. To conclude, Nixon spoke about his family's pet, a spaniel named Checkers: "And you know the kids love that dog, and I just want to say this right now – that regardless of what they say about it, we're going to keep it." The speech did its job.

It wasn't until after the mid 1960s that dogs became a more

standard sitcom feature or prop for easy humour (the English sheepdog on *My Three Sons*, for example), although they were conspicuously absent from dramatic, detective, and medical programs. One exception is the TV western, which may have found it easier to accommodate dogs since it already included horses and often showed an anonymous dog running about, a background detail like desert cactus. It's hard to imagine Ironside or Dr. Welby or Jessica Fletcher with a dog, which is puzzling because they all seem likely candidates for a canine buddy. And unlike many young women who live alone, Marlo Thomas (*That Girl*) and Mary Tyler Moore (*The Mary Tyler Moore Show*) never had dogs, nor did the young singles on *Friends*, nor any of the other numerous programs about finding a partner (day-time soap operas included); on the other hand, happily married couples, like the one on *Mad About You*, seemed to need a dog as a buffer zone. Canadians who grew up the the 1980s often fondly recall the CTV series *The Littlest Hobo*, with its wandering stray German shepherd who arrived weekly in new settings to help people in need. (The show, which ran from 1979 to 1985, was actually a revised version of an earlier series, from 1963–65.) Also in the 1980s, *The Golden Girls* occasionally made use of actress Betty White's well-known sympathy for animals (Dorothy and Blanche wouldn't let her have a dog, which never made sense because everyone spent a lot of time sitting around the kitchen table eating cheesecake, a good place for a dog), while *The Nanny* periodically included a Pomeranian named Chester as a standard sight gag, and Archie Bunker objected to dogs on *All in the Family* the way he objected to just about everything else. The list could go on.

Dog actors, who always come with the possibility of unexpected behaviour, may be harder on quick-paced television production than on the movies, accustomed as they are to more "takes" of an individual scene. In this sense television is closer to live theatre than to the movies. When Lucille Ball tried to recharge her career with the Broadway show *Wildcat* in 1960, a Yorkshire terrier named Mousy was part of the cast. During one try-out matinee, Lucy, who sometimes forgot her lines and ad-libbed them, saw that the dog had made a mess on stage. While singing and dancing, she cleaned up after it, and quipped to the audience, "It's in the small print in my contract, I have to clean up the dog shit!" Of course she got her laugh.

Hollywood, it would seem, no longer knows quite what to do with dogs. Several television networks recently acquired the rights to show two first-run movies that had never been released in North American theatres, as if television was a canine dumping ground. Jeff Bridges starred in *A Dog Year* (2009), the film version of one of Jon Katz's dog memoirs, on HBO It's the story of an angry man who adopts an abused and untrainable border collie, thus finding a subject for his next book. The dog, Devon, is wonderful, but he deserves a better filmscript. Though happily married and well-off, the human Jon is for no apparent reason a sour cuss, and his anger is equated by other characters in the movie with the dog's disruptive behaviour. But the dog was badly abused for the first two years of its life, so the equation between man and dog is an absurd and misleading plot convention. For Hallmark, Richard Gere starred in *Hachi: A Dog's Tale* (2010), which presents the story of the famous Japanese Akita who, during the 1920s, waited for his deceased master every day for nine years at a Tokyo train station. Updating the story to a Rhode Island town in the late 1990s destroys its unique nature; today, no decent family would abandon their dog to homelessness, as the film expects us to believe, and if they did, they would be charged with animal cruelty and the dog taken to a local animal shelter where, given its size, it would likely be destroyed. But not in this filmscript. However, the three Akitas – male and female – who play Hachi over the course of his life are so beautiful I wanted to run out and bring one home at once. (Some credit goes to trainer Boone Narr, who admitted that Akitas are a stubborn breed and not easily trained.) And the movie has one notable, redeeming feature: its director presents sections of the story through a dog's-eye perspective, even alternating the film's lush colour palette with near-nonchromatic scenes that mirror the way we now think dogs see the world.

Over time, dogs from some less familiar breeds have joined the list of the most popular canine stars, with Eddie, a Jack Russell terrier on *Frasier* (September 1993 to May 2004), perhaps the most popular, creating a fashion in Jack Russells after *Frasier* hit the TV screen. Given the popularity of "reality" programs, one with dogs was bound to happen. In the summer of 2008 *The Greatest American Dog* began its run on CBS. Like most reality-based television, the goal appeared to be to stir up emotion, humiliate people and get some of the contestants to cry. I managed to watch two episodes, charmed by several of the dogs but put off by many of their human companions and by the casual nastiness of it all. With the exception of Lassie, most TV dogs have been less significant to their programs than canine movie stars once were, as if the smaller world of television can't quite find a place for them when they're almost the size of the dog in your own living room.

THERAPY

We expect a lot from our dogs and in recent years have come to lump our needs under the term *therapy*. Individual dogs have always been valued for their heroic acts, but medical studies have shown that companion dogs can help people who live alone live longer. One study, from the Medical School of the State University of New York at Buffalo, even suggested that in a stressful situation a dog will be of more comfort than a spouse.

Such preoccupations are not only North American – in March, 2007, for example, the Taiwanese-produced magazine *Dog* ran an article, in Chinese, about the health benefits of walking your dog. Petting your dog lowers your blood pressure and heart rate, walking him provides exercise and social interaction – all obvious benefits. But there's more.

In the weeks after the 9/11 attack on the World Trade Center, a papillon named Annie, along with her handler, travelled on a ferry twice a day down the Hudson River to Ground Zero, comforting the mourners who petted and hugged her. Papillons seldom weigh more than ten or twelve pounds, so Annie packed a lot of consolation into a small frame. She wasn't the only dog to receive newspaper attention, nor the only therapy-trained dog that people turned to for a moment of speechless respite. One Associated Press article told of Mario Canzoneri, a plumbing contractor from Staten Island who regularly brought his dogs into Manhattan. A day after Jesse, his golden retriever, had comforted the sobbing widow of a firefighter, the dog collapsed with bloodshot eyes. "He was lying down. He wasn't the same dog. You'd think that dog had pulled 100 pounds on a sled for a month." The stress a therapy dog has to accept, and absorb, needs our recognition and respect. Their working time should be limited to several hours a day and only a few days a week. Dogs trained by Therapy Dogs International, the Delta Society, and the Good Dog Foundation, among other organizations, and also by individual trainers, provide services to individual owners as well as to institutions like hospitals and nursing homes. Founded in 1976, in Flanders, New Jersey, Therapy Dogs International is the oldest and largest group of its kind. In 2007, it had approximately eighteen thousand registered therapy dogs. National Service Dogs (NSD), a registered charity, began its program for therapy dogs and autistic children in 1996, and has now extended its work to include a program for skilled companion dogs and Canadian soldiers suffering from Post-Traumatic Stress

Disorder (PTSD) after serving in Afghanistan.

Dogs can provide a buffer zone between an individual and the world, even blocking it out temporarily, like the portable headphones that people wear on the street. This may not be the best use of dogs but it's a popular one. In the spring of 2006, the Sunday Styles section of *The New York Times* ran an article called "Wagging the Dog, and a Finger," by Beth Landman, with a large illustration of a dog wearing a tag that read: I'm an Emotional Support Dog: By order of the law, my owner is entitled to bring me * Into restaurants * Onto airplanes * To the office. *Emotional support dog* – that's the moniker. Now that dogs are commonly valued for the physical and psychological benefits of pet ownership, it was only a matter of time before people began to insist that they needed their dogs constantly at hand as support, just as a blind person might require a service dog. In 2003, the U.S. Department of Transportation had already ruled that airplane passengers who required the presence of their dogs to counteract conditions like depression and anxiety should be afforded the same rights as people with physical disabilities. Since the legislation didn't stipulate that these dogs must have special training, as seeing-eye dogs require, a legal gray area opened numerous possibilities for creative claims of entitlement. And the idea that any person can, or should, decide whether or not another individual is unhappy enough to need the emotional support of a dog, strikes me as downright frightening.

Dogs providing emotional support should be treated with special care. Their owners may need more training than the dogs themselves. Landman quotes a clinical social worker who insists that dogs "are major antidepressants." But a dog is a living being in itself, not a pharmaceutical. Therapy dogs never work 24/7, and an individual pet shouldn't have to either. In 1997, the writer Louise Rafkin was travelling in Japan and missing her dog at home, a yellow Lab. In Tokyo she went to a pet shop that rented dogs to tourists who were unhappy with their dogless state. Rafkin acquired a yellow Lab named, almost cynically, Love, for the afternoon. Of course she found the experience unsatisfying, though it gave her something to write about. I read her article with increasing discomfort: think of that poor dog, rented out like something from Avis or Hertz.

Dogs can work their therapeutic magic on almost everyone, the young, the old, the in-between. Cleveland's University Hospitals' Rainbow Babies and Children's Hospital has developed a pet therapy program called "Pet Pals" to "normalize the hospital experience as much as possible for each child," said the program's coordinator Alyson Grossman in the hospital's publication, *InHouse*. These dogs are checked for a range of diseases, including strep A, intestinal parasites, and salmonella, and wear a customized T-shirt that identifies them and cuts down on messy dog hair. (The testing is done because dogs can harbour germs that may be a threat to someone with a suppressed immune system – *Bordetella bronchiseptica*, or kennel cough, is one.) A success with children, the program has been extended to adult patients. It's a commonplace that elderly people, who can easily become isolated, benefit from dog companions as long as the dogs are manageable. Breeds often mentioned as good choices include several of my favourites – Boston terriers, Cavalier King Charles spaniels, and pugs – as well as cocker spaniels, corgis, French bulldogs, papillons, and West Highland white terriers. However, a dissenting voice in all this praise of therapy dogs came several years ago when two Finnish researchers, Leena K. Koivusilta and Ansa Ojanlatva, surveyed more than twenty thousand Finns and discovered that pet owners were not healthier than the non-pet population, but rather poorer, less-educated, older, and with higher blood-pressure rates, ulcers, and depression. I would assume that the first conditions may have been responsible for the latter – there are limits to what we should expect dogs to accomplish.

In our therapy-friendly society, dogs get to have their own therapists too. They can suffer from depression and "separation anxiety," one of the most common problems; demonstrate a range of phobias, from the fear of fireworks to thunderstorms; show unexplainable (to humans) likes and dislikes as well as emotions familiar to all of us, like jealousy and possessiveness. Some doctors, naturally, treat them with the same drugs that may be given to humans (Prozac is one). Nicholas Dodman, a professor of behavioural pharmacology at the Tufts University School of Veterinary Medicine, has written a lively account of this subject, *The Dog Who Loved Too Much: Tales, Treatments and the Psychology of Dogs.* The first part of his book focuses on aggressive canine behaviour, perhaps the most serious problem because a third of all dogs in animal shelters are given up because of unwanted behaviour, accounting for about 1.5 million of the dogs euthanized annually in the United States. "To put this in perspective," Dodman wrote, "about three times as many dogs are destroyed because they have behavior problems as die from cancer. From a veterinary perspective, this is a huge-scale problem and one that demands immediate attention." Anxiety, fear-related problems, and compulsive behaviour make up Dodman's remaining concerns, all treatable, although with varying degrees of success, if a troubled dog's owner is willing to take his own role seriously. As Dodman warns, dog owners report that 42 per cent of their dogs have some kind of behaviour problem. *Forty-two per cent.* Many of these people – even the most well-intentioned – may be unaware of the ways in which they are influencing and contributing to their pet's undesirable behaviour. In other words, everyone involved may need therapy too.

My own experience is that pugs are natural therapy dogs. While neither Zoli nor Rennie had formal training, both took to the job with ease. Zoli spent a great deal of his life on campus with me, attending classes and literary readings, and comforting students who were almost inevitably drawn to him. He prompted stories and often made it possible for strangers to tell them to each other; and storytelling is therapeutic. University campuses that allow the presence of dogs are more congenial places for everyone. Students have sat in my office laughing while they petted Zoli, taken consolation from him while telling an upsetting story or discussing a poor mark, even relaxed before a dreaded final exam or oral thesis defence. One young woman talked herself out of an unwanted abortion while stroking him, a young man with ADHD regularly dog-sat for Zoli and found it helped him to concentrate on his reading. Often students I'd never taught came up to me to ask, "Is that Zoli?" and then spoke about missing a family dog back home. Zoli always greeted them gustily, as if exclaiming, "Hey, a new friend." Dogs as therapists change public space, making it more humane.

In recent years I've spent less time on campus, so Rennie's therapy work had a different focus – he spent many long hours in my mother's nursing home, cheering patients with Alzheimer's and dementia. Evenings, when I went to feed my mother at her place in the dining room, the five other ladies at her table waited to see Rennie, who sat alertly on my lap as they offered their own stories and reached out to pet him. "Does he eat butter?" one woman asked every night before seguing into a memory about the kitchen adventures of a childhood dog, then someone else spoke of a remembered Chihuahua or poodle or sheltie. Most of the stories had humorous endings, and the ladies' eyes brightened with their memories and retellings. Another woman who never talked would sometimes make a remark or two in German about a childhood dachshund, and if my dog and I passed her several minutes later, she'd make the same remark again. Stroke victims leaned from their wheelchairs to catch Rennie's attention, and even the nurses and aides liked to give his head a pat. My mother still remembered Rennie's name when she forgot everyone else's, and smiled blissfully when he settled in her lap. While the nursing home had its own resident therapy dog, Ennis, a noisy black Lab-shar-pei mix who had received therapy training, Rennie's gentle personality won people to him immediately. Elderly residents who couldn't take care of themselves, as well as some of their families, often asked if I was going to breed him (no), and then who his breeder was. This, I think, is therapy at its best.

TIME

During one of many escapades in the novel *Lassie Come-Home*, the collie is stymied by a command given at an unexpected time of day, and Eric Knight wrote, "It was Lassie's time sense that did it – that curious sense in an animal which tells it exactly what time of the day it is." I want to linger here with a story of my own. In the fall of 1985, I took a three-month sabbatical from my job in publishing to work on a collection of short stories. My mother had just undergone surgery so I decided to spend a month at my parents' home to help out during her recovery, which meant I spent a lot of time with Buster, who was then a year old. It was a mild autumn and every night, about nine o'clock, I took Buster for a long walk. My parents never went for walks after dark, so the experience was a new one for the dog, and he took to it with enthusiasm. After two or three evenings I noticed that promptly at 8:55 p.m. he came to sit at my feet and looked up at me, awaiting our departure. But how, I wondered, did he know the exact time? When we turned back the clocks at the end of October, Buster somehow made the adjustment without consulting a watch. This puzzled me all the more. If he had an internal clock, how did it know to add an hour? Did he notice that night had fallen earlier?

Ten years later, when I had a dog of my own, I wasn't surprised that Zoli came to sit at my feet every evening at the same time, before his dinner hour. This made sense, as if there were a clock in his stomach, since pugs definitely love to eat. (I feed my dogs three times each day – breakfast, a small lunch, and dinner.) Unfortunately most writers about dogs skip the subject of time. As Clive D.L. Wynne wrote in *Do Animals Think?* the study of animal behaviour is "such a patchy affair that today's declarations about skills that all animals have could be proved wrong tomorrow." Still, he ventured that animals show a sense of time, "both the time of day and also the length of brief and arbitrary time intervals on the scale of seconds to minutes." This doesn't help explain Buster's nightly behaviour though it does confirm my sense that something interesting was going on. I've asked myself about signals I might have inadvertently been sending, clues that Buster may have picked up. As Stanley Coren has written, "If we want to learn the language of the dog's mind, we must learn the vocabulary provided by his senses." Time is, of course, linked to memory. Vicki Hearne addressed this in *Adam's Task: Calling Animals by Name*, when she wrote about training horses, an act she considered morally defensible because horses have a sense of time. While they lack a human sense of the past and future, they don't live only in the present. She suggested that their concept of time is best expressed by the ideas of "'not yet, here and gone.' You can't make appointments with such tenses, but you can remember, and you can anticipate the future with no little anxiety." In Hearne's terms, dogs are not unlike horses. Buster's memory knew that some time after dinner – but not immediately after it – we'd go for a long walk. Each night, if we hadn't yet taken the walk, if it wasn't here and happening, and if we hadn't just returned, the walk was out there waiting for us. The rest still remains a mystery. Perhaps Buster had reached the limits of his anxiety and wanted to remind me to get moving, as if we had an appointment.

TRAINERS AND TRAINING

There's a wonderful comic moment in *The Broadway Melody of 1938*, a black-and-white showbiz musical from 1937, when a dozen small dogs climb onto the dining-room table of a theatrical rooming house, and the landlady (played by the great borscht-belt singer Sophie Tucker) calls out to their master, who is one of her tenants: "Why did you allow those dogs to get on my table?" They're trained dogs, he retorts. "Did you train them that way?" she asks. "No, that was their own idea."

Dog trainers are like ice cream, with the flavour-of-the-month a sales feature. At the time of this writing, Cesar Millan and his dominance methods in *Dog Whisperer* may be on the way out, and Tamar Geller, a former Israeli army-intelligence officer, on the rise. Author of *The Loved Dog*, Geller advises positive-reinforcement training along with pampering, and she has criticized Millan as a man who "wants a dog to be a 'calm submissive.' I do not. I do not want anybody in relation with me to be a submissive." Her ascent on bestseller lists highlights one problem of advice about training – where to look? I'm not going to try to add to the wealth of available advice about dog training. I've mentioned some admirable books, and make no claim to professional expertise in this area, with its vague professional standards. Fashions in training styles are cyclical, and the publishing industry is alert to the next new approach. We're a society with serious problems around learning, self-discipline, and motivation – just look at the increasing figures for the high-school dropout rate over the last decade. Why would we do a better job with dog training? But you have to start somewhere. At least avoid training books and videos sporting celebrity names and endorsements – they're beside the point. Millan was advertised as a trainer to the stars (Oprah, Nicolas Cage, and Will Smith) while Bashkim Dibra's video *Simple Solutions* touted Kim Basinger and Henry Kissinger; so what?

When buying a training manual, the names to look for are not those of celebrities with troubled dogs but trainers who've made a serious contribution to the subject. In July, 2007, *The New York Times* ran a deservedly long obituary for Laurence Mancuso, the founding abbot of the Monks of New Skete, an abbey north of Albany, New York, renowned for its holistic approach to dog training as well as the breeding of exceptional German shepherds; in the previous July, the paper ran an equally impressive obituary for Arthur J. Haggerty, a former army captain and the most famous American dog trainer in recent memory. Haggerty, who had trained dogs for more than 150 feature films, 450 television commercials and Broadway plays like *Annie*, as well as military dogs and police dogs, also founded his own training academy, first on Manhattan's Upper East Side and then, after thirty years, relocating to Los Angeles and later to Florida. Unfortunately he never wrote a book. Mancuso, on the other hand, left behind a rich tradition of training and one of the true modern dog classics, *How to Be Your Dog's Best Friend*, published in 1978 and now in its fortieth printing. Like Tamar Geller, the Monks of New Skete think that dog-training should involve tremendous positive reinforcement; they encourage cuddling and massaging, and even sleeping with your pet (there's that dog on the bed once more).

A few dogs, however, need more than cuddles. An aggressive dog can become dangerous; inappropriate training might make the situation worse. Choke collars and the like should never be the first resort. Begin instead with a visit to your dog's veterinarian in case the problem has a medical basis. If the dog hasn't been socialized at obedience classes, blame yourself, not your pet, for some of its troubling behaviour. It may be hard to admit but a dog's problems often stem from its humans. Almost all trainers and training manuals emphasize patience, difficult to hear in our fast-moving culture. An untrained dog is as easily distracted as its owner. Yet a dog can teach us patience if we slow down to its rhythm. This is an exciting part of the human/ dog bond, an exchange that's not valued enough; dogs can be good trainers, too.

The idea of training a dog presupposes a goal, or a set of them, and training manuals alone can't convey all the possibilities. An unusual novel comes to mind here because it takes the idea of training into a new dimension. *The Dogs of Babel* by Carolyn Parkhurst is the story of a man – a linguist by training – whose wife was murdered in the presence of the family dog Lorelei, a Rhodesian ridgeback. Parkhurst builds on the premise that "dogs are witnesses" as the narrator attempts to find ways for his dog to reveal what she knows. Their experiments and training sessions depend on the man's precise observations of his dog, but communication is, all said, a kind of training of the self and the other. An unconventional page-turner, Parkhurst's novel tempts us to wonder if we may ask too little of ourselves and our pets.

If people tried to think like a dog, they'd have fewer problems with training. I've seen friends frustrate themselves over housebreaking a new puppy while ignoring an obvious aspect of their problem, like the weather. If you live in the northeast or midwest, for instance, don't get a dog in the middle of the snowy cold winter, which makes housebreaking much harder. And don't start with paper training indoors and expect your puppy to make an easy springtime adjustment to the lawn or sidewalk. Morgan, the sweet-tempered Cavalier, drove everyone to distraction when he refused to be housebroken in January or February or March. With Toronto's streets full of snow, icy patches and rock salt, who could blame him? Zoli and Rennie, on the other hand, took to the late-spring and early-summer weather without a problem. So if you live where the winter climate can be severe, wait until May, if at all possible, before you get a pet. That's what I mean by thinking like a dog.

TRAVEL

In the Greek-Orthodox tradition many old icons show St. Christopher, patron of travellers, in profile with a dog's head instead of a man's. This mysterious image may reassure anyone contemplating a trip with a dog, but what does it mean? In Eastern Christianity, Christopher is regarded as a descendant of the Cynocephali, giants with human bodies and dog heads. Western Christianity, in keeping with the tradition, includes the legend that St. Christopher once carried the Christ child across a stream, hence, another common image of the saint with a baby in his arms. As a reward, Christopher's head was apparently changed to match his body. However you see it, travel and dogs have an ancient link.

One autumn, during a book tour, I checked into a splendid Vancouver hotel with Zoli. A few minutes after settling in our room, there was a soft knock on the door. I never expected to find a middle-aged man carrying a large tray with two white china dog bowls, a dog treat and bottled water, everything to make Zoli welcome. Earlier that summer, however, during a stormy car trip from Toronto to Boston, I decided to stop just after crossing the New York-Massachusetts state line and take a room for the night, to avoid the increasingly severe rain. None of the motels I found – all, to my eye, rather seedy – would allow a dog on the premises, so I had to drive the Mass Pike on to Boston in pretty rough weather, arriving long after midnight. High- and low-end travel? Unlike the pet-food industry, which has grown dramatically in the last half century, the travel industry has discovered dogs only in recent years, and one can wonder what it will eventually provide.

Before heading out on any trip, it's important to consider why your dog is coming along and what you'll find ahead. If you won't leave your dog in a kennel (and I won't), and you don't have friends or family you can trust to watch it, sometimes it's easier – though not necessarily desireable – to stay home. But not always. While dogs are pack animals, idyllic images of travelling with a pet can quickly collapse against reality. What, after all, is best for the dog? And why do some travel writers seem vaguely uncomfortable with this subject, or amused by it? In an "Escape" section of *The New York Times*, Wendy Knight regarded travelling with dogs as an expression of a culture where "dogs and cats have become surrogate children (and grandchildren)." Surrogate *grandchildren*? Her remark says more about a common embarrassment before human affection for animals than it does about the pet-travelling phenomenon. On the other hand, journalists who regularly focus on dogs are far more matter-of-fact about pet travel in their columns.

A dog's size and age can determine its travelability, along with health conditions and other variables only its human guardian can know. Air travel takes planning in advance, and in the post-9/11 world most airlines are less cooperative than they once were about bringing a pet into the cabin. (When we flew economy, Zoli was always comfortable in his soft-sided Sherpa bag under the seat in front of me, though during one business-class trip to New York City the stewardess allowed him to sit on my lap and even fed him bits of warm blueberry muffin – something I never expect to see again.) A dog's size matters for cabin travel, but I can't imagine putting any dog into the cargo hold and forcing it to undergo unexplainable stress at the very least, while taking the risk that you might never see your pet again. Both the American Society for the Prevention of Cruelty to Animals and the Humane Society warn of the dangers of cargo holds. Flat-faced dogs like my pug might not even survive the trip.

Car travel is another matter, and a dog needs its own seat belt or portable kennel or crate for safety's sake. A dog moving about any car freely is a risky prospect. And what to do with the dog when you need to stop for a restaurant or bathroom break? Travel sections of most newspapers now regularly print articles on travelling with pets, which suggests that the issue is a serious one deserving attention. On road trips in the middle of summer I've often spotted panting dogs locked alone in cars, and I can't imagine how any dog owner can be so thoughtless. Most bus and train lines do not allow dogs on board, so cars remain the inevitable choice for many travellers with dogs. (The American Kennel Club offers a free AKC Travel Kit, and similar guides are available from a wide range of sources, including the AAA and the CAA.)

Luxury accommodations belong to a rarified world – the famous Parisian Four-Seasons-George V will provide a coverlet embroidered with your dog's name if it's custom-ordered in advance, as long as your dog fits the fifteen-pound limit, or is a guide dog – but every dog owner faces the same problem when suitcases come out: will the dog tag along? According to 2002 statistics from the Travel Industry Association of America, almost 30 million adults claim that they've travelled with a pet for a trip of 80 kilometres or more, and dogs made up nearly 80 per cent of these pets. In 2007, BringYourPet.com, a website for travellers with dogs, noted that in a survey of 100,000 of its users, 75 per cent had taken their pets along on trips. Many of these trips were probably visits to relatives, with a familiar destination. Trickier are the holidays that involve new cities, sightseeing, and hotels. Leaving a dog alone in a hotel room can be extremely stressful, and even the most accommodating staff will not tolerate prolonged barking and other disturbances. If you're travelling with family or friends, someone can always keep an eye on the dog. In *The Difficulty of Being a Dog*, a book I've mentioned several times, Roger Grenier described travelling with his dog Ulysses, a Saint-

Germain pointer. Along with the dog's pleasurable company, "He spared me the burdens of culture." Looking after the dog instead of visiting museums and churches, Grenier and Ulysses stayed outside comfortably – "And sometimes we even fell asleep, happy as clams." If you're travelling alone, as I usually do, you need to think carefully about the way your dog will change your trip, and what you're willing to give up for canine companionship.

Some of my happiest memories are of wandering about a damp beach in Ogunquit, Maine, on a misty August morning, with Zoli on leash, pulling ahead to explore, and Morgan carried snugly under my left arm because he refused to step on the wet sand, covered as it was with ocean debris; of driving to Florida through the West Virginia mountains on a clear March afternoon, Zoli at my side and Gluck's *Orfeo* on the CD player; of exploring bookstores in Cambridge, Massachusetts, with Rennie, before we sampled a pint of take-out clam chowder from Boston Chowdra; I could go on and on. Though I'm not a suntanning type, there are more beaches in my list than I might have thought. Dogs like beaches, so why not? You adapt. I have one university colleague who has smuggled her toy poodle into the Louvre in a large shoulder bag, though I'm not up for such subterfuge, and anyway pugs are too large and lively for such concealment. If you're persistent, however, it's amazing how many places will welcome a well-behaved dog. And there are always more beaches.

UNCANNY

In his postwar essay of 1919, known in English as "The Uncanny," Sigmund Freud wrote about a group of subjects that have often been pushed to the side of scientific inquiry and linked to the world of psychic phenomenon and the paranormal: ambiguous feelings of what is eerie, unsettling and frightening, and "anything to do with death, dead bodies, revenants, spirits and ghosts." This essay has recently caught the attention of scholars working in the humanities. Although many aspects of Freud's writing have now been debunked as unscientific, and he has lost much of his medical appeal – at its zenith in North America in the 1950s – as a literary figure Freud appears to be in the ascent.

At the risk of sounding like a new-age guru, I'm going to borrow Freud's "uncanny" as an umbrella term for the paranormal, parapsychology, and telepathy – all of the strange happenings that traditional science eschews. Freud, as one might predict, traced the uncanny back to infantile desires and fears, but his thoughts still allowed for complex tensions between the unconscious life and observable, material reality. Even the least superstitious person has heard stories of exceptional and mysterious canine behaviour, though too often it happens to other people and seldom to ourselves and our own dogs. These are the kinds of stories about a sixth sense that Rupert Sheldrake, a British biochemist and former research fellow at the Royal Society, has collected in *Dogs That Know When Their Owners Are Coming Home and Other Unexplained Powers of Animals*. Sheldrake, however, is no pushover for mumbo-jumbo. He argues that a complex memory system, which he calls "morphic fields," is part of the bond between humans and animals, and that the bond is "not just metaphorical but real, literal connections." Dogs who know when their owners are coming home, who can warn of epileptic fits and have premonitions about earthquakes, who can find their way home alone from distances of hundreds of miles – it's puzzling stories like these that Sheldrake examines in the context of quantum physics, where space and time are not the simpler chronological pattern we normally experience without much thought. Sheldrake has a name for this phenomenon, *morphic resonance*, which allows memory of past events to come alive, across time, in the present.

Sheldrake's approach is far more elaborate than the common-sense views of Desmond Morris, at one time the Curator of Mammals at the London Zoo, in *Dogwatching*. In "Do Dogs Have a Sixth Sense?" Morris explains the traditional link between dogs and ghosts quite simply. When dog owners claim that their dog has "seen a ghost" because the animal is staring at nothing the owner can see, perhaps growling or whining, the hair on its back rising, the pet refusing to move, an assumption that the cause is a ghost is understandable but unfounded. "The truth is that it probably detected a particularly strong scent deposit, not from another dog, but from some other animal species." Other incidents of sixth-sense behaviour are explained in a similar, matter-of-fact manner, and Morris is always convincing. Yet I don't like to stop there. At the end of Sheldrake's book, he invites readers to send him the unique and puzzling results of their own observations of their animals. Good scientists always remain on the lookout for corroboration as well as for new challenges. It's important to remember that the study of animal consciousness is a relatively new field of research. As Sheldrake once put it, "Scientists are beginning to take a look at what pet owners already know." In 1922, Albert Payson Terhune published the novel *His Dog* about a dirt-poor farmer named Link Ferris whose life is changed for the good after he saves a wounded collie. In one episode, when the dog's behaviour puzzles his new master, Terhune wrote:

> And, all suddenly, Link Ferris understood. He himself did not know how the knowledge came to him. A canine psychologist might perhaps have told him that there is always an occult telepathy between the mind of a thoroughbred dog and its master, a power which gives them a glimpse into the other's processes of thought.

The image of "occult telepathy" is a telling one. It's humbling to think how little we've learned since this passage was written.

Many pet owners seek to understand their dogs through our

popular culture, which thrives on the uncanny while simplifying and packaging it. Sonia Fitzpatrick, the host of the popular cable-television series *The Pet Psychic* on the Animal Planet network, manages to be simultaneously both fascinating and a little creepy. With her sculpted eyebrows she resembles the sketch of a stylish praying mantis drawn by Al Hirschfeld. Though she's based in Houston, Texas, Fitzpatrick has maintained her clipped British accent, which makes her sound less like a new-age nut than a sophisticated grande dame. In her memoir, also called *The Pet Psychic*, she writes of her idyllic childhood in the Midlands countryside with her family and at her grandmother's cottage, a time when she could hear animals speaking to her and speak back to them in telepathic communion. But only her grandmother believed her stories. After her father killed several pet geese for the Christmas dinner of 1950, when Fitzpatrick was ten years old, a kind of curtain descended between the girl and the animal world. A year later, her problems with hearing loss were finally discovered by doctors. What to make of this? Had the animal voices been a kind of compensatory sensation for partial deafness? Eventually, after "an angelic visitation" in 1994 and some words from St. Francis, Fitzpatrick reconnected with her voices – or the ability to hear them – and she launched a career.

Watching Fitzpatrick console grieving pet owners about the loss of a beloved animal companion can be curiously disheartening (reincarnation appears to be one message, along with communion from the beyond). Yet Fitzpatrick brings her skills – whatever they are – to the aid of troubled animals in numerous veterinary clinics and animal shelters. She has described her abilities as something far more elaborate than simply hearing voices, but rather seeing images or physical pictures as well as receiving sensations on her body that correspond to an animal's energy ("It is easier to communicate in this way with animals than with other humans because animals are receptive to telepathic transmissions, whereas most humans, through years of conditioning, are not."). Since we project our wishes and fears onto our animals, as anyone who has even heard of Freud and transference will know, it isn't necessary to sound as reductionist as Desmond Morris sometimes can and dismiss Fitzpatrick altogether. Where the trouble starts, for me at least, is when she moves from observing living animals, often in distress, to communicating with animals after their death. But her advice on housebreaking and various other behaviour problems is as sensible as her thoughts on being "a responsible pet parent." She might have been popular with Canada's eccentric tenth prime minister, William Lyon Mackenzie King (in office from 1935 to 1948), who held regular seances, using a crystal ball or ouija board, to contact his favourite deceased dogs, all Irish terriers. Running a government during the Second World War must have been extremely stressful, but that may not be sufficient explanation of Mackenzie King's psychology.

Communing with dogs takes a spiritual turn in Jean Houston's *Mystical Dogs*, the right book for anyone who wants to read about dogs as well as Mexican spirit guides, bodhisattvas and the mystic path in William Blake's poetry. Drawn to ecstatic states of an exotic nature, Houston loves the word *mystery*, which she particularly associates with her dog Luna, "perhaps in part because of her wolf lineage." (Here again is the preference for wolfish dogs, as if they're somehow purer than ordinary purebreds, let alone mutts.) The spirit world is always giving Houston gifts in the form of special dogs – she might get along very well with Shirley MacLaine. People without such generous gifts can look to animal communicators like Fitzpatrick and Dr. Doolittle, who aren't alone in their claims to have conversations with animals. In fact, Fitzpatrick is part of a growing community that makes a business of it. Pet psychics, also referred to as animal communicators, are finding a lucrative niche for themselves in the ever-growing marketplace aimed at pet owners. Word of mouth travels across the continent, with the

better-known communicators charging fees ranging from $100 to
$200 per hour. Anyone with cash enough can ask about a dog's
problems or learn about its past lives. Long-distance telephone
consultations are optional (one West Hollywood communicator
offered sixty minutes for $100, in 2001), while another, near San
Francisco, even runs training courses. And new-age California
isn't the only host to animal communicators – prominent ones
practise in smaller towns across North America, from Kitchener,
Ontario (Beata Pillach), to Gilbertsville, Pennsylvania (Anita
Curtis and Carlos Jiminez, a chiropractic veterinarian). No, I've
never consulted one. For the curious, Donna Ball includes a self-
doubting animal communicator in her mystery novel *Smoky
Mountain Tracks*.

It would be too easy to dismiss these people – and their work
– as charlatanism and be done with the subject. While traditional
science and orthodox religion offer their versions of reality,
legitimate questions about the human/animal connection remain
unanswered. Surveys suggest that contemporary Americans like
to think of themselves as among the most religious people on the
planet, with a majority belief in angels (and some occult notions
that traditional religions seldom espouse), so it's not a big leap
of faith to animal telepathy. As more people live with dogs and
cats, they will inevitably wonder what their companions might
have to say to them, or about them. Meanwhile, the increasing
social isolation of our techno-savvy life exacerbates this situation.
Alternative science, like alternative medicine, may be the last
hope of the desperate, but the desire to explain the unknown is
as old as human consciousness and present in our earliest myths
about human and animal transformations.

All said, I'm frustrated by reductionist explanations of dog
behaviour. This leaves me sometimes taking refuge in the
anecdotal – an interesting place to rest because it's open-ended.
One example: the great French writer Colette, known to North

"Colette with Dog" (1935), photographed by Walter Limot. Here she holds her French bulldog Souci.

Americans mainly for a novella that was the basis of the movie musical *Gigi*, claimed to be able to communicate with animals. One night in 1926, during a beach holiday at Saint-Tropez with her husband, Maurice Goudeket, she awoke with a start. Colette appeared to be listening to something that Maurice could not hear, and she said, "He's drowning." When her husband asked "Who?" she replied, "A dog." In her nightgown and robe, Colette suddenly hurried out of their room, ran down into the water and saved a fox terrier from drowning. Although it's true that Goudeket adored his famous older wife, and gladly contributed to her legend in his memoir, *something* must have happened that night. Colette was not a foolish woman given to sentimentality. In fact, she wrote pointedly about dogs and cats, tolerating little nonsense. In her novel *Break of Day*, she made several remarks that show how carefully she had observed her many pets over the years: "Shall we never have done with that cliché, so stupid that it could only be human, about the sympathy of animals for man when he is unhappy? Animals love happiness almost as much as we do," and "All animals who are well treated choose whatever is best in us and in their surroundings." If I were a dog, I'd probably want to talk to someone that wise.

Dogs do make choices though we don't always understand them, no matter how hard we try. I want to relate an incident that still puzzles me and has left me asking, What *really* happens at death? During the Christmas holidays of 2007, my mother's illness worsened. Like many people suffering from dementia, she had forgotten how to swallow, a life-threatening situation. I was fortunately able to be at her side and help with her care. Rennie was with us too, during her visits to the hospital and also back in the nursing home, when, in January, she began what is called active dying.

On her last night, Rennie slept beside me in a chair next to my mother's bed, and shortly after 4:00 a.m. he jumped from my lap onto her bed (he'd spent time there before) and curled up at her feet, his head on her ankle. She died peacefully in less than half an hour, and when the nurses asked us to leave the room while they prepared my mother's body for the undertaker, Rennie remained behind in his place on the bed. I can't emphasize enough how unusual this was for him, since Rennie ordinarily acts like my shadow. Waiting in the corridor, with the door to my mother's room half-open, I expected him to hurry out any moment. But he didn't appear. Twenty-five minutes later he emerged, followed by the nurses. They said that he'd remained on the bed the entire time and once even growled when he'd been motioned away. In the years I've lived with Rennie I've never heard him growl, and I can't explain his behaviour.

Since that night I've mentioned the incident to several veterinarians, other doctors, dog trainers and, of course, friends and family. None of their well-intentioned explanations satisfy me. Rennie, it's been said, was protecting my mother, or watching her soul depart, or observing her astral body take leave, or finding himself paralyzed by the scents of death. Whatever happened, it did not frighten him, at least not enough to cause him to leave the room; in fact, the experience was one that made him overcome his ordinary instincts and remain beside my mother instead of following me. I like to think that he was guarding her. From what? I can't put myself in his mind so I won't venture an explanation. I'll just have to live with the uncanny.

UNDERWORLD

Cosmologically speaking, the underworld is a place in the geography of the human imagination. Whether it's seen as a spiritual location in mythology and religion or a symbolic one in philosophy and poetry, this troubling piece of real estate has, from the start, managed to accommodate the human/dog bond. The ancient Egyptians worshipped Anubis, the jackal-headed god also sometimes represented with a dog's head. Anubis indicated the roads to the other world that the dead might take, presided over embalmments and played an important role in funeral prayers. The ancient Chinese had the Celestial Dog (Tian gou), who helped the Second Lord drive evil spirits from the palace of the August Personage of Jade in the highest level of heaven. And the Greeks had Cerberus, probably the most familiar of mythological dogs, the three-headed dog who guarded the entrance to Hades. They also had the Dog Star – as did the ancient Persians – as well as the Lesser Dog Star, which was, in fact, the transformation of the faithful dog companion of the daughter of Icarius, who had been carried into the heavens by her father after Dionysus took revenge on the Attican women for...well, the story goes on and on. Similar mythological dogs have an important place in many old legends, among the endless cycles of mating and generation, aristocratic horses, and soaring birds. In the Norse epics, chained dogs guard the palace of the giant Gymir in the kingdom of the giants (dogs frequently appear in their working mode as guards), and Garm, a dog from the kingdom of the dead, was killed in a battle with Tyr during the twilight of the gods, but not until he had fatally mauled that warrior. In Africa, the Ugandan Nandi blamed death on a dog that had been sent to inform mankind of human mortality. Poorly received, the dog warned that humans would die and not be reborn like the moon unless they fed him well. When they mocked him instead, he announced that all men would die and only the moon would be reborn.

This link between dogs, death, and appetite was written into two seminal books of the Western literary canon. In Book VI of Virgil's *Aeneid* (lines 478-88), an epic poem about the founding of Rome, the Sybil, Aeneas's guide to the underworld, approaches Cerberus, the three-headed guard of "the Kingdom of Death," with a piece of doped honey-cake. Despite the serpents writhing around his neck, Cerberus gulps down the dangerous treat and falls into a deep sleep, letting Aeneas and the Sybil pass by. Some guard dog! Nearly fourteen centuries later Dante Alighieri picked up on Cerberus's weakness for his *Inferno*, the first section of his epic account of medieval cosmology, *The Divine Comedy*. In Canto VI (lines 13-33), devoted to the circle of hell marked for gluttons, the ravenous barking dog is now fed a handful of dirt by Dante's guide, Virgil; of course, Cerberus swallows it at once. But in defence of Cerberus – if that's possible – despite his tenure in the horrific underworld, he does not revert to wild, wolfish behaviour. Instead, he continues to embody the human/dog bond and, oddly enough, trust a human hand outstretched with food, or something that resembles it. Though Virgil and Dante probably wouldn't approve, you almost have to feel sorry for him.

Without books like these it's difficult to reach back into the canine myths of the past, but the work of anthropologists can sometimes get us close to ancient beliefs through a living oral tradition. At the end of the nineteenth century Sir James George Frazer, one of the pioneers of folklore studies and comparative anthropology, included superstitions about dogs in his encyclopedic history, *The Golden Bough: A Study in Magic and Religion*. Dogs have been sacrificed to tree spirits, to war gods, and at bear feasts; they have been used in ceremonies for rain-making, fertility, and against madness, illness, and sin; they were eaten in sacred rites, feared as witches, and treated as suitable scapegoats for kings and other humans. Such activities build on the association of dogs and mortality. This convention is still with us today, and has become a commonplace in books and movies about the supernatural. There's a particularly horrifying scene in *The Omen* (1976), which starred Gregory Peck as the American ambassador to England who is caught up in the activities of the anti-Christ. Near the end of the film, Peck visits an ancient Etruscan cemetery north of Rome where four monstrous, black hell hounds guard the graves of the mother of the anti-Christ and the ambassador's kidnapped son. It won't spoil things to say that one of the graves contains the skeleton of a jackal. Good superstitions seldom die.

Are such beliefs simply to be lumped together under the heading of "mythology" and set aside, or left to folklorists and anthropologists? Perhaps one alternative occurs in the writings of the eighteenth-century British poet and satirist Alexander Pope, who included such beliefs in his long poem "An Essay on Man" (1733-34). Examining ideas about natural religion, he had this to say regarding religious systems and practices then thought of, and dismissed, as pagan:

> Lo, the poor Indian! Whose untutored mind
> Sees God in clouds, or hears him in the wind;
> His soul, proud Science never taught to stray
> Far as the solar walk, or milky way;
> Yet simple Nature to his hope has given,
> Behind the cloud-topped hill, an humbler heaven;
> Some safer world in depth of woods embraced,
> Some happier island in the watery waste,
> Where slaves once more their native land behold,
> No fiends torment, no Christians thirst for gold.
> To Be, contents his natural desire,
> He asks no Angel's wing, no Seraph's fire;
> But thinks, admitted to that equal sky,
> His faithful dog shall bear him company.

Often associated with the philosophy of deism, where God is seen as a creator but absent from the universe and its workings or laws, Pope barely conceals his sympathy for his "poor Indian!" and his "faithful" dog, who, at least in "natural desire," appear bound for eternity together. Pope was not a predecessor of our new-age gurus – in fact, he would probably have enjoyed mocking them – but his emphasis on what is "natural" in the heart of man is worth remembering. Myths, after all, explain the things that otherwise elude everyday language.

In the face of death we're loathe to leave our dogs behind. They sometimes accompany us, lead us and even serve as guards; they're there. And like Cerberus, they do not let us return to the world of the living. Only Orpheus was able to charm the hell hound Cerberus – with the music of his lyre – and return to earth. In time, his story also ended badly. It's as if the short life of a dog has become so deeply embedded in the human psyche that it is associated with the mysteries of death itself.

UNLEASHED

Unleashed or off lead, whatever one calls it, this state can be dangerous for a dog. Dangerous, but all too common. In an early scene in Virginia Woolf's *Flush*, when her canine hero is taken for a walk in Regent's Park in London, threatening men marched about ominously and Flush kept close to his walker – "he gladly accepted the protection of the chain." *Protection* is the key word.

First, some personal anecdotes. Wherever I've travelled, there's a pattern among other dog walkers. Large dogs roam off lead more often than small and mid-sized dogs, who are usually leashed. In my Toronto neighbourhood I've seen several unleashed dogs run over. One man regularly walked his Chihauhaus off lead, and they would dash across the street to other dogs, so it was essential to keep on eye on them. I saw one hit by a car in a nearby intersection, the other's death I heard about later. Another family had a mangy white poodle who wandered the streets not only unleashed but uncollared. One spring morning, after the dog was nearly killed in front of me, I tried to find its owners, and when I eventually learned who they were I notified the Humane Society. That summer, collared, the dog continued to wander alone until it ended its life under some car's wheels. Anyone who has unintentionally run over a dog will know how painful it can be for the driver. On a bright summer evening in the early 1980s, my parents and I were returning from some shopping, my father at the wheel, when a black Lab made a wild run across the street in front of our car. There was no way to spot it until the moment of collision, and nowhere to turn. Dogs can't be trusted to wander unleashed and unattended even in their own yards and driveways. We never knew what that dog had suddenly decided to chase – a squirrel, the occasional wild rabbit that sometimes appears in the city, or just a shadow? – but it was only acting like a dog.

Not all stories of unleashed dogs end in death, although they can include other problems. A neighbour of mine has a ten-year-old mixed breed named Jenny who resembles a small sheepdog. One afternoon, while she was walking her with a leash, another neighbour passed by with her golden retrievers off lead. The smaller of them attacked and bit Jenny. I saw the incident, and watched the owner of the retrievers walk on, as if she had no part in the episode. My neighbour called out to her but she only walked faster. We followed the woman around the block to her house, to learn her address in case there were veterinary bills. But biting isn't the only trouble unleashed dogs cause or face. Over the years Teresa Stratas and I have spent a lot of time talking about our various dogs, and commiserating about their health problems, but this story of hers is unique. In the early 1960s, when she was first singing at the Metropolitan Opera, Teresa rented an apartment on West 69th Street in New York City's Upper West Side, where she frequently walked her white toy poodle, Pudgy, off lead. The dog would follow after her, enjoying their outing, but on several occasions a local cop-on-the-beat teased Teresa about leashing-up her dog. One evening, on their usual walk, Teresa turned to see that Pudgy was missing. In a panic she retraced her steps, but the poodle was nowhere in sight. She hurried at once to the nearby police precinct, where Pudgy was sitting on a glass-topped counter ledge, surrounded by admirers. Under the glass, Teresa remembers, were posters and photographs of most-wanted criminals. The policeman had shown one potential danger an unleashed pet might face, and since then Teresa has always leashed her dogs before walking them anywhere.

Sometimes the unleashed are lucky. Spotty, my childhood fox terrier, was a gentleman but also a wanderer who enjoyed spurts of independence. A few times a year, during the first decade of his life, if he could sneak out an open door he ran off for the day as fast as the proverbial bat out of hell. This made everyone frantic with worry. Once his absence was noticed I'd take my bike and ride around the neighbourhood, my sister might be on hers, and when my father got home from work he would drive us about in the family car. In winter, we went on foot. I can still remember carrying Spotty home in knee-high snow because I'd forgotten his leash. Usually he wandered back by himself, exhausted, but if any of us came upon him during his adventures, he followed willingly. Over the years he'd been spotted by neighbours several miles away, and how he managed to avoid oncoming cars still amazes me. One summer he vanished overnight and we were certain he'd been run over. The next evening, when my father drove around, I saw him several blocks from our house, hooked to a chain in someone's backyard; we claimed him immediately. Another time he slunk home at the end of his day and went to sit quietly beside my mother, who was at her sewing machine. When she looked down she saw that one of his ears was bloody – he must have been in some sort of fight. He never concerned himself with our anxieties and never learned any lessons, he just got older and apparently lost the taste for a good run.

There is, of course, a counter-view in favour of unleashed dogs, and it's argued by Ted Kerasote in *Merle's Door: Lessons from a Freethinking Dog.* According to Kerasote, a wildlife writer, time off leash is essential to a dog's well-being. He shares this position with San Francisco's SPCA and New York City's FIDO, a dog advocacy group, and no doubt there's some truth to it. But most dogs do not have a rural, outdoor life in northwestern Wyoming, like Merle's, and even those that do remain at risk if they adventure onto a nearby highway. In recent decades some city parks have set aside areas for off-leash dogs, and these have become popular recreation spots, though not without contention. (Like most dog owners, Kerasote cares about his pet's needs, but he still sought to subordinate the golden Lab's instincts to his own own. His pages about "acclimatizing" Merle to the sounds of gunshot from pistols and a high-powered rifle – in order to train him as a hunting dog – were, to me, frankly troubling.)

Each of these stories embodies a warning, but unfortunately the people who need to hear are probably not listening. Every year countless dogs are killed in traffic accidents, while others are maimed and some, who run off, are lost. There's a fine sense of freedom involved in walking down the street with a dog off lead, but a city street isn't the country path Timmy wandered on with Lassie.

VETERINARIANS

Imagine a snowy Christmas eve – a heavy downfall. The streets haven't been cleared, yet a middle-aged couple heads out to their local pharmacy to fill a prescription. Not far from their front steps they spot a puppy buried to his neck in the snow. There's no choice but to save the abandoned dog and, after the rescue, to tend to it.

A veterinarian is needed and fortunately the couple has a good friend to call on, despite the holiday. This scene takes place in Magda Szabó's novel *The Door*, and it has an archetypal quality to it – that first moment between a dog and its prospective master – which is soon followed by an inevitable visit to the veterinarian. Only a few people, however, can count one as a friend.

Today we're quick to trust experts of almost any kind, relying on their opinions rather than thinking for ourselves. This may sometimes be necessary, and if the expert is sound we're indeed lucky. The commonest way to chose a veterinarian is to look about one's neighbourhood, but it's wise to speak to friends or neighbours with pets since their experiences may not only be helpful but could save some unhappy moments later. Finding the right vet begins with a recognition that the relationship should be one of ongoing trust in order to achieve the best possible care. Many people my age who remember childhood dogs in the 1950s and 1960s, recall a time when the family pet went to the vet once a year for annual shots, and seldom in between. Advances in veterinary medicine have given today's dogs longer lives just as our deteriorating environment has brought them life-threatening diseases at earlier ages.

Veterinary medicine and training is now a sophisticated and popular field, and it's sometimes said that it's harder to get into a good veterinary program than into a standard medical school, at least in Britain and Canada. Recent statistics show that the twenty-eight schools of veterinary medicine in the United States graduate about 2,100 students annually (with about 8,500 enrolled at any one time). Accurate figures are hard to find, but one statistic from Britain – where there are seven colleges of veterinary medicine – suggests that for every single place in a veterinary college there are fourteen applicants, while for every two places at medical school there are five applicants. Furthermore, in recent decades the field has increasingly drawn more women, a change that will also leave a mark on the profession. In "Economic Emergency," Jennifer Fiala, a senior editor at *dvm Newsmagazine*, reported that the high debt acquired during veterinary training, along with modest salaries, was changing the future of veterinary medicine. (Starting American salaries are less than $55,000 a year while educational loans often total $150,000. Data from the American Veterinary Medical Association shows that education debt for entry-level salaries for new graduates more than doubled from 91.6 per cent in 1980 to 184 percent in 2007.) There are many reasons for this percentage increase but what matters in the end is that the cost-earnings ratio may make careers in veterinary medicine out of reach or particularly subject to economic distress. Veterinary medicine's debt-to-income ratio, Fiala wrote, can negatively influence a graduate's important decisions about buying a practice or a home, or even getting married. It can also result in flat application numbers to veterinary schools, lower-quality but wealthier candidates, and graduates who need to leave general practice for higher-earning specialties.

Veterinarians have to treat patients who can't describe their symptoms while dealing with their owners as well. Increasingly, they cover the same territory we expect from our own doctors, using the latest medical advances we want for ourselves: cleaning teeth to prevent not only dental damage but other diseases (80 per cent of dogs over the age of two have some periodontal disease); performing difficult surgeries, such as kidney transplants, as well as more common biopsies; administering anaesthesia, chemotherapy, blood transfusions, ultrasounds, MRIs, and that dreaded moment of euthanasia; handling chronic conditions such as arthritis, diabetes, epilepsy, blindness, and deafness; administering diet drugs to overweight patients who are underexercised and overfed – about 35 per cent of all American dogs, according to FDA statistics; and keeping up on new health scares, such as the life-threatening dog flu during the fall of 2005, which was contracted in some kennels, parks, animal shelters, and at dog shows. While a few vets specialize, most have to be a jack-of-all trades. The work must be among the more stressful of occupations, and statistics support this thought. The suicide rate for veterinarians is significantly higher than for other health-care professionals. In the United Kingdom, for example, it is nearly four times the national average. Richard Halliwell, a former president of the Royal College of Veterinary Surgeons, has even suggested a relation between these figures and the difficult task of euthanasia that is a common part of a veterinarian's life.

What is the working day of a veterinarian like? One place to find out is *Tell Me Where It Hurts: A Day of Humor, Healing and Hope in My Life as an Animal Surgeon* by Nick Trout, a British-trained surgeon at Angell Animal Medical Center, one of the most prominent and largest animal hospitals in North America, located in a suburb of Boston. Trout compresses twenty-five years of experience into a page-turning account of twenty-four hours in his life. Unlike the rural stories of James Herriot, the gentle Yorkshire veterinarian of the popular *All Creatures Great and Small*, Trout's stories focus mainly on dogs and cats, which take up 95 percent of his attention, but he does include some exotics like iguanas and snakes. For every success it seems there is a death. Trout writes movingly about euthanasia, and has a sharp eye for the human strengths and foibles of his clients; the stories of his canine patients always take into account the situations and personalities of their owner-companions, reinforcing the importance of the human/dog bond.

A straight talker, Trout speaks out against the cosmetic practice of ear-cropping and tail-docking (outlawed in Britain and much of Europe, along with Australia and New Zealand), as well as debarking and declawing, and he writes with passion about the nature of his profession. In our status-conscious society, veterinarians are seldom held in the same esteem as other medical doctors. He offers a spirited defence for a profession that is sometimes misunderstood. And he is justly troubled by an article in the July 2003 *Consumer Reports*, "Veterinary Care without Bite," which focused on the cost of animal health-care. "What has been happening to my profession's time-honored reputation for ethics and honesty?" he asks. "Why am I being made to feel like an ambulance-chasing lawyer?" (Lawyers won't like the comparison, but that's another matter.) Attempting an answer, Trout reminds his readers that a veterinary life today is not like Herriot's rural romance but one of stressful contemporary medicine, and "some of the alleged distress of pet owners" may come from a nostalgic view of the profession's origins. I'm not convinced. When this passage occurs, around page 250, Trout seems to have forgotten that his book began with a middle-of-the-night phone call to him because a surgical resident was making a botch of an emergency procedure. Many people have ambivalent feelings about all doctors – including veterinarians – because they seem to have power over life and death. While we know they aren't infallible, we wish they could be, and we fear risks, errors, and medical complications.

Given the number of books about dogs published each year, one might expect more of them to be written by veterinarians. Nick Trout is one of the exceptions, along with Louise Murray and Allen M. Schoen. Murray's book *Vet Confidential: An Insider's Guide to Protecting Your Pet's Health*, offers brief medical tips written for a general reader. More ambitious, Schoen puts his emphasis on alternative healing practices in *Kindred Spirits: How the Remarkable Bond Between Humans and Animals Can Change the Way We Live*. Schoen is a natural-born storyteller, and unlike many dog books that offer slight variations on a common body of information, *Kindred Spirits* covers unfamiliar, holistic ground, from Chinese herbs to chiropractic evaluation to touch therapy. Influenced by Buddhist thought and new-age writers like Deepak Chopra, Schoen emphasizes the way a pet's health relates to the spiritual bond with its guardian-owner. He often mentions "negative energy," which may put off some readers, and he advises his clients to "Learn to love without being attached." If such remarks strike you as too pat, too easy – my own reaction – Schoen's book can still be enjoyed for the stories he tells.

As is the case with any health professional, second opinions about more serious health issues should be considered. When he was several years old, Zoli had an irritation in his nose wrinkle, the part of a pug's face that includes the flap of skin known as the nose fold, which gives the breed its distinct appearance and needs to be regularly cleaned. One American veterinarian suggested "a little surgery," which he wanted to perform, to "trim back" the nose fold. Not only would it have altered the dog's appearance in the strangest of ways, but more important, it was medically unnecessary. Common sense told me not to listen, and in several weeks, with the use of a topical cream, the problem was resolved. Less dramatic was an incident after Zoli needed to have his teeth cleaned during an August I spent away from Toronto and was unable to take him to his regular vet. The doctor, who disappeared after lunch, left the message that she'd had to remove half a dozen of Zoli's teeth. Her clerk told me to go ahead and feed him his regular supper, I mentioned that he ate dry food, and she insisted that this would not pose a problem. Bad advice. I already knew enough to make Zoli a scrambled egg and avoid the bleeding that might have occurred if he'd chomped away on his regular food. Experience with dogs teaches you to think proactively. Just ask questions, since your dog can't, and keep asking them until you're satisfied. Occasionally there's no choice but to weather a distracted or thoughtless vet. Every profession has a share of people to avoid and it's sentimental to think that veterinary medicine would be the exception just because it involves animals.

Since it can be frustrating to read a praise-filled portrait of someone you're not likely to meet, I'll confine myself to only a few words. Rennie (and before him, Zoli and Morgan) and I have had the great good fortune to know one of those medical paragons you hope to find but rarely do: Dr. Richard Medhurst of Toronto's Rosedale Animal Hospital. While there are a number of excellent doctors at this clinic, Rich has been involved with it from its beginning, and neighbourhood pet owners speak of him with reverence. One story will have to suffice. During the winter of 2003, when Zoli was receiving chemotherapy, Rich planned a week's holiday with his wife in San Francisco. Before leaving he made a point of giving me the telephone number of his hotel in case I had any questions or needed to talk. I didn't have to phone him, but that number meant a great deal to me at the time, and still does when I look back on it. While Zoli was receiving his chemotherapy from Ian Sandler – another fine doctor at the same hospital, who answered my numerous questions with detail and care – Dr. Medhurst had become a special friend to Zoli and me, and his compassion gave me courage through Zoli's decline. In case of an emergency, a good dog guardian knows something about first aid, but it's equally important to recognize the limitations of such knowledge. Anyone taking proper care of a dog will, sooner or later, have to rely on a veterinarian. You'll be happier if you know and trust your dog's doctor.

WAR

As time passed since the start of the Iraq war in 2003, I found myself wondering more frequently about the plight of Iraqi dogs, which were not mentioned by the American media and probably considered – if thought of at all – as part of "collateral damage," that linguistic blindfold. Did the fact that Iraq is a Muslim society, where dogs have a different status than they do in North America and Europe, make any difference? In June of 2002, for example, Ayatollah Ali Khamene'i of Iran issued a ban against public dog-walking, and even the sale of dogs, as offensive to Muslims, in accordance with the Islamic idea that dogs are *haram*, or unclean; in the fall of 2006, the Saudi Arabian Muttawa, or religious police, banned the sale of pets as a sign of Western influence; and in April 2011, Iran's parliament passed a bill criminalizing dog ownership – only guard dogs and police dogs are considered legal. Yet in his admirable book *Animals in Islamic Tradition and Muslim Cultures*, Richard C. Foltz argues that animals are proof of God's creative power, and that the only Qur'anic reference to dogs (in süra 18, the Companions of the Cave) is a positive one. No matter; many religious bans in all traditions have been political or provincial at the core. I'm still left wondering about those Iraqi dogs.

Since humans have spent so much of their time on earth at war, the subject of war dogs is essential. In his account of the battle of Thermopylae, Greek historian Herodotus wrote that Xerxes's Persian army of almost six million men was accompanied not only by women camp followers who prepared the food, and concubines and eunuchs, but also by a range of animals including "the Indian dogs." While the number of soldiers is an exaggeration, the dogs – as guards at the very least – are a telling detail. (Herodotus gamely speculates on how everyone, as well as the dogs, was fed.) Of course the dogs of war come in many guises. Over the last centuries, dogs have served their countries well as specialized working dogs during periods of war. It's commonly thought that modern dog-training as we know it began with German handlers during the First World War. The famous movie dog Rin Tin Tin, an Alsatian who has been discussed earlier, began his life as a German-trained war dog, and dogs were also trained by the British, French, and Italian armies as messengers, scouts, and sentries. The most famous American dog of the Great War, as people like to call it, was the 102nd Infantry's Stubby, an untrained bull terrier who accompanied troops to France and was known for his ability to locate wounded doughboys, warn of gas attacks, and discover German soldiers in battles at the Marne and the Neuse-Argonne. Eventually Stubby returned to America, received a gold medal from General John "Black Jack" Pershing, and became a member of the American Legion and the Red Cross. After his death in 1926, his preserved body was kept on display in the Red Cross Museum in Washington, D.C., until it began to decay some decades later.

The Second World War saw its own military working dogs, also known as K-9s, trained by the newly organized Dogs for Defense – DFD – after the Japanese attack on Pearl Harbor in December 1941. Within six months, dogs were working as sentries in defence plants and government depots. By the summer of 1942, after Secretary of War Henry Stimson ordered all military branches to study the wartime use of dogs, it was estimated that 125,000 dogs would be necessary. One of the more famous was a mixed-breed named Chips, who was shipped overseas with the 30th Infantry and who played a significant role in the invasion of Sicily in July 1943. After exposing several Italian soldiers who wounded Chips but failed to kill him, the undaunted dog went back into battle the same evening and exposed another ten Italian soldiers, who were then captured. Chips was later awarded a Silver Star for valour and a Purple Heart for his wounds, but both medals were revoked after the commander of the Order of the Purple Heart complained to President Roosevelt that giving awards to dogs was demeaning to the human soldiers who also received them. Since then, no American war dogs have received military decorations, and no bureaucrat has been wise enough to create a special award for dogs, or for their handlers – dogs that have often supported the troops better than their human superiors.

The U.S. War Dogs Association, a nonprofit organization of

Vietnam veterans, has urged the Pentagon to create a new medal to acknowledge canine combat work, and the American Legion has no objection. In 2006, Ron Aiello, a Vietnam War dog handler and president of the association, wrote to Secretary of Defense Donald Rumsfeld about these lifesaving dogs deployed in Iraq and Afghanistan: "In some cases they are also wounded or killed in the line of duty, yet we give them no credit for their service." While there is no national memorial for them in Washington, D.C. – or anywhere else – in recent years local monuments have appeared across the country, spearheaded by veterans of the Second World War. In the Metroparks that ring Cleveland, for example, there's one called the Dogs of All Wars/Smoky Memorial, a four-foot-tall stone base topped with a life-sized bronze dog, cast in the likeness of Smoky, a four-pound Yorkshire terrier who sits alertly in an upturned bronze helmet. The original Smoky was found in an abandoned foxhole in the jungles of New Guinea in February 1944 (no one knows how the dog ended up there). An unofficial war dog, Smoky accompanied the soldiers of the 5th Air Force 26th Photo Recon Squad on numerous missions, survived gunfire, charmed the troops, and, during the building of an air base, managed to run a telegraph wire attached to her collar through a pipe that was seventy feet long and eight inches in diameter. At the end of the war she was brought back to the United States hidden in an empty gas mask.

During the years of the Vietnam War, some four thousand dogs served as scouts and bomb sniffers, though official recognition of their efforts, let alone humane treatment, was a thing of the past. Pulitzer Prize–winning journalist Richard Ben Cramer has written about this sorry episode. When the United States pulled out of Vietnam, the Pentagon referred to the dogs as "war equipment" and ordered them "abandoned in place." Cramer cites Michael Lemish, the official historian for the Vietnam Dog Handler Association (VDHA), who wrote: "Officially, no one knows what happened to them – the only questions that really remain are how many were killed, eaten or just simply starved to death." Soldiers who were also dog handlers have protested such disregard and formed the VDHA, which seeks to create a National War Dog Memorial. As well, Lemish noted that when the Vietnam dog handlers applied to plant a tree at Arlington National Cemetery, they were denied. The president of the VDHA, John Burnam, said "We wanted it to be a team memorial – for the war dogs and the men who served with them. But they just won't do it. The bias is simple 'Humans Only.'" *Humans Only* – this is the eternal, recurring prejudice in our treatment of dogs. Though not everywhere, and not always. By contrast, in Ottawa, Ontario, there is a stone wall at the entrance to the Memorial Chamber in the federal Parliament buildings that has carvings of animals (a Saint Bernard dog carrying a message in its mouth, and of course cavalry horses) with these words: The Humble Beasts that Served and Died. The wall dates from 1927, and is a moving reminder that human life is not the only cost of war.

In 2004, the publication of the notorious Abu Ghraib prison photographs of an American soldier in Iraq – an army dog handler tormenting a restrained prisoner with a Belgian shepherd – shocked the world. Whether he was following orders or not, in June 2006 this sergeant was convicted of dereliction of duty and aggravated assault, with a possible three-and-a-half-year prison sentence; another army dog handler-received a six-month sentence. The verdict included this description of the assault on an alleged Baathist general: "unlawfully threatening him with a means of force likely to produce death or grievous bodily harm, to wit: unmuzzled military working dog" – or, dog as weapon. Back in the United States, both of the following stories show a civilian face of the war. In one of her "About Animals" columns for the *Cleveland Plain Dealer*, Suzanne Hively discussed a local couple who decided not to adopt a soldier and send him care packages but rather to adopt a war dog. They eventually found the name of a dog handler and sent him a bed for his dog and care packages that included dog biscuits, liver treats, even eye wash and tennis balls. In time, U.S. Representative Dennis Kucinich's office gave them the names of other dog handlers, and the couple (who own a German shepherd) broadened their efforts, convincing other dog lovers to follow their example. That same year, the mother of a young marine killed in Haditha sought to honour her son by adopting a dog – a mixed-breed puppy named Beans – that he and his company had bought from Iraqi villagers for three jelly beans and a quarter (hence, her name). Initially the military refused to transport a pet from Iraq to the United States. But Kathy Wright persisted, and with the help of a local bank which set up a fund called the Beans Foundation to raise money for the dog, Beans arrived at her new home that fall; Wright then thought to remind reporters that "Beans is not a replacement for my son."

Wright's story isn't unique – Military Mascots, an organization of animal lovers, works to help soldiers bring military pets home with them. *From Baghdad, with Love: A Marine, the War, and a Dog Named Lava* by Lieutenant Colonel Jay Kopelman tells the story of the rescue from an abandoned house in Fallujah of a mongrel puppy who was "de-flea'd with kerosene, de-wormed with chewing tobacco, and pumped full of MRE's (Meals Ready to Eat)," even though military orders prohibit adopting domestic animals as pets or mascots. Eventually Lava came to California with Kopelman, who described how, when surrounded by death, dogs can give soldiers a sense of hope for the future, providing "routine" and "something to be responsible for." Of note is the fact that the initiatives to recognize the work of war dogs come from veterans who knew firsthand the bond soldiers make with working dogs, dogs that not only serve alongside them but that also remind them of a more normal life back home. As I've mentioned elsewhere, soldiers wear "dog tags," a means of identification but also a term that marks their change in status from free-agent civilians to obedient combatants who must follow rules they haven't set for themselves. A dog nearby reassures people of their humanity.

Inevitably, fiction writers have been drawn to the subject of war dogs for the potential drama and heroics. During the period of the First World War when the United States and Canada were joining the conflagration, fiction writers enlisted themselves in the literary-propaganda efforts by telling war stories with a canine twist. Albert Payson Terhune, in his most famous novel *Lad: A Dog* (1919), included a chapter titled "Speaking of Utility" that revolves around the efforts of a nouveau-riche farmer (dismissively called "the Wall Street farmer") who wants to address wartime rationing and food scarcity by having his New Jersey neighbours shoot or poison their dogs as unnecessary burdens. Nothing of the sort happens, but in a later chapter a shepherd who accuses Lad of killing several of his charges is revealed as an evil sheep poacher, and a German at that, with a stereotypical ethnicity ("With true Teutonic relish for pain-inflicting, he swung the weapon [a riding crop] aloft and took a step toward the lazily recumbent collie, striking with all his strength"). More conventionally, Canadian writer Charles G.D. Roberts produced a short story called "The Dog that Saved the Bridge" (first published in a magazine in 1915) about the heroic efforts of two war dogs, Dirck and Leo – "brindled dogs – mongrels, evidently, showing a dash of bull and a dash of retriever in their make-up" – who, alongside Belgian riflemen behind enemy lines, fight "the Bosches."

One book stands out as the most moving novel about dogs and war: Sheila Burnford's *Bel Ria: Dog of War* (1977). Intended for young adult readers, it's now more likely to be appreciated by adults. Born in Scotland, Burnford served as a volunteer ambulance driver during the Second World War before settling in Canada. She used her own experiences in the story of a mixed-breed poodle who is, at first, a nameless dog belonging to a Gypsy caravan heading south in France, on a June morning in 1940, to escape the Nazi advance. The dog eventually ends up on a ship of the Royal Navy, where he serves as a mascot. Later, after landing in England during the Blitz, Burnford's hero takes a final turn when he rescues an elderly woman and becomes her redemptive companion. A brief plot synopsis can't do justice to the novel, or to its portrait of wartime life. Burnford has the unique ability to show what a dog feels and thinks through her descriptions of its behaviour. She is also a keen human psychologist. While the novel generally avoids didacticism, one of its characters, a dour assistant to the ship's doctor, does reflect near the end that "Loss of life was an accepted gamble that men took when they went to war. But no animal went to war: caught up in man's lethal affairs, they were an irreconcilable aberration." Like the best war novels, *Bel Ria* almost inevitably becomes an anti-war testament.

Once movies became standard fare, Hollywood wasn't going to leave the war work to fiction writers, especially when there was money to be made. Movies such as *Son of Lassie* (1945) included an ingenious collie who follows his master (the young Peter Lawford) into war resistance in occupied Norway. Lassie here is the domestic pet who thinks like a wise old general. Somewhat nearer reality is the scene in Franco Zeffirelli's partially autobiographical film *Tea with Mussolini* (1999), where an aging British spinster, played by Judi Dench, is forced to give up her pet dog (actually Zeffirelli's own dog, Nikki) when she's taken into custody by Italian fascists. The brief, flamboyant scene made some viewers cry and others laugh. Such separations do not happen only in times of war. During the fiasco known as Katrina, when residents of New Orleans were evacuated without their family dogs, many TV viewers across North America watched the disaster and claimed that they wouldn't have abandoned their own pets. One wonders, though, what they would actually have done in similar dire circumstances – or in wartime.

Many of the war dogs mentioned here are military working dogs. It's difficult enough to get accurate figures for their numbers, which the armed services will not release, citing security concerns. (Ron Aiello estimates that about seven hundred have served in Iraq and Afghanistan.) The number of civilian dogs – pet, wild, and homeless – killed alongside humans, civilian or not, is another matter entirely. Since it's difficult to find accurate figures for human deaths in Iraq, we shouldn't be surprised that figures for dog losses are almost impossible to come by, and may seem to many people of considerably less significance. But fortunately not to everyone.

WILLS

In August 2007, the North American media was agog with the news that multi-billionaire Leona Helmsley had died. The notorious "Queen of Mean," who once ran her own luxury Manhattan hotel and had served a prison sentence for tax evasion ("Only little people pay taxes," she was reputed to have said), continued to draw attention by leaving in her estate a trust fund of $12 million for her nine-year-old white Maltese, named Trouble. The dog continued to enjoy her more-than-comfortable lifestyle, and will eventually be buried alongside Helmsley in the family mausoleum. That Helmsley left more money to her pet than to anyone in her family is no one's business but her own, despite the censorious chortling of newscasters. Helmsley and her lawyers had the foresight to provide for Trouble, and all dog owners can learn something from this, even if they aren't leaving million-dollar estates. But on April 30, 2008, a judge of the Manhattan Surrogate Court cut back the inheritance from twelve to two million dollars on the ground that Helmsley was "mentally unfit" when she made her will.

Wills are not always airtight, nor are deathbed wishes. As if Helmsley's bequest to Trouble wasn't enough, several weeks later came the news that Helmsley had left instructions regarding a charitable bequest of eight *billion* dollars for the care and welfare of dogs. Was this legal? Was it binding? some journalists cried, with an implication that it would be wasted money. Ray D. Madoff, professor from the Boston College Law School, even argued in the editorial pages of *The New York Times* that Helmsley's bequest would cost taxpayers $3.6 billion because of federal tax laws regarding charitable deductions, and warned against "whims of the wealthy." ("If this were only a matter of Leona Helmley wasting her own money," he lamented, "no one would need to care. But she is wasting ours too.") That Helmsley's money would be a great boon to animal welfare – that dogs, in fact, deserve humane care – was beside the point. Indignation ruled the press coverage. Could Helmsley be found "mentally unfit" again? A fortune was at stake, and a chunk of it would end up in legal pockets. (By the way, Trouble died on December 13, 2010, but news of her passing did not become a matter of public record until *The New York Times* published her obituary – Trouble, the Cosseted Heir of Leona Helmsley, Dies – on June 10, 2011. Although the obituary covered almost half a page, the cause of death had not been released.)

While Helmsley's situation is *sui generis*, anyone who wants to provide for a beloved dog needs to remember that his or her wishes may be criticized, although you won't be around to hear the objections. Still, it's essential to ask some basic questions. Who will take your dog? What will its life be like? Concerns such as these inevitably shadow the care all dog owners owe their pets. As one ages, and mortality weighs more heavily, lawyers can offer guidance. I've spoken with several who suggest that there are basically two ways to handle a will and a pet. First, you can simply treat your dog as you might a child and leave money to a guardian, giving him or her carte blanche about how to spend the money. A wise proviso here is that if or when the dog dies, the remaining money goes elsewhere. If this approach is chosen, you have no control over the money outside of the will itself – there are no rules or strings attached, despite any wishes you may have left behind. The second approach is to create a trust for your dog, with a trustee who will supervise the money and how it's spent. In this arrangement you've chosen a guardian for the pet *and* a trustee who pays for all of the dog's expenses, making certain that the caretaker gives your dog the kind of care you wish for it. The key in this arrangement is to separate the money from the caregiver. Differing situations will determine the approach to follow, which should be discussed with your lawyer and, of course, any prospective pet guardian and trustee.

Anyone arranging for his or her dog's future should be luckier than the dog who is left to a poorly chosen guardian in the darkly satiric novel *Philosopher or Dog?* by the nineteenth-century Brazilian writer Joaquim Maria Machado de Assis. A spin on the subject of canine inheritance, it's the story of a provincial schoolteacher named Rubião, who inherits a fortune from a mad philosopher, Quincas Borba, as long as he promises to care for the man's dog, also named Quincas Borba because, as the philosopher claimed, if he died first, he would survive through his dog's name. And along with such logic, "Since Humanity, according to my doctrine, is the principle of life and resides everywhere, it is present in the dog, and thus the latter can receive a person's name..." (The novel's title in Portuguese, *Quincas Borba*, can refer to either dog or philosopher, or both). Rubião, a lost soul in search of love, at first has trouble finding his charge, a pretty, medium-sized grey dog with black spots. Arriving at the home of the dead man, he calls out to no avail, and soon contemplates his inheritance and the missing dog – if there is no dog, alive and well, will there be an inheritance? Eventually man and dog come together, and the hapless Rubião runs through the inheritance without ever making a genuine connection with the dog, who remains an unwanted nuisance at his side. Neither of these characters understands the other, but the dog at least assumes that his new master has his best interests in mind – "He likes to be loved, and he gratifies himself with the belief that this is so." *Philosopher or Dog?* offers no assurances to anyone planning a will. Life, Machado de Assis suggests, always has its own way with our best intentions. Leona Helmsley might agree.

WORK

All dogs work, although we normally associate the word with the working breeds trained to specific tasks. Some of these are policing, patrol and guard jobs, seeing-eye care, bomb- and drug-sniffing, tasks for the disabled, search and rescue work known as SAR, therapy and war jobs, and even drug-smuggling. Still, I couldn't help but nod in agreement when I first read this sentence in Donna Haraway's *The Companion Species Manifesto*: "Being a pet seems to me a demanding job for a dog, requiring self-control and canine emotional and cognitive skills matching those of good working dogs."

Dogs like to have jobs or tasks, even if that means nothing more than sitting on your lap while you watch TV – think of the self-control this involves. Whenever I spend a long stretch of time at my computer, only taking a break to walk Rennie around the block, by the end of the day he's eager for attention, for something to do. Work means more than completing a task; it includes social contact, movement out of the self, even the busyness of a routine. Dogs understand this intuitively, which may be why, like humans, they can adjust to tasks that they haven't set for themselves. We often think of dogs as pack animals, with humans as part of the pack. Most work is a form of pack activity, sometimes directly concerned with immediate survival, often indirectly so. Why else are human retirees encouraged to find meaningful activity to replace their jobs? The idea of a "dog's life" as something easy, lacking stress, can only appeal to a person who hasn't taken time to observe his or her dog. Dogs are at the mercy of their owners' moods, and they know this. When the human/dog hero of Jean Doutourd's novel *A Dog's Head* refers to a dog's life as one of slavery, he's not exaggerating. Try looking at someone adoringly for more than five minutes and you'll want to scream. Try waiting for someone to take you to the bathroom and you'll have to admit that waiting is a dreadful occupation.

Occasionally the print media focuses on a working-dog story for its human-interest qualities: a French magazine relates the saga of a young disabled boy and his helper dog, Robot; an American newspaper runs an article with this eye-catching headline: Dogs and Discriminating Noses Are Following New Career Paths. These dogs are doing human work that dogs can do just as effectively and perhaps more cheaply. The components of these tasks are more complex than we care to admit. Sometimes they even make us smile, which reinforces our sense of superiority. In the fall of 1998, the Cleveland Museum of Art hired a border collie named Jack and his handler Donna Lumme to chase away the Canada geese that were spoiling the elegant lawn of its Fine Arts Garden. Border collies, bred to herd sheep, are natural herders, a job with its own dangers (in this case, city traffic, for one). Jack's project was to spend a month chasing the geese from the grass into the lagoon, until they migrated south. I know of cemeteries, too, that have employed dogs to chase away persistent geese. Not exactly life-and-death work, but how much work is? Jack probably enjoyed himself while fulfilling his nature.

We're quick to think of working dogs as specialized eyes and noses, dogs that sniff out drugs or lead the blind, but the history of working dogs is actually an agrarian story, with echoes of it in the seven AKC group divisions: herding dogs were essential to shepherds and farmers, many terriers served as ratters, chasing "vermin" from barns and fields, and sporting dogs (known in Britain as gundogs) such as hounds and retrievers were used not only for the pleasure of the hunt, but to help retrieve the family's next meal before we went off to supermarkets. As Graham Robb noted in his study of French historical geography, the role of dogs shifted significantly wherever industrialization occurred: "There are now more domestic dogs per person in France (one for every seven) than in the mid-nineteenth century (one for every seventeen)," a statistic that has non-French parallels. Most canine agricultural tasks are no longer necessary for contemporary dog owners, yet a preference for large working dogs, at least in North America, remains. As we've built our post-industrial society, we've expected our dogs to evolve socially alongside us. In a nod to the changing nature of human work, newspapers periodically print articles about bringing dogs into the workplace, as long as they don't interfere with productivity. Imagine the stress a dog might be under unless a workplace truly suits its nature (some smaller stores, a nursing home, the less-crowded parts of a university campus). There's a thin line between a pet dog accompanying its human to the workplace and a therapy dog, trained or not, at one's side. (Alternatively, in 2007 I read about a number of British companies that are purchasing a new kind of insurance, or "peternity," that allows employees to take time off to care for an ailing pet.)

Prolific dog writer Jon Katz, in *The New Work of Dogs: Tending to Life, Love, and Family*, has interviewed numerous dog owners in Montclair, New Jersey, who have emotional needs they expect their dogs to satisfy, including, for example, a group of women who formed the Divorce Dogs Club to help rebuild post-marriage lives thorough some dog/human socializing. Dogs have become family caregivers, the nuclear family's substitute for extended family members. Katz links the growth in the American dog population to the increased time spent before the television. His chapter "Dogville, U.S.A.," which surveys the recent work of psychologists on attachment theory – or how infants bond to the world – includes attachment to dogs and other pets. As the scope of research about dogs has widened, not only psychologists and psychiatrists, but also animal behaviourists, animal ethicists and sociologists, have observed shifts in the human/dog bond – we *need* our dogs as our forebears never did, or at least now mainly for personal psychological satisfaction. The bulk of Katz's book, anecdotes about daily life in Montclair, is a group portrait of people suffering from loneliness, aging, illness, and depression as they keep themselves alive through their dogs. ("Often," he wrote, "if you scratched a dog lover, you found some underlying pain, something that opens a vein of empathy, nurturing, and affection.") The cost to dogs, which Katz acknowledges and laments, was generally overlooked.

Humans, at least, can escape into books with dramatic cliff-hangers. Donna Ball has written several mystery novels with a working dog central to the plots. It's a golden retriever, a search-and-rescue dog named Cisco, and the dog's training, persistence, and intelligence, give an idea of the difficulty working dogs accept as part of their lot. I certainly wouldn't want to be crawling through the Smoky Mountains at four o'clock in the morning during a cold, wet, March spring, in pursuit of a missing child, and if my efforts only led to a long-abandoned can of baked beans and a corpse, I'm sure that my training would fail me the next time around. Novelists, like scientists, need to be good observers, and Ball's experience as a dog trainer comes across on every page, dramatizing emotional and cognitive skills. Carol Lea Benjamin's readable series about Rachel Alexander and Dash includes the detective's working pitbull in a Manhattan setting, with some flashy, last-minute canine rescues. Few non-specialized working dogs face such demanding tasks, though pleasing a master or mistress has its own high stakes. A dog lives at our human pleasure – can be abandoned, given away, neglected, at our will – and that kind of life is difficult work.

WRITERS' DOGS

Writers almost inevitably turn to their own lives – or aspects of them – for subject matter. This is pretty much true for writers who live with dogs, though "serious" writers don't always admit it. Still, writers who haven't included a dog or two somewhere in their work have, since the invention of the camera, often been photographed with them – the list seems endless, from Colette to Faulkner and Hemingway. (Many of these photographs appear in the biographies of various writers, and some were anthologized by Peter Dyer and Judith Watt in their appealing collections, *Men & Dogs* and *Women & Dogs*.) The connection between writers and dogs is an ideal one. Writers need to work alone, in silence, in a solitude that may sometimes be discomforting, and a dog nearby can provide wordless communion and distraction, or a presence that isn't likely to stop the flow of words. The kinds of demands a dog might make suit the endeavours of art. As I writer I'm naturally interested in writers' dogs. Yet in spite of our legacy from Homer, writers are no less likely to feel superior to their dogs than anyone else.

I've written about a lot of books in these pages and want to add a few more reflections before concluding. After looking at thousands of book jackets and covers over the years, it appears that the only writers who chose to include photographs of themselves with their dogs are writers of books about dogs – Stanley Coren and his Cavalier King Charles spaniels, Vilmos Csányi, Vicki Hearne,

Ted Kerasote, and Elizabeth Marshall Thomas. The list could go on, as if the dog's image helps to establish the writer's credibility, while any potential book purchaser is unlikely to find the image sentimental. Magazine or newspaper photographs of a writer with his or her dog suggest the mysterious nature of communication itself, as if writers, like their dogs, in the end remain mute about the nature of their craft – despite the accompanying interview. Only a few writers have dedicated books to their dogs, which might seem off-putting eccentricity. Agatha Christie, who wrote eighty novels and collections of short stories, did dedicate one of them, *Dumb Witness* (1937), to a canine companion: "To Dear Peter, most faithful of friends and dearest of companions, a dog in a thousand." Perhaps with so many books to her credit, Christie was running out of suitable human friends. The novel has a well-observed wirehaired fox terrier as a crucial character, so she may have only been showing proper gratitude. More recently, Raymond and Lorna Coppinger dedicated their rich study of canine evolution to nine of their dogs, each with a mini-biography on the dedication page.

In recent years feminist critics have concentrated on women writers, some long-neglected, and brought the domestic sphere into the foreground of literary history. In *Shaggy Muses: The Dogs Who Inspired*, Maureen Adams retells familiar stories about five writers and their dogs: Emily Bronte (and Keeper, a mixed-breed mastiff), Elizabeth Barrett Browning (and Flush, a spaniel), Emily Dickinson (and Carlo, a Newfoundland), Edith Wharton (and Mitou, a toy spaniel), and Virginia Woolf (and Pinka, a cocker spaniel). Adams favours writers popular with university courses, eschewing authors deemed old-fashioned or mass-market (Pearl Buck and Jacqueline Susann, to name only two). Yet reading *Shaggy Muses* brought back every detail of a trip I took some summers ago with Zoli to visit the house of one of my favourite writers, Marguerite Yourcenar, on Maine's

Mount Desert Island, including the large photograph of her spaniel Valentine that greeted anyone stepping into the living room. Though Yourcenar's work is easily available in translation, and she was the first woman writer inducted into the prestigious Academie Française, Adams doesn't mention her, or Valentine. This isn't just a quibble. Yourcenar preferred male narrators for her novels, like *Memoirs of Hadrian*, and her writing showed little interest in the domestic lives of women.

A more puzzling omission on Adams's part is the iconic writer Gertrude Stein, who was often photographed with one of her white standard poodles (Basket I, Basket II) and, less frequently, with Pépé, a Chihuahua. Famous for her Paris literary salon, where she entertained the artistic avant garde of the early twentieth century, Stein was known to have enjoyed her walks with her dogs, exploring the city; she often wrote about them in her experimental works as well as in her unique memoir *The Autobiography of Alice B. Toklas*, which mimics Toklas's voice (Toklas was Stein's life companion for over three decades). Using her Toklas persona, Stein described visiting her friend Pablo Picasso in his studio, where the two sat in low chairs, knee to knee, and "They talk about everything, about pictures, about dogs, about death, about unhappiness." It's a fascinating list, with *dogs* inserted prominently between the art that brought Picasso and Stein together and the metaphysical concerns that troubled both of them. Frequently quoted for her observation "I am I because my little dog knows me," which she repeated in slightly different forms in various works, Stein went on to ponder whether or not the dog's experience of her "only proved the dog was he and not that I was I." While some of Stein's remarks may seem cryptic to readers not interested in her cubist poems in *Tender Buttons*, she did include there a dense prose poem titled "A Dog," and here it is: "A little monkey goes like a donkey that means to say that means to say that more sighs last goes. Leave with it. A little monkey goes like a donkey." In the context of Stein's celebration of companionable domesticity – which is at the heart of *Tender Buttons* – and seen against the modernist still-lifes by Cézanne, Matisse, and Picasso that inspired some of her linguistic experiments, "A Dog" seems less like nonsense verse than a playful extension of Stein's interest in phenomenology, alongside a desire to find fresh language for daily life.

Most of Stein's words about dogs are more reader-friendly. In her memoir *Paris France* she discussed the national character of dogs with her penchant for big generalizations, claiming that dogs resemble not only the people who own them but also the nation that "creates" them. During the Second World War, when she and Toklas left Paris to live in the French countryside – a courageous act for two Jewish-American women – they fortunately took along Basket's pedigree, and when authorities gave a special food ration to pedigreed dogs, Basket, as Toklas later wrote, "was not too badly nourished during the years of restriction." In *Wars I Have Seen*, Stein related an incident from one of her country walks in the winter of 1943-44. When she was told that a woman in the town of Bourg had recently given birth to six puppies, Stein naturally objected:

> Not possible, I said, but yes, she said...in times like these women do console themselves with dogs and this does happen, of course the dogs don't survive they are kept in museums, but it does happen, not really I said, oh yes, she said, in Bourg they once had it happen to a nun, and when the doctor went to see her the dog would not let him come near her.

The inhabitants of Bourg may have been a strange lot, but the fact that Stein recorded this fantastical story shows how extreme stress nearly overwhelmed ordinary encounters during those years

"Gertrude Stein with Basket II" (1946), photographed by Horst. Gelatin silver print. On the wall in the background is an oil painting by Marie Laurencin, *Portrait of Basket II*, c. 1945.

of war and Nazi occupation. Six years after Stein's death, Basket II died, in November 1952, and Toklas, then sixty-five, wrote poignantly to a friend that "I have realized how much I depended upon him and so it is the beginning of living for the rest of my days without anyone who is dependent upon me for anything." Like Stein, Toklas obviously loved dogs, and could have easily echoed her remark, "I am I because my little dog knows me."

While many writers have discussed their writing habits, two Canadian novelists acknowledged the role that dogs played in their time at work. In her touching memoir *Portrait of a Dog* (1930), Mazo de la Roche described the almost symbiotic bond that she and her writing shared with a Scottish terrier: "You seemed to think that it could not go on rightly without you – and, indeed, this came to be so. I must have the support of your solid little presence, the intimacy of your eyes, the sympathy of your quick thudding tail on the floor when the pencil was laid down, the paper gathered up." Eighty years later, Marie-Claire Blais described a similar bond in her elegiac story "Homage to Scheila," written for *The Exile Book of Canadian Dog Stories*. Blais praised the dog who was "a dignified and peaceful companion" during her long writing hours, often asleep under the work table. Yet Scheila might turn morose when Blais didn't notice her, "when she seemed to say to me, isn't it time to go out, to go for a walk? although she did it discreetly, with longing in her eyes, with a rub on her muzzle against the table..." What writer with a companion dog doesn't recognize such moments?

The issue of gender, writers, and dogs deserves further study. Today, many women writers are redefining their relationship with the world and the written word, while too many male writers remain stuck in sports and sex, or crime and cartoons. Still, writers' memoirs and personal essays provide a good place to start the probing, and two examples may indicate a fruitful area for examination. On opening American poet August Kleinzahler's engaging memoir *Cutty, One Rock: Low Characters and Strange Places, Gently Explained*, a reader might reasonably expect – from its title – some tough-guy reminiscences. Instead the book starts like this: "It was the dog who raised me." While other family members made "nurturing gestures," which he admits, "it was the dog on whose ear I teethed and who watched me through countless hours...." Kleinzahler's portrait of Grand, the troubled family's purebred male boxer (usually called Granny), is more than a variation on boy-and-his-dog adventure yarns. The subtext of this chapter is the sorrow of a young boy without emotional connections. When Granny died, and young August watched his mother weep, he had to face some grim facts. He saw that the dog was "Kaput," and this made him conclude, "I was alone in the world; but far worse, alone with Mother and Father." It's no accident that *Cutty, One Rock* opens with a tribute to "the dog who raised me." Taking one's dog as a subject requires the writerly conviction that dogs matter, whether they are part of painful childhood memories or less complicated, happier times. In "Dog Story," a charming essay for the *New Yorker*, Adam Gopnik wrote about buying a Havanese puppy for his ten-year-old daughter, almost against his will. To Gopnik's surprise, he became a converted dog lover, and he concluded the essay this way: "How does anyone live without a dog? I can't imagine." Kleinzahler might agree.

All writers have a great deal to learn from their dogs. Foremost, patience. Any idea can be spoiled by a writer in a hurry. The urge to force one's will on a project, to push it this way or that, can result in poor decisions and wrong turns. Writing takes time. Dogs have a different relationship with time than humans do, they seem to luxuriate in stillness and know how to be quiet without being bored or impatient. They enjoy diversion but require more than mere distraction to be amused. Put simply, describing a dog and trying to enter its consciousness is harder than any writer might think. This may explain why only a few of the greatest writers have succeeded or even come close.

XYLOCAINE

Xylocaine is a local anaesthetic, valuable in surgery to remove a small lump from a dog's skin for a biopsy, a procedure known as a lumpectomy. It is initially applied in its spray form to the throat, in preparation for the endotracheal tube, and can be given under the skin as a local anaesthetic. As such, it's a means to an end, not an end in itself. I first came to hear about Xylocaine when it was used on Zoli in the fall of 2003 for one of several biopsies. Xylocaine is actually the trade name for its derivative Lidocaine, produced for humans (where it is most commonly used for dental surgery) by AstraZeneca, and in its veterinary form by Bimeda-MTR. However, this anaesthetic opens the door to the larger subject of pharmaceuticals and dogs. Xylocaine was administered to Zoli by Dr. Ian Sandler of Toronto's Rosedale Animal Hospital, the lively veterinarian who also gave him his chemotherapy and who has recently become the designated veterinary spokesperson for a survey of Canadian pet owners conducted by an Ipsos-Reid poll and funded by the pharmaceutical giant Pfizer.

Since we've become a pharmaceutically oriented society, it follows that our dogs and our drugs frequently pair off. We've come a long way since surgery was done without anaesthetic. In her novel *Restoration*, British writer Rose Tremaine tells the story of a fraudulent court surgeon to King Charles II, who was asked to save the life of one of his monarch's spaniels, a breed that eventually came to be known as the Cavalier King Charles spaniel. The roguish "doctor" is locked into a room with the sick dog where, terrified, he gets drunk and passes out while nature takes its course, curing the animal. (The novel's movie version contains a memorable scene when a pack of the spaniels run through the palace corridor toward the camera, overwhelming the screen with their Cavalierness.) All this, of course, happened centuries ago. Many contemporary medical advances that have benefited humans are now available to our pets, from MRIs for diagnosis to chemotherapy. At the same time, researchers and drug companies have included dogs in their trials of new cancer drugs, hoping that both humans and dogs will reap the benefits. (Figures from the American Veterinary Medical Association suggest that cancer causes nearly half of the deaths in dogs over ten years old.) The human/dog bond extends to certain cancers as well. As *Scientific*

American reported in a compelling article, "Cancer Clues from Pet Dogs" by David J. Waters and Kathleen Wildasin, humans and their pet dogs are the only two species that develop lethal prostate cancers, the kind of breast cancer that affects dogs and humans can spread to their bones, and osterosarcoma, the most common bone cancer in dogs, also affects teenagers. The National Cancer Institute of the United States has even established a consortium of more than a dozen veterinary teaching hospitals to conduct this research. The medical potential seems limitless.

What complicates the subject is the way that successful research turns into big business, determining who has access to its benefits. Nicholas Dodman, author of *The Dog Who Loved Too Much,* and a professor of behavioural pharmacology at Tufts University in Boston, said in an interview with Helen Henderson of the *Toronto Star*: "Twenty-five years ago, we basically had clunker drugs, mainly sedatives. Today, the pet industry is more lucrative than ever." (Dodman, who suggests behaviour modification as the first resort, has prescribed a wide range of well-known drugs to dogs with problems, including Valium, Prozac, and Xanax.) According to statistics from the Animal Health Institute, a Washington, D.C.-based organization that represents companies producing animal health-care products, the U.S. pet industry is worth more than $3 billion a year (Canadian figures are a fraction of that, at $300 million). Some of the key players include familiar names like Eli Lilly, which in the spring of 2007 released through its animal health division a drug winningly named Reconcile to treat canine separation anxiety. Pfizer's offerings, in addition to the drug for human cancer that was first tested on dogs, include Anipryl, for canine cognitive dysfunction; Cerenia, for canine carsickness; Rimadyl, for arthritis pain; and Slentrol, for obese dogs, approved for sale in the United States in January 2007 by the Food and Drug Administration. And there's also Novartis International, which manufactures Clomicalm for separation anxiety, in direct competition with Reconcile.

The matter of potential side effects from any drug should make us pause. Like many pharmaceuticals, Slentrol carries a warning label, and even cautions that the drug is not intended for human consumption. There is some question of whether it may cause liver problems, though one of Pfizer's executives, who is also a veterinarian, claims this is not an issue. As modern dogs take on the sedentary habits of their owners, canine obesity has become a serious problem. A few dogs may suffer from hypothyroidism, an underactive thyroid responsible for weight gain without increased appetite, but they are not the norm (and they can be diagnosed and treated). Pet owners who have paid little attention to the various lower-fat, weight-loss foods available on the market, may resort to the latest drug's quick fix. Dogs like their treats and know how to tempt us to feed them. The health risks to an overweight dog are considerable – arthritis, cardiovascular disease, diabetes – and it's estimated that at least a third of all American dogs are overweight, if not obese. As a pug guardian, I'm particularly sensitive to this concern. Pugs approach a plate of food as if they were industrial-powered Hoovers, but it's their human's responsibility to protect them from themselves. When people with overweight pugs ask how Rennie stays trim, I'm usually amazed to hear what, and how much, they feed their pets.

Dogs in chronic pain, or post-surgical pain, should of course be helped with medication, but not with over-the-counter drugs for humans. Ibuprofen, for example, can kill a dog. In such cases trust your veterinarian, though veterinarians, like doctors for humans, can be tempted by pharmaceutical companies that are glad to supply them with free samples. Since a dog can't speak directly of pain, a dog's owner has to be observant. Watching a dog, however, is part of the pleasure of caring for it. This may be difficult when a dog is unwell, but an illness is all the more reason to keep a sharp eye on your pet. For dogs in good health there are many situations when drugs can be avoided. The notion of sedating a dog before an airplane trip, for example, may at first seem like a sensible one (even a kindness, if not a convenience), but it's always better to train a dog to be comfortable in advance of changes in routine. Zoli and Morgan became good travellers because time was spent helping them adjust to their carry-on Sherpa kennels as well as speaking to them reassuringly on rides to the airport. I'm not a particularly patient person, which means that if I could do it, anyone can manage it with a little forethought.

Finally, for behavioural problems, first determine if a dog can be helped with some form of behaviour modification and retraining. This will take more time than administering a pill, but no one need worry about side effects. The announcement of every new drug is greeted as gleefully today as the coming attractions at the movies or the fall previews of new automobile models. Good merchandising on the part of drug companies, perhaps, but don't be duped and turn your dog into a guinea pig.

YAPPING

My next-door neighbours have a twelve-year-old Chihuahua named Chico, and when anyone steps into the hallway, he barks hysterically – a persistent yapping. Occasionally someone inside the apartment calls "ssh," but if the dog hasn't listened in twelve years he's not likely to start now. Chihauhaus are a breed whose appeal I've never understood. When I was growing up our neighbours acquired one who resembled a large beige rat with the personality of a concentration-camp guard, and they named it Pixie. She yapped continually and, unspayed, drew the attention of the street's male dogs. Our fox terrier Spotty fathered one of Pixie's litters, apparently not put off by her yapping; everyone else was.

To yap or *yapping* is defined by Webster's as "a snappish bark." The word can be both a verb (to yap) and the base of a noun (yapper, yapping). In his translation of a Latin prose bestiary from the twelfth century, novelist T. H. White, known for his much-loved retelling of the Arthurian legends in *The Once and Future King*, gave new life to a remarkable compendium of ancient knowledge. Written anonymously, bestiaries were important works of medieval natural history; as one might expect, they have much to say about dogs. The canine section in White's *The Bestiary: A Book of Beasts*, begins with some linguistic history. *Canis*, the Latin name of the dog, has an etymology from the Greek, from *canos*, but "some hold it to be named from the melody (*canor*) of its barking, since it howls deeply and is said to sing (*canere*)." As engaging as this may be, a yapping dog probably reminds few people of a singer with a melody. Yapping is usually associated with smaller breeds, like Chihauhaus and Yorkies, whose vocal chords are shorter and thinner than those of a collie or German shepherd. The sharp nature of the sound, however, is not the only issue, and the word also suggests a persistent act – a repeated plea for attention that somehow lacks dignity. (This may be part of the North American prejudice against smaller dogs in general and a kind of macho preference for larger breeds.) There is also an unstated gender bias to the term, more commonly associated with women than men. Just imagine this variation on an old truism – "his yap is worse than his bite" – without laughing. In fact yapping always suggests a decline in status from barking. When the word is applied to a human being, it's a reverse kind of anthropomorphism.

Like barking, yapping is a form of communication. While the distinction between the two is a fine one, it has to do with repetition. Yapping repeats a point ad infinitum. Often a territorial marker, a kind of vocal version of canine urination, yapping can degenerate into a bad habit that may drive everyone to distraction except the yapper's owner. Yapping may also indicate a greeting, though in this manifestation it's seldom prolonged; a demand for food or attention, at any rate something desired at once; and also a protest, as in "I want out of this kennel!" The intensity and frequency of the yap contain information, if one listens. And if rewarded by food, a place on the sofa or bed, even soft words of displeasure – that gentle shushing – yapping has been reinforced as a strategy for dealing with the world. White relates an anecdote about a Roman dog in the time of the consuls Appius and Junius Pictimus. The loyal dog had followed its master to prison, and even went along to the man's execution, where it stood howling. When Romans pitied the animal and gave it some food, the dog took it to the mouth of its dead master. A bittersweet story. Behaviour manuals suggest various ways to stop yapping and barking, from special collars, to muzzles, to sprays of water from a plastic bottle. Sooner or later all dogs "speak" their needs, and it's best to listen and think about what they're telling us from the first bark. In his memoir *Merle's Door*, Ted Kerasote, who told of finding a stray dog in the Utah desert and training him as a companion for his outdoor pursuits, used this apt metaphor about canine communication: "...they're speakers of a foreign language and, if we pay attention to their vocalizations, ocular and facial expressions, and ever-changing postures, we can translate what they're saying." Dogs, alas, don't come with subtitles. Whenever I hear a yapping dog, I wonder what the other half of the dog/human bond is – or isn't – doing.

YEARS

Almost everyone has heard that one year of a dog's life equals seven of a human's. On an episode of the popular television comedy series *The Golden Girls*, the raunchy character Blanche described a much younger man whom she planned to date, remarking that he was five years her junior, and her sharp-tongued housemate Dorothy replied, "What, Blanche, in dog years?" The figure seven is actually inaccurate. A truer comparative guide works something like this: the first year of a dog's life equals fifteen human years; the second year's human equivalent would be twenty-four; and every subsequent dog year equals four more human years, in other words: 3 = 28, 4 = 32, 5 = 36, 6 = 36, etc. The calculation is simple, though there is no exact equivalency. Stanley Coren, for example, suggests that the first two years of a dog's life are equivalent to twenty-four human years, and every additional dog year equals five. But however many years of life a dog may have, they aren't enough.

ZOLI

How else could I end this book? As long as my mind still works, the great pleasure of Zoli's company – and the pain of his loss – will be with me. I wouldn't have it any other way.

SOURCES AND BIBLIOGRAPHY

The following bibliography of books and articles I've read and consulted for *The Dog on the Bed* includes works from which I have made short quotations or cited for facts or opinions. Rather than filling the pages of my book with seemingly endless footnotes – which can distract many readers – I've noted the authors of relevant work and have given here full bibliographic details. For some classic and/or popular books (for example, Mary Shelley's *Frankenstein*) many editions are available; other works are long out of print and found mainly in libraries, or through used bookstores reached by various internet sites.

BOOKS

Ackerley, J. R., *My Dog Tulip*. 1956. New York: New York Review Books, 1999.

Adams, Cindy, *The Gift of Jazzy*. New York: St Martin's Griffin, 2004.

Adams, Richard, *The Plague Dogs*. New York: Knopf, 1978.

Aiello, Susan E., ed., *The Merck Veterinary Manual*. Eighth edition. Whitehouse Station, N.J.: Merck & Co., Inc., 1998.

Albers, Patricia, *Joan Mitchell: Lady Painter, A Life*. New York: Knopf, 2011.

Allcott, Louisa May, *Under the Lilacs*. 1878. Akron, Ohio: Saalfield Publishing, 1935.

Allen, Mary, *Animals in America Literature*. Urbana: University of Illinois Press, 1983.

Armstrong, William H., *Sounder*. 1969. New York: Scholastic, 2005.

Atkinson, Eleanor, *Greyfriars Bobby*. 1912. London: Penguin, 1996.

Austen, Jane, *Mansfield Park*. 1814. Middlesex, UK.: Penguin, 1966.

Auster, Paul, *Timbuktu*. New York: Henry Holt, 1999.

Baker, Steve, *Picturing the Beast: Animals, Identity, and Representation*. Urbana: University of Illinois Press, 2001.

Bakis, Kirsten, *Lives of the Monster Dogs*. New York: Warner, 1997.

Ball, Donna, *Rapid Fire*. New York: Signet, 2006.

-----, *Smoky Mountain Tracks*. New York: Signet, 2006.

Barthes, Roland, *A Lover's Discourse: Fragments*. Translated by Richard Howard. New York: Hill and Wang/Farrar, Straus and Giroux, 1978.

Basinger, Jeanine, *Silent Stars*. New York: Knopf, 2004.

Beach, Laura, *The Art of Stephen Huneck*. New York: Abrams, 2004.

Belben, Rosalind, *Hound Music*. London: Vintage, 2002.

Bell, Quentin, *Virginia Woolf: A Biography*. Volume Two, *Mrs Woolf, 1912-1941*. London: Hogarth Press, 1972.

Benjamin, Carol Lea, *Fall Guy*. New York: Avon, 2005.

-----, *This Dog for Hire*. New York: Walker and Company, 1996.

-----, *The Wrong Dog*. New York: Avon, 2005.

Berenson, Laurien, *Underdog*. New York: Kensington, 1996.

Bickerton, Derek, *Language and Human Behavior*. Seattle: University of Washington Press, 1995.

Bierce, Ambrose, *The Collected Writings of Ambrose Bierce*. New York: Citadel Press, 1974.

Bioy Casares, Adolfo, *Asleep in the Sun*. Translated by Suzanne Jill Levine. New York: Persea, 1978.

Bonaparte, Marie. *Topsy: The Story of a Golden-Haired Chow*. 1940. New Brunswick, New Jersey: Transaction Publishers, 1994.

Bondeson, Jan, *Amazing Dogs: A Cabinet of Canine Curiosities*. Ithaca, New York: Cornell University Press, 2011.

Bowron, Edgar Peters, Carolyn Rose Rebbert, Robert Rosenblum, and William Secord, *Best in Show: The Dog in Art from the Renaissance to Today*. New Haven: Yale University Press, 2006.

Bradbury, Ray, *Fahrenheit 451*. 1953. New York: Ballantine, 2003.

Brandow, Michael, *New York's poop scoop laws: dogs, the dirt, and due process*. West Lafayette, Ind: Purdue University Press, 2008.

Bromfield, Louis, *Animals and Other People*. New York: Harper & Brothers, 1944.

Brown, Rebecca, *The Dogs: A Modern Bestiary*. San Francisco: City Lights Books, 1998.

Budiansky, Stephen, *The Truth About Dogs: An Inquiry into the Ancestry, Social Conventions, Mental Habits, and Moral Fiber of Canis familiaris*. New York: Viking, 2000.

Bulanda, Susan, *Boston Terriers: Everything About Purchase, Care, Nutrition, Breeding, Behavior and Training*. Hauppauge, N.Y.: Barron's Educational Series, Inc., A Complete Pet Owner's Manual, 1994.

Bulgakov, Mikhail, *The Heart of a Dog*. Translated by Michael Glenny. New York: Harcourt, Brace & World, 1968.

Burnford, Sheila, *Bel Ria: Dog of War*. 1977. New York: New York Review Books, 2006.

-----, *The Incredible Journey: A Tale of Three Animals*. New York: Little, Brown, 1961.

Bush, Barbara, *Millie's Book: As Dictated to Barbara Bush*. New York: William Morrow, 1990.

Burt, Jonathan, *Animals in Film*. London: Reaktion, 2003.

Carr, Emily, *Emily Carr & her dogs – flirt, punk & loo*. 1944. Toronto: Douglas & McIntyre, 1997.

Carroll, Lewis, *Alice's Adventures in Wonderland* and *Through the Looking-Glass*. 1897 revised editions. Oxford: Oxford University Press, 2008.

Carroll, Willard, *I, Toto: The Autobiography of Terry, the Dog who was Toto*. New York: Stewart, Tabori & Chang, 2001.

Cervantes, Miguel de, *Don Quixote*. Translated by Edith Grossman. New York: HarperCollins, 2003.

Chandler, Charlotte, *The Girl Who Walked Home Alone: Bette Davis – A Personal Biography*. New York: Simon & Schuster, 2006.

Chekhov, Anton, *The Essential Tales of Chekhov*. Translated by Constance Garnett. New York: Ecco Press, 1998.

Christie, Agatha, *Dumb Witness*. 1937. New York: Berkley/Penguin, 1984.

Ciment, Jill, *Heroic Measures*. New York: Pantheon, 2009.

Ciuraru, Carmela, ed., *Doggerel: Poems About Dogs*. New York: Knopf, 2003.

Clothier, Suzanne, *Bones Would Rain from the Sky: Deepening Our Relationships with Dogs*. New York: Warner, 2002.

Coetzee, J. M., *Disgrace*. London: Vintage, 2000.

-----, *The Lives of Animals*. Princeton, New Jersey: Princeton University Press, 1999.

Colette, *Break of Day*. 1928. Translated by Enid McLeod. New York: Farrar, Straus and Giroux, 2002.

-----, *My Mother's House & Sido*. Translated by Una Vicenzo Troubridge and Enid McLeod. New York: Modern Library, 1995.

Collins, Ace, *Lassie: A Dog's Life – The First Fifty Years*. New York: Penguin, 1993.

Conant, Susan, *Stud Rites*. New York: Doubleday, 1996.

Conrad, Barnaby, *Les chiens de Paris*. San Francisco: Chronicle, 1995.

Coppinger, Raymond, and Lorna Coppinger, *Dogs: A Startling New Understanding of Canine Origin, Behavior & Evolution*. New York: Scribner, 2001.

Coren, Stanley, *How Dogs Think: What the World Looks Like to Them and Why They Act the Way They Do*. New York: Free Press, 2005.

-----, *The Intelligence of Dogs*. New York: Free Press, 1994.

-----, *The Modern Dog: A Joyful Exploration of How We Live with Dogs Today*. New York: Free Press, 2008.

Coren, Stanley, *The Pawprints of History: Dogs and the Course of Human Events*. New York: Free Press, 2003.

Corey, Mary F., *The World through a Monocle: The* New Yorker *at Midcentury*. Cambridge: Harvard University Press, 1999.

Craske, Matthew, and Stephen Feeke, et al., *Hounds in Leash: The Dog in 18th and 19th Century Sculpture*. Leeds, England: Henry Moore Institute, 2002.

Crespin, Régine, *On Stage, Off Stage: A Memoir*. Translated by G. S. Bourdain. Boston: Northeastern University Press, 1997.

Csányi, Vilmos, *If Dogs Could Talk: Exploring the Canine Mind*. Translated by Richard E. Quandt. New York: North Point, 2000.

Cuddy, Beverley, *Cavalier King Charles Spaniels*. Neptune City, N.J.: T.F.H. Publications, 1991.

Dante Alighieri, *The Divine Comedy*. Translated by H. R. Huse. New York: Holt, Rinehart and Winston, 1953.

Darwin, Charles, *The Expression of the Emotions in Man and Animals*. 1872. Chicago: University of Chicago Press, 1999.

de la Roche, Mazo, *Portrait of a Dog*. Boston: Little, Brown, 1930.

Derr, Mark, *A Dog's History of America: How Our Best Friend Explored, Conquered, and Settled a Continent*. New York: North Point Press/Farrar, Straus and Giroux, 2004.

-----, *Dog's Best Friend: Annals of the Dog-Human Relationship*. New York: Henry Holt, 1997.

Derrida, Jacques, *The Animal That Therefore I Am*. Translated by David Wills. New York: Fordham University Press, 2008.

Déry, Tibor, *Love and Other Stories*. 1955. New York: New Directions, 2005.

----, *Niki: The Story of a Dog*. Translated by Edward Hyams. 1958. New York: New York Review Books, 2009.

de Waal, Frans, *Good Natured: The Origins of Right and Wrong in Human and Other Animals*. Cambridge, Mass.: Harvard University Press, 1996.

Dickens, Charles, *Oliver Twist*. 1838. New York: Oxford University Press, 1999.

Dodman, Nicholas, *The Dog Who Loved Too Much: Tales, Treatments, and the Psychology of Dogs*. New York: Bantam, 1996.

Doty, Mark, *Dog Years: A Memoir*. New York: HarperCollins, 2007.

Doyle, Sir Arthur Conan, *The Hound of the Baskervilles*. 1902. London: Penguin, 2004.

Dratfield, Jim, *Pug Shots*. New York: Viking Studio/Penguin, 1999.

-----, *Pugnation: The Bark Is Back!* New York: Gotham, 2009.

Duemer, Joseph, and Jim Simmerman, eds., *Dog Music: Poetry about Dogs*. New York: St. Martin's, 1996.

Dunbar, Ian, ed., *The Essential Pug*. New York: Howell House Book/Macmillan, 1999.

Duncan, David Douglas, *Picasso and Lump: A Dachshund's Odyssey*. New York: Bulfinch Press, 2006.

Dutourd, Jean, *A Dog's Head*. 1951. Translated by Robin Chancellor. Chicago: University of Chicago Press, 1998.

Dye, Dan, and Mark Beckloff, *Amazing Grace: A Dog's Tale*. New York: Workman, 2003.

The Editors of *Bark*, *Dog Is My Co-Pilot: Great Writers on the World's Oldest Friendship*. New York: Three Rivers, 2003.

Eighner, Lars., *Travels with Lizbeth: Three Years on the Road and on the Streets*. New York: Fawcett Columbine, 1994.

Ellison, Harlan, *The Essential Ellison*. Las Vegas: Morpheus International, 2006.

Encyclopedia Americana, Vol. 28. New York: Americana Corporation, 1949.

Esenin, Sergei, *Selected Poetry*. Translated by Peter Tempest. Moscow: Progress Publishers, 1982.

Falk, Peter Hastings, ed., *Who Was Who in American Art 1564-1975*, Vol. III: P-Z. Sound View Press/Institute for Art Research & Documentation, 1999.

Fekete, István, *Bogáncs*. 1957. Budapest: Móra Könyvkiadó, 1973.

-----*Thistle*. Translated by Gyula Gulyás, revised by Elisabeth West. Budapest: Corvina, 1970.

Fisher, M. F. K., *An Alphabet for Gourmets*. 1949. San Francisco: North Point Press, 1989.

-----*The Boss Dog*. New York: Pantheon, 1991.

Fitzpatrick, Sonia, *The Pet Psychic: What Animals Tell Me*. New York: Berkley, 2003.

Foltz, Richard C., *Animals in Islamic Tradition and Muslim Cultures*. Oxford, UK.: Oneworld, 2006.

Foster, Stephen, *Walking Ollie*. New York: Perigee/Penguin, 2008.

Francis, Claude, and Fernande Gontier, *Creating Colette: From Baroness to Woman of Letters, 1921-1954*, Volume II. South Royalton, Vermont: Steerforth, 1999.

Frazer, James George, *The Golden Bough: A Study in Magic and Religion*. Twelve volumes. 1915. London: Macmillan and Company Limited, 1966.

Freud, Sigmund, *The Uncanny*. 1919. Translated by David McLintock. London: Penguin, 2003.

Freud, Sigmund, *The 'Wolfman' and Other Cases*. Translated by Louise Adey Huish. London: Penguin, 2003.

Gaita, Raimond, *The Philosopher's Dog: Friendship with Animals*. New York: Random House, 2002.

Gallant, Mavis, *The Selected Stories of Mavis Gallant*. Toronto: McClelland & Stewart, 1996.

Garber, Marjorie, *Dog Love*. New York: Simon & Schuster, 1996.

Geller, Tamar, with Andrea Cagan, *The Loved Dog: The Playful Nonaggressive Way to Teach Your Dog Good Behavior*. New York: Simon Spotlight Entertainment, 2007.

Gerstenfeld, Sheldon L., *ASPCA Complete Guide to Dogs*. San Francisco: Chronicle, 1999.

Gipson, Fred, *Old Yeller*. 1956. New York: Harper Trophy, 2004.

Givner, Joan, *Mazo de la Roche: The Hidden Life*. Toronto: Oxford University Press, 1989.

Grandin, Temple, with Catherine Johnson, *Animals in Translation: Using the Mysteries of Autism to Decode Animal Behavior*. New York: Simon & Schuster, 2005.

Gray, Harold, *Little Orphan Annie: Bucking the World*. New York: Cupples and Leon Co, 1929.

-----, *Little Orphan Annie: Never Say Die!* New York: Cupples and Leon Co., 1930.

Grenier, Roger, *The Difficulty of Being a Dog*. Translated by Alice Kaplan. Chicago: University of Chicago Press, 2000.

Grier, Katherine C., *Pets in America: A History*. Chapel Hill: University of North Carolina Press, 2006.

Grogan, John, *Marley & Me: Life and Love with the World's Worst Dog*. New York: Morrow, 2005.

Grosskurth, Phyllis, *Byron: The Flawed Angel*. Toronto: Macfarlane, Walter & Ross, 1997.

Guirand, Felix, ed., *The New Larousse Encyclopedia of Mythology*. Translated by Richard Aldington and Delane Ames. New York: Prometheus Press, 1968.

Hall, Libby, *These Were Our Dogs*. London: Bloomsbury, 2007.

Haraway, Donna, *The Companion Species Manifesto: Dogs, People, and Significant Otherness*. Chicago: Prickly Paradigm, 2003.

Hardy, Thomas, *Far from the Madding Crowd*. 1874. New York: Oxford University Press, 1998.

Hargrove, Brian, *My Life as a Dog*. New York: HarperCollins, 2000.

Hattersley, Roy, *Buster's Diaries: The True Story of a Dog and His Man.* New York: Warner, 2000.

Hausman, Gerald and Loretta, *The Mythology of Dogs: Canine Legend and Lore through the Ages.* New York: St. Martin's, 1997.

Hawtree, Christopher, ed., *The Literary Companion to Dogs: From Homer to Hockney.* London: Sinclair-Stevenson, 1993.

Hearne, Vicki, *Adam's Task: Calling Animals by Name.* New York: Knopf, 1986.

Hempel, Amy, and Jim Shephard, eds., *Unleashed: Poems by Writers' Dogs.* New York: Crown: 1995.

Hergé, *The Adventures of Tintin: The Blue Lotus.* 1946. London: Egmont UK, 2008.

Herodotus, *The Landmark Herodotus: The Histories.* Translated by Andrea L. Purvis. New York; Pantheon, 2007.

Herriot, James, *James Herriot's Dog Stories.* 1986. New York: St. Martin's Griffin, 2006.

Highet, Gilbert, *The Classical Tradition: Greek and Roman Influences on Western Literature.* 1949. New York: Oxford University Press, 1976.

Homer, *The Odyssey.* Translated by Robert Fitzgerald. 1961. New York: Vintage, 1990.

Hornung, Eva, *Dog Boy.* New York: Viking, 2010.

Horowitz, Alexandra, *Inside of a Dog: What Dogs See, Smell, and Know.* New York: Scribner, 2009.

Hotchner, Tracie, *The Dog Bible: Everything Your Dogs Wants You to Know.* New York: Gotham, 2005.

Houston, Jean, *Mystical Dogs: Animals as Guides to Our Inner Life.* Makawao, Maui, Hawaii: Inner Ocean Publishing, 2002.

Jackson, Frank, ed., *Faithful Friends: Dogs in Life and Literature.* New York: Carroll & Graf, 1997. (Reprinted as *The Mammoth Book of Dogs: A Collection of Stories, Verse and Prose*, 1999.)

Jönsson, Reidar, *My Life as a Dog.* Translated by Eivor Martinus. New York: Farrar, Straus, Giroux, 1989.

Kafka, Franz, *Selected Short Stories of Franz Kafka.* Translated by Willa and Edwin Muir. New York: Modern Library, 1952.

Kanfer, Stefan, *Ball of Fire: The Tumultuous Life and Comic Art of Lucille Ball.* New York: Knopf, 2003.

Katz, Jon, *The Dog Year: Twelve Months, Four Dogs, and Me.* New York: Random House, 2003.

-----, *The New Work of Dogs.* New York: Villard, 2003.

Kaufman, Margo, *Clara, The Early Years: The Story of the Pug who Ruled My Life.* New York: Penguin/Plume, 1999.

Keene, Carolyn (pseud.), *The Whispering Statue.* New York: Grosset & Dunlop, 1937.

Kelley, Lee Charles, *To Collar a Killer.* A Jack Field Mystery. New York: Avon, 2004.

Kerasote, Ted, *Merle's Door: Lessons from a Freethinking Dog.* New York: Harcourt, 2007.

Kete, Kathleen, *The Beast in the Boudoir: Petkeeping in Nineteenth Century Paris.* Berkeley: University of California Press, 1994.

Kilcommons, Brian with Sarah Wilson, *Good Owners, Great Dogs: A Training Manual for Humans and their Canine Companions.* New York: Warner, 1992.

King, Stephen, *Cujo.* New York: Signet, 1982.

Kipling, Rudyard, *The Complete Verse.* London: Kyle Cathie Limited, 1996.

Kleinzahler, August, *Cutty, One Rock: Low Characters and Strange Places, Gently Explained.* New York: Farrar, Straus and Giroux, 2005.

Knapp, Caroline, *Pack of Two: The Intricate Bond Between People and Dogs.* New York: Dial, 1998.

Knight, Black (pseudonym of Sir Alfred Munnings), *The Diary of A Freeman.* London: Cassell, 1953.

Knight, Eric, *Lassie Come-Home.* 1940. New York: Henry Holt, 2003.

Konik, Michael, *Ella in Europe: An American Dog's International Adventures.* New York: Delta, 2006.

Koontz, Dean, *The Darkest Evening of the Year.* New York: Bantam, 2008.

Kopelman, Lt. Col. Jay, with Melinda Roth, *From Baghdad, With Love: A Marine, the War, and a Dog Named Lava.* Guilford, Conn.: Lyons, 2006.

Korman, Gordon, *No More Dead Dogs.* New York: Hyperion, 2002.

Kuzniar, Alice A., *Melancholia's Dog: Reflections on Our Animal Kinship.* Chicago: University of Chicago Press, 2006.

Lansbury, Coral, *The Old Brown Dog: Women, Workers and Vivisection in Edwardian England.* London: University of Wisconsin Press, 1985.

Laurents, Arthur, *Original Story By.* New York: Applause, 2000.

Lee, Hermione, *Edith Wharton.* New York: Vintage, 2008.

Leigh, Janet, *There Really Was a Hollywood.* Garden City, New York: Doubleday, 1984.

Leonard, R. Maynard, ed., *The Dog in British Poetry.* San Francisco: Chronicle Books, n.d.

Lerman, Leo, *The Grand Surprise: The Journals of Leo Lerman*. New York: Knopf, 2007.

Lessing, Doris, *The Memoirs of a Survivor*. 1974. New York: Vintage, 1988.

-----, *The Story of General Dann and Mara's Daughter, Griot and the Snow Dog*. 2005. New York: Harper Perennial, 2007.

Levine, Nancy, *The Tao of Pug*. New York: Viking Studio/Penguin, 2003.

Lloyd, Ann, *Hollywood Dogs*. Hauppauge, New York: Barron's, 2004.

London, Jack, *The Call of the Wild and White Fang*.1903 and 1906. New York: Barnes & Noble Classics, 2003.

Lorenz, Konrad, *Man Meets Dog*. Translated by Marjorie Kerr Wilson. 1953. New York: Kodansha, 1994.

Lovejoy, Arthur O., *The Great Chain of Being: A Study in the History of an Idea*. 1936. New York: Harper & Row, 1965.

Machado de Assis, *Philosopher or Dog?* Translated by Clotilde Wilson. New York: Noonday Press, 1954.

MacLaine, Shirley, *Out on a Leash: Exploring the Nature of Reality and Love*. New York: Atria, 2005.

Maggitti, Phil, *Pugs: Everything About Purchase, Care, Nutrition, Breeding, Behavior, and Training*. Hauppauge, N.Y.: Barron's, 1994.

Malcolm, Janet, *Two Lives: Gertrude and Alice*. New Haven: Yale University Press, 2007.

Man-ho, Kwok, *Dog: The Chinese Horoscopes Library*. Scarborough, Ont.: Prentice Hall Canada, 1994.

Mann, Thomas, *Bashan and I*. Translated by Herman George Scheffauer. 1923. Philadelphia: Pine Street Books/University of Pennsylvania Press, 2003.

-----, "A Man and His Dog" in *Stories of Three Decades*. Translated by H. T. Lowe-Porter. New York: Modern Library, 1930.

Marshall Thomas, Elizabeth, *The Hidden Life of Dogs*. Boston: Houghton Mifflin, 1993.

-----, *The Social Lives of Dogs: The Grace of Canine Company*. New York: Simon & Schuster, 2002.

Masson, Jeffrey Moussaieff, *Dogs Never Lie About Love: Reflections on the Emotional World of Dogs*. New York: Crown, 1997.

-----, and Susan McCarthy, *When Elephants Weep: The Emotional Lives of Animals*. New York: Delta, 1996.

Martin, Ann N., *Food Pets Die For: Shocking Facts About Pet Food*. Troutdale, Oregon: NewSage, 1997.

Martin, Charles L., *Ophthalmic Disease in Veterinary Medicine*. Softcover edition with revisions. London, UK: Manson Publishing/The Veterinary Press, 2010.

Mayle, Peter, *A Dog's Life*. New York: Vintage, 1996.

McCaig, Donald, *Eminent Dogs, Dangerous Men: Searching Through Scotland for a Border Collie*. New York: Lyons, 1991.

McCann, Evelyn, *Bibliographic Index of Artists in Canada*. Toronto: University of Toronto Press, 2003.

McConnell, Patricia B., *The Other End of the Leash: Why We Do What We Do Around Dogs*. New York: Ballantine, 2002.

Merrill, James, *Collected Poems*. New York: Knopf, 2001.

Merritt, Raymond, and Miles Barth, *1000 Dogs: The Presence of the Dog in the History of Photography 1839 to Today*. New York: Taschen, n.d.

Merwin, W. S., *The Shadow of Sirius*. Port Townsend, Washington: Copper Canyon, 2008.

Michaelis, David, *Schulz and Peanuts: A Biography*. New York: HarperCollins, 2007.

Millan, Cesar, *Cesar's Way: The Natural Everyday Guide to Understanding & Correcting Common Dog Problems*. New York: Harmony, 2006.

Mitchell, Vanessa, *Best-Loved Dog Stories*. New York: Barnes & Noble, 1998.

Monks of New Skete, *How to Be Your Dog's Best Friend: A Training Manual for Dog Owners*. Boston: Little, Brown, 1978.

Montaigne, Michel de, *The Essays: A Selection*. Translated by M. A. Screech. London: Penguin, 2004.

Montgomery, Lee, ed., *Woof! Writers on Dogs*. New York: Viking Penguin, 2008.

Morris, Desmond, *Dogwatching: Why dogs bark and everything else you ever wanted to know*. New York: Crown, 1986.

Morris, Willie, *My Dog Skip*. New York: Vintage, 1996.

Mowat, Farley, *The Dog Who Wouldn't Be*. Boston: Little, Brown, 1957.

Murray, Louise, *Vet Confidential: An Insider's Guide to Protecting Your Pet's Health*. New York: Ballantine, 2008.

Naylor, Phyllis Reynolds, *Shiloh*. 1991. New York: Aladdin Paperbacks, 2000.

Nestle, Marion, and Malden C. Nesheim, *Feed Your Dog Right: The Authoritative Guide to Feeding Your Dog and Cat*. New York: Free Press, 2010.

The New Yorker Book of Dog Cartoons. New York: Knopf, 1997.

Nicolson, Nigel, and Joanne Trautmann, eds., *The Letters of Virginia Woolf, Volume V: 1932-1935*. New York: Harcourt Brace Jovanovich, 1979.

O'Hagan, Andrew, *The Life and Opinions of Maf the Dog and of his friend Marilyn Monroe*. Boston: Houghton Mifflin Harcourt, 2010.

Ollivant, Alfred, *Bob, Son of Battle*. New York: Garden City Publishing, 1898.

Orde, A. J., *Death and the Dogwalker*. New York: Doubleday, 1990.

Orwell, George, *Animal Farm*. 1945. London: Penguin, 1989.

Owens, Carrie, *Working Dogs*. New York: Prima, 1999.

Pace, Alison, *Pug Hill*. New York: Berkley Books/Penguin, 2006.

Pacelle, Wayne, *The Bond: Our Kinship with Animals, Our Call to Defend Them*. New York: William Morrow/HarperCollins, 2011.

Page, Jake, *Dogs: A Natural History*. New York: HarperCollins/Smithsonian Books, 2007.

Parkhurst, Carolyn, *The Dogs of Babel*. Boston: Little, Brown, 2003.

Pascal, Blaise, *Pensées: Thoughts on Religion and other subjects*. Translated by William Finlayson Trotter. New York: Washington Square Press, 1965.

Perenyi, Eleanor, *Green Thoughts: A Writer in the Garden*. New York: Random House, 1982.

Pickeral, Tamsin, *The Dog: 5000 Years of the Dog in Art*. New York: Merrell, 2008.

Pitcher, George, *The Dogs Who Came to Stay*. New York: Dutton, 1995.

Pletzinger, Thomas, *Funeral for a Dog*. Translated by Ross Benjamin. New York: Norton, 2011.

Poortvliet, Rien, *Dogs*. New York: Abrams, 1983.

Pope, Alexander, *Alexander Pope: Selected Poetry & Prose*. Edited by William K. Wimsatt, Jr. New York: Holt, Rinehart and Winston, 1965.

Pound, Ezra, *ABC of Reading*. New York: New Directions, 1960.

Pryor, Karen, *Don't Shoot the Dog! The New Art of Teaching and Training*. New York: Bantam, 1985.

Pushkin, Alexander, *Eugene Onegin*. Translated by Charles Johnston. London: Penguin, 2003.

Quinn, Spencer, *Dog on It*. New York: Atria, 2009.

Rawls, Wilson, *Where the Red Fern Grows*. 1961. New York: Bantam Doubleday Dell, 1996.

Regan, Tom, *The Case for Animal Rights*. Berkeley: University of California Press, 2004.

Rhees, Rush, *Moral Questions*. New York: St. Martin's, 1999.

Ritter, Erica, *The Hidden Life of Humans*. Toronto: Key Porter, 1997.

Robb, Graham, *The Discovery of France: A Historical Geography from the Revolution to the First World War*. New York: Norton, 2007.

Roberts, Lilian M., *Almost Human*. New York: Fawcett Gold Medal, 1998.

Roiphe, Anne, *1185 Park Avenue*. New York: Free Press, 1999.

Rose, Elisabeth, *For the Love of a Dog*. New York: Harmony, 2001.

Rosen, Michael J., ed., *The Company of Dogs: 21 Stories by Contemporary Masters*. New York: Galahad, 1996.

Rosenblum, Robert, with Edgar Peters Bowron, Carolyn Rose Rebbert, and William Secord, *The Dog in Art from Rococo to Post-Modernism*. New York: Abrams, 1988.

Rosenfelt, David, *Play Dead*. New York: Warner, 2007.

Roth, Melinda, *The Man Who Talks to Dogs: The Story of America's Wild Street Dogs and Their Unlikely Savior*. New York: Thomas Dunne Books/St. Martin's, 2002.

Rothfels, Nigel, ed., *Representing Animals*. Bloomington: University of Indiana Press, 2002.

Salisbury, Joyce E., *The Beast Within: Animals in the Middle Ages*. London: Routledge, 1994.

Sárkány, Pál, and Imre Ócsag, *Magyar kutyafajták*. Budapest: Mezögazdasági Kiado, 1987.

Sarton, May, *Journal of a Solitude*. New York: Norton, 1973.

Saunders, Marshall, *Beautiful Joe: A Dog's Own Story*. 1894. New York: Grosset & Dunlap, 1920.

Schine, Cathleen, *The New Yorkers*. New York: Farrar, Straus & Giroux, 2007.

Schinto, Jeanne, ed., *The Literary Dog: Great Contemporary Dog Stories*. New York: Atlantic Monthly, 1990.

Schnur, Leslie, *The Dog Walker*. New York: Atria Books, 2004.

Schoen, Allen M., *Kindred Spirits: How the Remarkable Bond between Humans and Animals Can Change the Way We Live*. New York: Broadway, 2002.

Schwartz, Marion, *A History of Dogs in the Early Americas*. New Haven, Conn.: Yale University Press, 1997.

Secord, William, *The American Dog at Home*. Woodbridge, Suffolk: Antique Collectors' Club, 2010.

-----, *A Breed Apart: The Art Collections of the American Kennel Club and The American Kennel Club Museum of the Dog*. Woodbridge, Suffolk: Antique Collectors' Club, 2001.

-----, *Dog Painting: The European Breeds*. Woodbridge, Suffolk: Antique Collectors' Club, 2000.

Secord, William, *Dog Painting, 1840-1940. A social history of the dog in art*. Woodbridge, Suffolk: Antique Collectors' Club, 1992.

Sendak, Maurice, *Higglety Pigglety Pop! or There Must Be More to Life*. New York: Harper & Row, 1967.

Serpell, James, *The Domestic Dog: Its Evolution, Behaviour, and Interactions with People*. Cambridge: Cambridge University Press, 1995.

Shaw, George Bernard, *Six Plays with Prefaces*. New York: Dodd, Mead & Company, 1948.

Sheldrake, Rupert, *Dogs That Know When Their Owners Are Coming Home and Other Unexplained Powers of Animals*. New York: Crown, 1999.

Shelley, Mary, *Frankenstein*. 1818. Oxford: Oxford University Press, 1969.

Sherrill, Martha, *Dog Man: An Uncommon Life on a Faraway Mountain*. New York: Penguin, 2008.

Sherwood, Patricia M., ed., *The Greatest Dog Stories Ever Told*. New York: Gramercy Books, 2001.

Shevelow, Kathryn, *For the Love of Animals: The Rise of the Animal Protection Movement*. New York: Henry Holt, 2008.

Sife, Wallace, *The Loss of a Pet: A Guide to Coping with the Grieving Process When a Pet Dies*. New York: Wiley, 1998.

Sills, Beverly, and Lawrence Linderman, *Beverly: An Autobiography*. New York: Bantam, 1987.

Silverman, Stephen M., *Movie Mutts: Hollywood Goes to the Dogs*. New York: Abrams, 2001.

Singer, Peter, *Animal Liberation*. 1975. New York: HarperCollins, 2002.

Smith, Alexander McCall, *Corduroy Mansions*. Toronto: Knopf, 2009.

Smith, Liz, *Natural Blonde: A Memoir*. New York: Hyperion, 2000.

Smith, Sheila, *Cavalier King Charles Spaniels Today*. New York: Howell/Macmillan, Inc., 1995.

Souhami, Diana, *Gertrude and Alice*. New York: HarperCollins, 1991.

Stapledon, Olaf, *Odd John and Sirius: Two Science Fiction Novels*. 1935 and 1944. New York: Dover, 1972.

Stein, Gertrude, *Paris France*. 1940. New York: Liveright, 1970.

-----, *Selected Writings of Gertrude Stein*. New York: Vintage, 1990.

-----, *Wars I Have Seen*. New York: Random House, 1945.

Steinbeck, John, *Travels with Charley (in Search of America)*.1961. New York: Penguin, 2002.

Stern, Jane and Michael, *Dog Eat Dog: A Very Human Book about Dogs and Dog Shows*. New York: Scribner, 1997.

Suarès, J. C., ed., *Hollywood Dogs*. San Francisco: Collins, 1993.

Summers, Judith, *My Life with George: What I Learned about Joy from One Neurotic (and Very Expensive) Dog*. New York: Hyperion, 2007.

Susann, Jacqueline, *Every Night, Josephine!* 1963. New York: William Morrow, 1974.

Szabó, Magda, *The Door*. 1987. Translated by Len Rix. London: Vintage, 2006.

Tawada, Yoko, *The Bridegroom Was a Dog*. Translated by Margaret Mitsutani. 1998. New York: Kodansha, 2003.

Teleky, Richard, ed., *The Exile Book of Canadian Dog Stories*. Toronto: Exile Editions, 2009.

Terhune, Albert Payson, *A Dog Named Chips*. New York: Harper & Brothers, 1931.

-----, *Buff: A Collie*. New York: Grosset & Dunlap, 1921.

----, *A Highland Collie*. 1925. New York: Grosset & Dunlap, 1927.

-----, *His Dog*. New York: E.P. Dutton, 1922.

-----, *Lad: A Dog*. 1919. New York: E.P. Dutton, 1934.

-----, *Lochinvar Luck*. New York: Grosset & Dunlap, 1923.

-----, *Real Tales of Real Dogs*. Etchings by Diana Thorne. Akron, Ohio: Saalfield, 1935.

Thomas, Shirley, *The New Pug*. New York: Howell Book House/Macmillan, 1990.

Thompson, Colin, *Unknown*. New York: Walker & Company, 2000.

Thorne, Diana, and Albert Payson Terhune, *The Dog Book*. Akron, Ohio: Saalfield, 1932.

Thorne, Diana, *Drawing Dogs*. New York: The Studio Publications, Inc., 1940.

Thurber, James, *Thurber's Dogs*. New York: Fireside, 1992.

Thurston, Mary Elizabeth, *The Lost History of the Canine Race: Our 15,000-Year Love Affair with Dogs*. Kansas City: Andrews and McMeel, 1996.

Toklas, Alice B., *Staying on Alone: Letters of Alice B. Toklas*. Edited by Edward Burns. New York: Liveright, 1973.

Tolstoy, Leo, *Anna Karenina*. Translated by Richard Pavear and Larissa Volokhonsky. New York: Penguin, 2001.

-----, *War and Peace*. Translated by Richard Pavear and Larissa Volokhonsky. New York: Knopf, 2007.

Trout, Nick, *Tell Me Where It Hurts: A Day of Humor, Healing. and Hope in My Life as an Animal Surgeon*. New York: Broadway, 2008.

Turgenev, Ivan, *First Love and Other Stories*. "Mumu." Oxford: Oxford University Press, 1999.

Uglow, Jenny, *Hogarth: A Life and a World*. New York: Farrar, Straus and Giroux, 2002.

Virgil, *The Aeneid*. Translated by Robert Fagles. New York: Penguin, 2008.

Vitebsky, Piers, *The Reindeer People: Living with Animals and Spirits in Siberia*. Boston: Houghton Mifflin, 2005.

von Arnim, Elizabeth, *All the Dogs of My Life*. 1936. London: Virago, 1995.

Watson, Brad, *Last Days of the Dog-Men*. New York: Norton, 1996.

Watt, Judith, and Peter Dyer, *Men & Dogs*. New York: Atria, 2005.

-----, *Women & Dogs*. New York: Atria, 2005.

Webb, Stephen H.., *On God and Dogs: A Christian Theology of Compassion for Animals*. New York, Oxford University Press, 1998.

Welch, Frances, *A Romanov Fantasy: Life at the Court of Anna Anderson*. New York: Norton, 2007.

Wershler-Henry, Darren, *The Iron Whim: A Fragmented History of Typewriting*. Toronto: McClelland & Stewart, 2005.

Weschler, Lawrence, *Mr. Wilson's Cabinet of Wonders*. New York: Pantheon, 1995.

West, Beverly, and Jason Bergund, *Pug Therapy: Finding Happiness, One Pug at a Time*. New York: Broadway, 2006.

White, T. H., editor and translator, *The Bestiary: A Book of Beasts*. 1954. New York: Capricorn Books/G.P. Putnam's Sons, 1960.

Wolfe, Cary, *Animal Rites: American Culture, the Discourse of Species, and Posthumanist Theory*. Chicago: University of Chicago Press, 2003.

Woloy, Eleanora M., *The Symbol of the Dog in the Human Psyche: A Study of the Human-Dog Bond*. Wilmette, Illinois: Chiron Publications, 1990.

Woolf, Virginia, *Flush*. 1933. Oxford: Oxford University Press, 1998.

Wroblewski, David, *The Story of Edgar Sawtelle*. New York: Ecco/HarperCollins, 2008.

Wynne, Clive, *Do Animals Think?* Princeton, N.J.: Princeton University Press, 2004.

ARTICLES

Abu-Nasr, Donna, "Saudis ban sale of dogs, cats," *Toronto Star*, Sept. 9, 2006, A17.

Aksyonov, Vassily, "Around Dupont." Translated by Alla Zbinovsky. *New Yorker*, Nov. 20, 1995, 92-100.

Albert, Dora, "Dogs Made Her Famous," *Saturday Night*, Dec. 28, 1929, 13-14.

Bennett, Drake, "Lawyer for the dog," *Boston Sunday Globe*, Sept. 9, 2007, D1, D2.

Bragg, Rick, "An Artist and a Staring Dog that Became a Cultural Icon," *The New York Times*, Sept. 16, 1998, B3.

Briggs, David, "Who Let the Dogs In?" *Plain Dealer*, Oct. 13, 2007, E1, E3.

Brody, Jane E., "The Truth about Cat and Dog Food," *The New York Times*, June 1, 2010, D7.

Brown, Clifton, "Vick Faces Federal Charges on Dogfighting," *The New York Times*, July 18, 2007, C13.

Buckley, Cara, "Trouble, the Cosseted Heir of Leona Helmsley, Dies," *The New York Times*, June 10, 2011, A18.

Budiansky, Stephen, "The Truth about Dogs," *Atlantic Monthly*, July 1999, 39-53.

Bulliet, C. J., "Respectability in Chicago," *The New York Times*, Feb. 22, 1931, 105.

Bumiller, Elizabeth, "Through 7 Presidents, Thousands of Bulbs and a Few Dogs, the Keeper of the Trowel," *New York Times*, April 25, 2005, A18.

Chivers, D. J., "A Brutal Sport Is Having Its Day Again in Russia," *The New York Times*, Feb. 9, 2007, A1, A10.

Cramer, Richard Ben, "They Were Heroes Too," *Parade/Boston Sunday Globe*, April 1, 2001, 4-6.

Cranston, Meg, "Every Dog in the Pound." Exhibition brochure. Toronto: Mercer Union, 2008.

d'Hauthuille, Christine, "La belle histoire d'Alexis et de son chien, Robot," *Paris Match*, Dec. 10, 2003, 58-63.

Dekoven, Marianne, "Guest Column: Why Animals Now?" *PMLA*, Vol. 124, No. 2, March 2009, 361-69.

Dempsey, Amy, "Getting the scoop on whose dog pooped," *Toronto Star*, June 28, 2011, A1, A4.

Derr, Mark, "Pack of Lies," *The New York Times*, Aug. 31, 2006, A27.

-----, "The Politics of Dogs: How Greed and AKC Policies are Endangering the Health and Quality of American Dogs," *Atlantic Monthly*, March 1990, 49-72.

Dubner, Stephen J., and Steven D. Levitt, "Dog-Waste Management: Can Technology keep New York City Scooped?" *The New York Times Magazine*, Oct. 2, 2005, 32-34.

Dunne, Dominick, "The Queen and I," *Vanity Fair*, March 2007, 248-52.

Editorial, "Dog Days Indeed," *The New York Times*, July 20, 1997, E14.

Edwards, Peter, "Two die trying to save dog," *Toronto Star*, Jan. 22, 1996, A1, A8.

Fassihi, Farnaz, "A Craze for Pooches in Iran Dogs the Morality Police," *Wall Street Journal*, July 18, 2011, A1, A10.

Fiala, Jennifer, "Economic Emergency: Crisis looms as debt-to-salary statistics paint bleak outlook for veterinary medicine's future, experts say," *dvm Newsmagazine: The Voice of Veterinary News*, March 2008, 1, 18-20.

Fischer, Julia, "Behavior: Can a Dog Learn a Word?," *Science*, Vol. 304, No. 56777, 11 June 2004, 1605-06.

Fountain, Henry, "An Artist's Best Friend? Giraffe, Monkey, Etc.," *The New York Times*, July 18, 2006, Arts-28.

Fox, Margalit, "Arthur Haggerty, 74, Master Dog Trainer, Dies," *The New York Times*, July 18, 2006, A22.

Gill, Alexandra, "If we could talk to the animals," *Globe and Mail*, Dec. 11, 1999, R31.

-----, "Bow Wow," *Globe and Mail*, March 4, 2000, R1, R6.

Gilmer, Maureen, "Create a dog-friendly haven out back," *Plain Dealer*, Feb. 22, 2007, F12.

Glueck, Grace, "Out of the Kennel and into the Gallery: The Artist's Best Friend," *The New York Times*, July 7, 2006, B29.

Gopnik, Adam, "Dog Story," *New Yorker*, Aug. 8, 2011, 46-53.

Grognet, Jeff, "Canadian cancer research," *Dogs in Canada*, Oct. 2007, 37-40.

-----, "Golden Years: Adopting a Dog When You Are a Senior," *Dogs in Canada*, May 2006, 56-7.

Grossfeld, Stan, "Touched by an Angell," *Boston Globe Magazine*, Aug. 20, 2000, 10-15, 23-28.

Harpaz, Beth J., "Dogs help ease the pain of grieving victims," (Associated Press), *Toronto Star*, Oct. 28, 2001, F8.

Harris Poll, "Pets and the holidays," *Plain Dealer*, Dec. 8, 2007, B9.

Henderson, Helen, "Why pooches pop more pills," *Toronto Star*, June 30, 2007.

Henri, Veronica, "Owner Drowns Trying to Save Dog," *Toronto Sun*, March 30, 1998, 1, 4.

Hevesi, Dennis, "Laurence Mancuso Dies; New Skete Abbot Was 72," *New York Times*, July 1, 2007, 23.

Hively, Suzanne, "Art museum uses dog to say 'Keep off the grass,' to geese," *Plain Dealer*, Oct. 30, 1998, E1-2.

-----, "Lakewood couple help dogs in war zones," *Plain Dealer*, Nov. 24, 2005, F19.

-----, "Researchers probe similarity of auras for people, animals," *Plain Dealer*, July 6, 2006, E13.

Hoffman, Lisa, "Group seeks recognition for four-legged war heroes," *Plain Dealer*, Aug. 6, 2006, A12.

Hone-McMahan, Kim, "Canine Artistry," *Akron Beacon Journal*, Aug. 23, 2009, E1.

Hookway, James, "Historian Won't Let Scotland's Most Famous Dog Lie," *Wall Street Journal*, Sept. 3-4, 2011, A1, A12.

Iovine, Julie V., "A Dog Biscuit for Your Thoughts," *The New York Times*, July 23, 2001, B7.

-----, "The Healing Ways of Dr. Dog," *The New York Times*, Oct. 28, 2001, 8.

Jewett, Eleanor, "There are Dog Days at Show by this Artist," *Chicago Daily Tribune*, May 23, 1930, 37.

Johnson, Kevin V., "Love on a leash knows no limits at Chicago ER," *USA Today*, Aug. 2, 1999, 6D.

Kaufman, Leslie, "Owners in a Bitter Dispute over Dog Attacks," *The New York Times*, Sept. 2, 2004, A20.

King, Carol, "Boldly, Where No Dog Had Gone Before," *The New York Times*, Nov. 4, 2007, Art 22.

Kluger, Jeffrey, "Inside the Minds of Animals," *Time*, Aug. 18, 2010, 36-43.

Knight, Wendy, "No Pet Left Behind," *The New York Times*, March 30, 2007, D1, 7.

Koppel, Lily, "Today He Is a Dog; Actually, He Always Was," *The New York Times*, Dec. 20, 2004, A23.

Krivel, Peter, "This years goes to the dogs," *Toronto Star*, Jan. 26, 2006, J2.

Lacey, Marc, "Hero Dog from Afghan Base Is Killed by Mistake in Arizona," *The New York Times*, Nov. 19, 2010, A1, 14.

Landman, Beth, "Wagging the Dog, and a Finger," *The New York Times*, May 14, 2006, Section 9, 1, 6.

Lane, Anthony, "A Boy's World: The Tintin century," *New Yorker*, May 28, 2007, 47-53.

Lederer, Susan E., "Political Animals: The Shaping of Biomedical Research Literature in Twentieth-Century America," *Isis*, Vol. 83, No. 1, March 1992, 61-79.

Leetaru, Lars, "Metropolitan Diary" (cartoon), *The New York Times*, June 20, 2005, B2.

Light, Alison, "Hitchcock's *Rebecca*: A Woman's Film?" in *The Daphne Du Maurier Companion*, edited by Helen Taylor. London: Virago, 2007.

Liptak, Adam, "Justices Reject Ban on Depicting Animal Cruelty," *The New York Times*, April 21, 2010, A1, 17.

Madoff, Ray, "Dog Eat Your Taxes?," *The New York Times*, July 9, 2008, A25.

Malanca, Ettore (photographs) and Jane Perlez (text), "Romania's Lost Boys," *The New York Times Magazine*, May 10, 1998, 26-29.

Marko, Natasha, "Cancer Care: Advances in treatment," *Dogs in Canada*, Oct. 2007, 32-36.

McGreevy, Patrick, "Bill requiring owners to spay or neuter pets dies," *Los Angeles Times*, July 12, 2007, B1, B9.

Mooallem, Jon, "The Modern Kennel Conundrum," *The New York Times Magazine*, Feb. 4, 2007, 42-49, 78-84.

Myrone, Martin, "George Stubbs' Noble Creatures," *Bark*, No. 40, Jan./Feb. 2007, 74-81.

Neff, Mark, et al., "Breed Distribution and History of Canine *mdr 1-1*, a Pharmacogenetic Mutation that Marks the Emergence of Breeds from the Collie Lineage," *Proceedings of the National Academy of Sciences*, Vol. 101, No. 32, Aug. 10, 2004, 11725-11730.

Newman, Cathy, "Cesar Millan the Dog Whisperer," *National Geographic*, Dec. 2006, 33-37.

Orlean, Susan, "The Dog Star: Rin Tin Tin and the making of Warner Bros," *New Yorker*, Aug. 29, 2011, 34-39.

Ostrander, Elaine, and Leonid Kruglyak, et al., "Genetic Structure of the Purebred Domestic Dog," *Science*, Vol. 304, May 21, 2004, 1160-1164.

Pearce, Tralee, "Resuscitating Rover," *Globe and Mail*, Aug. 9, 2003, F1, F6.

Pennisi, Elizabeth, "Genome Resources to Boost Canines' Role in Gene Hunts," *Science*, Vol. 304, May 21, 2004, 1093-1095.

Pew Research Center Poll, "Dogs edge cats, and dads trail both!" *Plain Dealer*, March 11, 2006, B9.

Pollack, Andrew, "In Trials for New Cancer Drugs, Family Pets Are Benefiting, Too," *The New York Times*, Nov. 24, 2006, A1, A19.

Pratt, Laura, "Pet-traits," *National Post*, April 17, 1999, 22.

Quiñonez, Ernesto, "Dog Days," *The New York Times Magazine*, Nov. 26, 2000, 152.

Rafkin, Louise, "Rent-a-Dog," *The New York Times Magazine*, April 20, 1997, 86.

Rhoden, William C., "An Elusive Quarterback Takes His Hardest Hit," *The New York Times*, July 20, 2007, C13.

Rich, Motoko, "Pet Therapy Sets Landlords Howling," *The New York Times*, June 26, 2003, D1, D8.

Richman, Josh, "California Deploys K-9s with a Nose for Hebrew," *The Forward*, May 11, 2007, A1, A6.

Rozhon, Tracie, "The Market for Dog Paintings Refuses to Play Dead," *The New York Times.*, Feb. 17, 2000, B16.

Sangiacomo, Michael, "Mom on quest to bring son's 'best friend' home: Marines bought, cared for puppy in Iraq," *Plain Dealer*, Aug. 20, 2005, A1, A11.

Schorow, Stephanie, "Rembrandt's Dog," *Bark*, No. 37, July/Aug. 2006, 84-89.

Schultz, Stacey, "Pets and their humans," *U.S. News & World Report*, Oct. 30, 2000, 53-55.

Siebert, Charles, "The Animal-Cruelty Syndrome," *The New York Times Magazine*, June 13, 2010, 42-51.

Siebert, Charles, "The Animal Self," *The New York Times Magazine*, Jan. 22, 2006, 48-87.

-----, "Citizen Canine," *The New York Times Magazine*, March 26, 2000, 46-49.

-----, "New Tricks," *The New York Times Magazine*, April 8, 2007, 46-51.

Slater, X., "Mike Wallace: The Clintons' Lapdog" (cartoon), *The New York Times*, July 20, 1997, E16.

Solomon, Deborah, "The Dogged Approach: Questions for Tamar Geller," *The New York Times Magazine*, May 27, 2007, 13.

-----, "Leader of the Pack," *The New York Times Magazine*, May 7, 2006.

Spector, Kaye, "Dog park has neighbors barking," *Plain Dealer*, June 12, 2006, A4.

Staff, "Dog Quits Modeling to Lead her Own Life," *The New York Times*, March 6, 1928, 29.

Staff, "A Soldier's Best New Friend," *cottagedog*, Winter 2011, Vol. 2, Issue 1, 18-20.

Staff, "That Was Then & This Is Now," *Vanity Fair*, Aug. 2007, 114.

Staff, "Window on a cruel world," *USA Today*, July 20, 2007, 10A.

Stevens, Mark, "Puppy Love," *New Yorker*, April 3, 2006, 84.

Swenson, Kyle, "Breeding Contempt: Rescuers insist an Amish way of life is torture for the dogs in their care," *Scene*, Vol. 41, Issue, 3, July 21-27, 2010, 12-19.

Tangley, Laura, "Animal Emotions," *U.S. News & World Report*, Oct. 30, 2000, 48-52.

Teleky, Richard, "In Search of Diana Thorne," *Queen's Quarterly*, Vol. 116, No.4, 520-33.

Thorne, Diana, "Look Doggish, If You Please," *Christian Science Monitor Magazine*, July 15, 1936, 8-9.

Trilling, Diana, "A Visit to Camelot," *New Yorker*, June 2, 1997, 54-65.

Turnbull, Barbara, "The Scoop on Poop," *Toronto Star*, April 6, 2006, K1, K6.

Updike, John, "The Changeling," *New Yorker*, April 16, 2007, 154-157.

Van Dam, Peggy, "Owners must keep firmer leash on dogs in parks," *Toronto Star*, Feb. 4, 2004, A17.

Van Wyck, Morgan, "The Meaning of Dog," *Shambhala Sun*, July 1998, 30-35.

Vilà, Carles, *et. al.*, "Multiple and Ancient Origins of the Domestic Dog," *Science*, Vol. 276, June 13, 1997, 1687-1689.

Waters, David J. and Kathleen Wildasin, "Cancer Clues from Pet Dogs," *Scientific American*, Dec. 2006, 94-101.

Watson, Julie and Sue Manning, "Dogs of war look forward to a peaceful retirement," *Toronto Star*, May 28, 2011, A26.

Wells, D. L., L. Graham, and P. G. Hepper, "The Influence of Auditory Stimulation on the Behaviour of Dogs Housed in a Rescue Shelter," *Animal Welfare* (2002)11: 385-393.

Williams, Joy, "The Inhumanity of the Animal People." *Harper's*, Aug. 1997, 60-67.

Wood, Skip, "Quarterbacks face harsh reality," *USA Today*, July 20, 2007, 1A, 2A.

Yardley, William, "As Racing Ends, What About the Dogs?" *The New York Times*, May 5, 2005, A23.

Zezima, Katie, "Tracing Unscooped Dog Waste to the Culprit, with Science," *The New York Times*, July 3, 2011, A9.

Zimmer, Carl, "Viral Outbreak in Dogs Yields Clues on Origins of Hepatitis C.," *The New York Times*, May 31, 2011, D3.

CREDITS

We are grateful for permission to reprint short extracts from previously published works as well as selected paintings, drawings, engravings and photographs. Every effort has been made to determine copyright owners. In the case of any omissions, the publisher will be pleased to make suitable acknowledgements in future editions.

BONAPARTE, MARIE. From *Topsy: The Story of a Golden-Haired Chow*. Originally published by the Pushkin Press, 1940. © 1994 by Transaction Publishers. Reprinted by permission of the publisher. BURNFORD, SHIELA. Extracts from *Bel Ria: Dog of War* by Sheila Burnford. New York Review Books. © 1977. By permission of Harold Ober Associates Incorporated. CERVANTES. From *Don Quixote* by Miguel de Cervantes. A new translation by Edith Grossman. Translation © Edith Grossman; introduction © Harold Bloom. Reprinted by permission of HarperCollins Publishers. COLETTE. "Colette with Dog" (1935). By permission of akg.-images/Walter Limot. CRESPIN, RÉGINE. © Régine Crespin. Published by Northeastern University Press, c/o University Press of New England, Lebanon, NH. Reprinted by permission. DUTOURD, JEAN. From *A Dog's Head*. Translated by Robin Chancellor. By permission of the University of Chicago Press. GRENIER, ROGER. From *The Difficulty of Being a Dog*. Translated by Alice Kaplan. By permission of the University of Chicago Press. HOGARTH, WILLIAM. "Self Portrait," engraved by J. Mollison (engraving) by William Hogarth (1697-1764). Private Collection/The Bridgeman Art Library. HORST. "Gertrude Stein with Basket II" (1946). © Estate of Horst P. Horst / Art + Commerce KOBAL COLLECTION. From First National/The Kobal Collection "A Dog's Life" (1918); 20TH-Century Fox/The Kobal Collection *Call of the Wild* (1935); MGM/The Kobal Collection *Lassie Come Home* (1943) and *After the Thin Man* (1936). LANDSEER, SIR EDWIN. *Attachment*. Saint Louis Art Museum. Gift of Mrs. Eugene A. Perry in memory of her mother, Mrs. Claude Kilpatrick by exchange. LESSING, DORIS. From *The Memoirs of a Survivor* by Doris Lessing, © The Octabon Press. Used by permission of Alfred A. Knopf, a division of Random House Inc. MALANCA, ETTORE. From "The Lost Boys" series. By permission of Ettore Malanca and Sipa Press USA. MCCAIG, DONALD. From *Eminent Dogs, Dangerous Men*. Copyright © Donald McCaig. Reprinted by permission of The Lyons Press. MITCHELL, JOAN. *George Went Swimming at Barnes Hole, but It Got Too Cold* (1957), by Joan Mitchell. Courtesy of the Albright-Knox Art Gallery, Buffalo, New York. © Estate of Joan Mitchell. RHEINGOLD ADVERTISEMENT. By permission of the Rheingold Brewing Company. WEBB, STEPHEN. From *On God and Dogs: A Christian Theology of Compassion for Animals* by Webb, Stephen (1998). By permission of Oxford University Press, Inc.

Comic strips

Zoli